The Treatment of Criminal Offenders

ALSO BY MICHAEL DOW BURKHEAD

The Search for the Causes of Crime:
A History of Theory in Criminology (McFarland, 2006)

The Treatment of Criminal Offenders

A History

Michael Dow Burkhead

McFarland & Company, Inc., Publishers
Jefferson, North Carolina, and London

LIBRARY OF CONGRESS CATALOGUING-IN-PUBLICATION DATA

Burkhead, Michael Dow, 1946–
    The treatment of criminal offenders : a history /
Michael Dow Burkhead.
        p.   cm.
    Includes bibliographical references and index.

    ISBN-13: 978-0-7864-3020-8
    softcover : 50# alkaline paper ∞

    1. Criminals — Rehabilitation — United States — History.
    2. Corrections — United States — History.   3. Recidivism —
    United States — Prevention — History.   I. Title.
    HV9304.B866   2007
    365'.66 — dc22   2007014425

British Library cataloguing data are available

Cover photograph ©2006 Design Pics

Manufactured in the United States of America

*McFarland & Company, Inc., Publishers
  Box 611, Jefferson, North Carolina 28640
    www.mcfarlandpub.com*

To my parents, L.D. and Virginia Burkhead,
who value family and education,
and who led the way.

Acknowledgments

I owe debts to many people who enabled my career and who directly contributed to this book. I would like to especially mention Richard Franklin, friend and colleague, who has years of experience treating sex offenders and who reviewed that section of this book and made many helpful comments. I also wish to thank the Reverend Bud Walker, former Chief of Chaplaincy Services, North Carolina Department of Correction, who provided me with helpful information about religious programming and its issues in prison settings. I also wish to acknowledge Dr. Paul Gendreau who contributed a great deal to my understanding of correctional treatment and its evaluation and Dr. Richard Rolfe, my former clinical supervisor, now retired, who nourished my career in corrections. Dr. Mickey Braswell encouraged my writing career early on and contributed helpful suggestions to my publishing efforts.

Finally, without the support and encouragement of my wife, Jan, I would not have succeeded at anything that I have been able to achieve. Whatever credit this book may deserve must, by all means, be shared.

Table of Contents

Preface

The Carolinas are hot in July. So my family went every summer of my childhood to the shore for a two-week vacation. We usually stayed at one of the family beaches which stretched from the North Carolina state line to Myrtle Beach in South Carolina. Sometimes we stayed at Edisto Island, a shell-strewn beach with an Old South ambience. I loved going on these beach vacations where I felt excitement and freedom.

One of those hot summer vacations, when I was eight years old and my brother was four, there was a disastrous fish kill. Hundreds of dead fish washed up from the sea and covered the sand, so thickly in some places that you could not make a path across the beach without stepping on them. Soon the ugly sight of rotting fish was accompanied by a terrible stench. Nearly everyone abandoned the beach, disappointed over a spoiled vacation. But my brother and I could not resist returning periodically during the next few days to see if anything had changed, in hopes that our anticipated pleasures might yet be recovered.

One afternoon, our little patrol marched over the line of dunes and saw two large trucks on the beach and a group of men fanning out from the trucks in a ragged line. They were all dressed alike, in white T-shirts and long black-and-white striped pants, little round caps, and work boots. They walked with an odd gait, as if they had to pull their feet away from the sand at each step and had to be careful not to slip and fall down. Each one carried a long stick. My brother and I ran down for a closer look.

They were stabbing the dead fish with their sticks, picking them up, and putting them into canvas sacks which hung from their sides. We were made bold by curiosity at their peculiar appearance and gradually we edged within a few feet of the nearest one.

"Hello," I said, feeling brave. "What're you doing?"

He was young, with a sunburned face and blond hair sticking out from beneath his odd cap. I saw that his legs were chained together, which caused his awkward way of walking. He looked at me with a pained expression on his face and then returned his gaze to the sand and the dead fish.

"You don't want to talk to me," he said. He kept on walking, dragging his feet, and spearing the fish with his sharp-pointed stick.

We began following him down the beach. I wanted to ask him questions, but he steadfastly ignored me. Since I was watching the prisoner instead of where I was going, I did not notice the guard until I nearly collided with him. I was face-to-face with his belt buckle, which was shining silver, and was canted over from the pressure of all that flesh pushing it outward. He was exactly the archetypal Southern sheriff, with a huge hanging potbelly, reflecting sunglasses, boots, and a white cowboy hat. He carried a shotgun that looked six feet long to my eight-year-old eyes. The butt of the weapon was pressed against his right hip, the barrel pointing skyward. He said to me, quietly, in a rolling drawl, "Boy, you all better get out of heah."

I had been taught not to defy adult authority, but I didn't want to leave. I wanted to stay and see what was going to happen.

"Go on. Git."

There had been a small knot of anxiety inside of me since I had first addressed the prisoner, and at the guard's stern tone, it twisted into panic.

"Yes, sir," I stammered, and turned and ran as fast as I could up the beach towards the rows of cottages behind it, my brother racing behind me. We paused for breath and I looked back across the sand towards the sea and saw the prisoners, spreading apart now, scuttling along in their leg chains and stabbing the fish, looking like little crabs in black-and-white striped shells. This was a strange happening in my boyhood world and I was dismayed and disturbed. I could not have known then that I would choose a career, lasting over 25 years, in which the principal activity would be talking to prisoners.

On this side of those 25 years, I wanted to obtain, for myself as much as for anyone else, a "long view" of the rehabilitation of prisoners. So it is the purpose of this book to present a discussion of the treatment of criminal offenders with an historical perspective. It is my hope that these chapters will help the reader to form a more knowledgeable and a more critical view of the public debate on the rehabilitation of offenders, but this historical summary will not, by any means, conclude that debate.

In taking an historical perspective, we can see more clearly the exaggerated claims which often accompany new treatment methods for criminals and the rapidity with which they vanish. We can see the roller-coaster trends in public opinion which influence our specific efforts to prevent and reduce crime, to create informed and practicable public policy, and to reform the criminal law. A central point of this book, and the reason that an historical perspective is important, is that we keep repeating ourselves, recycling old ideas as if they were brand new, and then discarding them before we have found out if they are effective or not, only to bring them up again later. So we never really learn from them. We act like this because we are, as a culture, deeply conflicted about punishment and treatment. Should we punish them? Should we help them? Should we do both? Can we do both? It is our ambivalence on these issues, not a lack of technical knowledge, which is the main impediment to our progress in reducing crime.

The American founding fathers thought that the 18th-century British criminal law was too harsh and arbitrary and set out deliberately to reform it. One of the first ideas that they adopted, an idea which was Continental in origin, was to sentence criminals to a period of solitary confinement so that they could reflect upon their wrongdoing, come to know God, and reform. Today solitary confinement is our chief means of punishment, not treatment, and our penal system is the harshest among all first-world nations. We have the highest incarceration rate in the world. What happened? The "nothing works" literature of the 1970s was a gunshot across the bow of prisoner rehabilitation and, even though there is a healthy and growing body of "what works" literature, which we will review in chapter six, the debate is far from over. Political partisans can marshal "scientific evidence" for almost any point of view in this great debate, but, no matter how you try to address the measurement problems, data, as Stevens Clarke has said, is no substitute for thinking. It will help us in our decision making to have the historical background, the context, the scientific sophistication, and the skepticism with which to assess the validity of claims to treatment efficacy. To this end, and to those concerned citizens who care about the problems of crime and justice, this book is dedicated.

Chapter One

The Principal Issues

It is better to prevent crimes than to punish them.
—Cesare Beccaria, 1764

"Corrections is one hundred and fifty years of undocumented fads," said Professor George Beto, a former Commissioner of Corrections in Texas. He made this remark at a conference in 1978. With the growth of a "what works literature" and the advent of "evidence-based practice" in the last twenty-five years or so, we can report some progress in documenting the results of rehabilitative programs, but not enough to render Beto's summary as no longer true. Doris MacKenzie writes in 2005, "Despite researchers' continual calls for evidence-based corrections, many policy makers and correctional administrators follow the latest fad or what feels appropriate in their guts" (2005, p. 249). From the workhouse to the boot camp, from psychosurgery to Depo-Provera, from transactional analysis to Scared Straight, from Cherry Hill to Marion, from P.R.A.C. to D.A.R.E, the history of corrections is the history of one fad about treatment after another.

What to do with criminal offenders is an enormous problem. In the United States, prison and jails held 2.1 million people in mid–2004. One in every 138 residents in the United States was in jail or prison in 2004 (Bureau of Justice Statistics, 2005). According to the Justice Policy Institute (2005), the United States has the highest incarceration rate in the world. The best available recidivism data says that 67 percent of prison inmates in the United States are rearrested, almost exclusively for a felony or a serious misdemeanor, within three years of their release from prison (Langan and Levin, 2002). When this recidivism rate is applied as an estimate to our present prison population, the resulting sum strongly suggests that our problems with crime will continue on a large scale.

The main reason for the steady growth in the prison population is the widespread use of "mandatory sentencing" for drug offenders, "three strikes and you're out" laws for repeat offenders, and "truth in sentencing" laws which restrict early release of prisoners from their sentences. These laws were enacted in the 1980s and 1990s as a "get tough" response to the growing crime rate of those decades and to the perceived failure of rehabilitation programs of the 1960s and 1970s ("nothing works"). Malcolm Young of the Sentencing Project, reports: "We're working under the burden of laws and practices that have developed over thirty years that have focused on punishment and prison as our primary response to crime" (Associated Press, 2005).

With a high crime rate, a high incarceration rate, and a high recidivism rate, nearly everyone agrees that our system is not working, though there is considerable disagreement about the reasons that it is not. There are three core issues in considering crime, and to review those issues here may help to place our discussion of treatment in a realistic context. The three core issues in the study of crime are: (1) the issue of free will and determinism, (2) the issue of studying crimes versus studying criminals, and (3) the issue of a single, "root" cause of crime versus multicausal explanations of crime.

The issue of free will and determinism is one which I refer to as the mighty opposites, "opposites" because we tend to think of them as a strict dichotomy, instead of as a continuum, and "mighty" because both sides have eloquent and convincing proponents. I like to use, as a learning aid, and not with any claim that it reflects the true nature of reality, a continuum of choice. This continuum of choice has fate on one of its ends and choice on the other. These are the mighty opposites, choice and fate, free will and determinism. They each have powerful arguments in their behalf, and we have investigated and debated their respective contributions to criminal behavior, indeed, to all of human behavior, with much passion and for such a long time.

Aristotle thought that a science of human behavior was not possible because such a science could never account for the unpredictability of free will. Herbert Spencer, a 19th-century philosopher credited with extending evolutionary theory into the realm of human social behavior, argued that no free will is possible if human behavior conforms to scientific laws (Spencer, 1862). Stephen Hawking, the famous contemporary physicist, suggests we say that people have free will whenever we cannot predict what they will do (Hawking, 1998). But, perhaps, choice and fate do not represent such a sharp dichotomy and exists along a continuum. I prefer a middle path between these two extremes: that no science of human behavior is possible or that no free will exists. The continuum of choice is a visualization of this middle path; it portrays the concept that choice and causation may coexist in a single action.

Figure 1. <u>The Continuum of Choice</u>

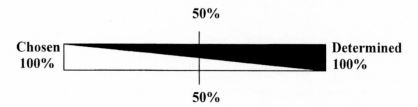

Any behavior of an individual may be understood as falling at some point along this continuum, though for our purposes we are thinking of criminal behavior. The advantage of conceiving behavior in this way is that a person's behavior may be seen as having some element of choice and some element not entirely under the person's control. For what behaviors are so freely chosen that there are no determining factors *at all*? Any behavior can be analyzed as a chain of cause-and-effect leading backwards through a person's life until some element not under his control is encountered, though it may be, perhaps, only a very small influence on the behavior under analysis. On the other side, what behaviors are so completely determined that there is no choice *at all*? There are some behaviors that we understand as completely determined, muscle reflexes, for example, but it certainly has not been demonstrated that any *criminal* behaviors would fall in this category. Though a case might be made for some types of human behavior to fall at either extreme, complete choice or complete determination, the preponderance of criminal behavior would not fall at either extreme. Even if I could imagine a criminal act that would be an exception to this point of view, it would not destroy the usefulness of the continuum as a way of organizing our thinking about the causes of crime.

This issue is important for treatment partly because most treatment providers believe that successful treatment requires choice on the part of the offender. The classical criminologists thought that crime was a calculated choice and that certain, swift, and equitable punishment was needed to prevent it. Positivist criminologists believed that crime had a cause and that the discovery of it would lead to the treatment necessary to change it. To them, criminal behavior was, to a large extent, determined.

The second core issue involves the study of crime versus the study of criminality, an issue which I like to refer to as "the acts and the actors." It is important to know that crime and criminality are not the same thing. Criminality is the propensity of an individual person to commit crimes. Thus, the study of criminality focuses on the individual offender, while the study of crime focuses on the offenses, such as aggregated crime rates. Having this distinction clearly in mind helps in understanding and evaluating explanations of crime, many of which are really explanations of criminality. Studying why crime increased during Prohibition and why it increased more in Chicago than in other cities results in a different kind of explanation, and suggests different courses of action, than does studying why certain individuals became bootleggers during the years of Prohibition. The first is a study of crime (crime rates) and the second is a study of criminality (the tendency of individuals to commit crimes). Lombroso is generally credited with having changed the focus of criminology from crime to the criminal, which Piers Bierne (1993) refers to as "the rise of *homo criminalis*," but neither kind of study is entirely satisfactory in isolation from the other.

For example, Chaiken and Chaiken (1983) suggest the following. If a city has 3,000 burglars per 100,000 population, and on average each committed two burglaries a year, the city's burglary rate would be 6,000 per 100,000 population. Alternatively, if a city has 300 burglars per 100,000 population and each committed an average of 20 burglaries per year, the burglary rate would also be 6,000 per 100,000 population. In this example, at the level of aggregate crime rates, the two cities are nearly identical.

However, this study would miss a significant difference in criminality at the level of individual analysis; criminality among the offenders in the two hypothetical cities is quite different and could very well suggest different courses of corrective action.

Studying criminality in isolation from other factors is also insufficient. Gottfredson and Hirschi (1990) call this isolation "the fundamental mistake of modern theory." As an example, they summarize a theory of crime proposed by Cohen and Felson (1979). The theory is that the commission of a crime requires: (1) a motivated offender, (2) the absence of a capable guardian, such as a vigilant parent or a police officer and (3) a suitable target. A study of the motivated offender, which would be a study of criminality, is not sufficient in itself to explain the burglary rate. We must attend to contextual and situational factors as well, such as suitability of the target and absence of a capable guardian. On the other hand, leaving out the study of the motivated offender would also lead to an insufficient understanding of the crime of burglary. "Crime and criminal behavior are confused," writes Jeffrey (1973). Are we explaining the acts or the actors? As we have seen, the classical school tended to focus on the acts and the positivist school tended to focus on the actors. To refine our thinking about the causes of crime, we must be alert to this particular confusion. Yet treatment as we are conceiving it in this book is about criminality, the propensity of an individual to commit crimes and the factors which may change or, at least, influence this propensity.

The third core issue is that of the root cause of crime. The classical criminologists were not much concerned with discovering the cause of crime as they assumed that it was a calculated choice and did not inquire further. The positivists, however, believed that criminal behavior is determined or caused by something. The search for this "thing that causes crime" has produced a very long list of candidates including, for example, poverty, genes, gangs, climate, poor parenting, low self-control, head injury, racism, the full moon, body type, role models, mental illness, childhood trauma, brain waves, peer pressure, class struggle, substance abuse, unemployment, illiteracy, social alienation, biological inferiority, the shape of the skull, low self-esteem, rejection, boredom, lead poisoning, labeling, neurotic guilt, TV, IQ, and the devil. But the search so far has not led to a single destination.

There is a complication in identifying the cause of crime, namely, that there may be more than one. In thinking about crime, or any human behavior for that matter, there is often a strong tendency to oversimplify, to seek a single underlying principle or explanation. This is the problem of the one and the many: is there a single cause of crime or are there multiple causes of crime? And if there are multiple causes of crime rather than a single cause of crime, what is to be our method of discovery?

It is my inclination to argue against a "root cause of crime." I admit that this bias is the result of my own personal experience with crime and criminals as well as my reading of the data. There have been some good efforts at a single theory of crime, most notably Sutherland's theory of differential association (1966), mainly of historical significance now, and Gottfredson and Hirschi's self-control theory, a valiant attempt at a general principle which I admire and which has much to recommend it. And there have been other efforts as well. Sutherland says:

> Just as the germ theory of disease does not explain all diseases, so it is possible that no one theory of criminal behavior will explain all criminal behavior. In that case, it will be desirable to define the area to which the theory applies, so that the several theories are coordinate and, when taken together, explain all criminal behavior [Sutherland, 1966, p. 74].

Still one might choose to search for the single cause of crime. Committed scientists certainly desire to discover universal laws. A unified theory of the universe is the grand challenge of physics, but who can name the Isaac Newton, the Max Planck, or the Albert Einstein of criminology? It may be that we cannot so name because criminology is such a young science, but it may also be because proof in the scientific sense does not answer many of the problems in criminology.

One approach is to categorize the offenders rather than the offenses. Categorizing offenders, or classification, is such a popular pastime that a good deal of the criminological literature is taken up with it. Offenders are placed into like groups in order to apply different explanations for their behavior, but also in order to make prison management more efficient, or in order to deliver treatment services more effectively. Sometimes, however, this classification is simply a way of organizing multiple explanations for crime. Looking at the problem in this way, as a problem in classification, does not eliminate all possibility of choice by the offender.

In reviewing these three core issues, we are trying to point out some fundamental difficulties with which the experts struggle, to suggest some limitations that apply to the science of crime, and to help the reader to sharpen his or her own judgment about the current state of our knowledge of the causes of crime and the treatment of criminals. We especially wish to inculcate a healthy skepticism concerning dramatic announcements of the latest cure for crime, not to mention public policies that are based upon them.

In addition to these three core issues in criminology, we will also address a number of significant treatment issues including program integrity, informed consent, treatment provider competence, and offender rights. But for now we will consider two treatment-specific issues of fundamental importance to our understanding of the treatment of offenders:

1. Is criminal behavior a mental illness?
2. When has a treatment been proven effective?

These two issues are important because they underpin all of our treatment efforts in corrections, yet they remain very debatable. The first one is an ancient debate and the second is a modern one.

Is crime a mental illness? Socrates claimed that criminals suffered from a disease of the soul, being unable to distinguish between the just and the unjust. Plato wrote that the criminal is a sick man whose recovery is a matter of importance (Eriksson, 1976). Aristotle believed that the criminal was not a sick man but made voluntary choices which were a direct outcome of his appetites and desires (Drapkin, 1989). These ancient points of view are readily apparent in contemporary debate on the treatment of criminal offenders.

A 17th-century point of view may be found in Shakespeare's *Macbeth*. The play is one of the great tales of ruthless ambition, crime, and murder. Contained within the larger plot of the play is a small dialogue on crime as illness. It is in the form of two conversations with the court physician, a "doctor of physic."

Macbeth has committed terrible crimes in pursuit of his political ambition, a string of crimes, commencing with the bloody murder of Duncan. Lady Macbeth has been an instigator, since she kindled the flame of ambition in him and then suggested the crimes. She was a coconspirator and a willing accomplice to murder. But she suffers guilt and remorse, cannot sleep, engages in compulsive hand washing, and talks out loud to herself. Her servant calls the doctor to assess and offer treatment for this strange behavior. This court physician observes Lady Macbeth, questions her servant about her, and finally concludes, "This disease is beyond my practice."

In a later passage, the doctor is questioned by Macbeth regarding his assessment of Lady Macbeth.

> MACBETH. Canst thou not minister to a mind diseased,
>   Pluck from the memory a rooted sorrow,
>   Raze out the written troubles of the brain,
>   And with some sweet oblivious antidote
>   Cleanse the stuffed bosom of that perilous stuff
>   Which weighs upon the heart?
> DOCTOR. Therein the patient
>   Must minister to himself.
> MACBETH. Throw physic to the dogs; I'll none of it.

Today few physicians would make the same assessment as the Scottish doctor in *Macbeth*. Lady Macbeth would be a good candidate for Prozac, which likely would succeed in reducing her symptoms. Lord Macbeth would be pleased and not so quick to "throw physic to the dogs." He seeks treatment for himself as well and hopes for some "sweet oblivious antidote" to cure "a mind diseased." The doctor understands that Macbeth is seeking treatment for himself as well as for Lady Macbeth because he answers that "therein the patient must minister to *him*self." With this statement, he is rejecting the concept of crime as illness. The doctor states his own view: "unnatural deeds do breed unnatural troubles/Infected minds to their deaf pillows will discharge their secrets." The doctor sees her "infected mind" as the result, not the cause, of her crimes. The play leaves Macbeth also without excuse, "the author of his proper woe." Shakespeare is generally considered to have written this play in 1606 and so I consider Macbeth's physician to be the deliverer of 17th-century views on crime as illness. Out of date? It is an old subject to be sure, antique, but not, I would argue, antiquated. Unlike Macbeth, we would not "throw physic to the dogs"; medicine has helped us too much. Yet, perhaps, this disease is beyond our practice, that is to say, that ultimately the question of crime is not a scientific question, and so there is no scientific answer. Science cannot fully account for the individual decision to commit or not to commit a crime. Therein the patient must minister to himself.

Yet, "crime is a disorder," proposes Adriane Raine in an excellent book on biology and crime: "*many* instances of repeated criminal behavior, including theft and burglary, may represent a disorder or psychopathology in much the same way that depression, schizophrenia, or other conditions currently recognized as mental disorders represent psychopathologies" (Raine, 1993, p. 2). Raine emphasizes *many* because he recognizes that not all crime is related to a mental disorder, but he thinks that much of it is. If so, it can treated. This is the approach of many psychologists and psychiatrists and is based on their observations that criminals, especially repeat offenders, differ from ordinary people in important ways, including both biological and psychological differences (for more on this subject, see Raine, 1993; Millon et al., 1998; and Burkhead, 2006). It is also based on the conclusion of many average citizens: "A person has got to be *sick* to do some of those things." Raine concludes that we need to increase our research and clinical efforts to understand and treat crime.

The modern debate about criminal offenders, like the ancient Greek one, has two sides. For example, Stanton Samenow, in his work on the criminal personality, states that the offender has freely chosen his irresponsible lifestyle and that he supports this lifestyle with thought processes which justify these choices. Criminals choose to commit crime and it is their choices which are the cause of crime (Samenow, 1984). We will not resolve the "mad or bad" debate here and now; it is sufficient for our purposes to remind the reader that this debate, "is criminal behavior a mental illness?" continues in the background of any discussion of offender treatment and its effectiveness.

When is a treatment for criminal offenders proven effective? Understanding recidivism is important for our purposes because the effectiveness of treatment is usually determined by measuring and comparing recidivism rates. *Recidivism* means the rearrest, reconviction, or reimprisonment of former inmates. Recidivism is the critical outcome variable in corrections, but assessing recidivism is a complex measurement problem.

The phrase *recidivism rate* is something of a misnomer since the recidivism rate as usually reported is the *proportion* of released offenders who reoffend, such as 60 percent or 51 percent, and not the *rate* at which they reoffend. Nevertheless, a reduction in the recidivism rate of offenders, or a specified group of offenders, is the universally accepted way of measuring the effectiveness of treatment.

A criminal offender may reoffend, may be rearrested, may be reconvicted, and may be reimprisoned. The reoffense rate, the true rate of recidivism, is unknown since, unless the offender has been rearrested, we don't know what he has or has not done. Rearrest is generally considered to be the best measure of recidivism because it is closest to the reoffend rate, or true rate. There are some problems, however, with using the rearrest rate, not only because it doesn't include offenses which did not result in an arrest, but also because one arrest may be the result of multiple charges, because an arrest may not result in a conviction, and because, of course, an innocent person may be arrested. Reconviction or reimprisonment rates can be of interest, for example, if you want to project and estimate of the cost of crime, or how many new prison beds will be needed in the future, or what the burden of recidivists on the court system might be. Reimprisonment rates are the most conservative estimate of recidivism and reimprisonment data are often easier for researchers to obtain.

There are four important issues in determining what a reported recidivism rate is really telling us.

The definition of *recidivism* is important as there are several choices. "Rearrest" is the most common definition of *recidivism*, but "reimprisonment" is also often used. Some studies include such definitions as prison rule violations and probation or parole violations which result in reimprisonment even though these violations are not in themselves crimes.

How the recidivists are identified is also important. Some studies only search rearrest or reincarceration in the same state in which the offender was originally incarcerated. This, of course, leaves out reimprisonment in another state, reimprisonment in the federal prison system, and incarceration in a local jail (where some offenders serve short sentences), and would certainly produce a dubious recidivism rate. It is important to note what databases were searched in determining the reported recidivism rate.

Another vital issue is the length of the follow up period. How long must an offender go before he can be considered a nonrecidivist? Three months? Six months? Two years? Twenty years? To be totally accurate, we must follow him to the end of his life. But, besides being impracticable, this is not really necessary. While one-year recidivism studies can produce meaningful data (Mackenzie et al., 1995), most rearrests occur within two years of release, so that studies reporting recidivism rates that used follow-up periods of two to five years are considered to be reasonably accurate and worth paying attention to (Schmidt and Witte, 1989). Follow-up periods less than a year are frequently reported in the literature, but these should not be considered as strong evidence of treatment effects.

The size of the sample is important in weighing the value of a reported recidivism rate. Those responsible for treatment programs are often anxious to report reduced recidivism as a result of their programs and too often report recidivism rates with very small samples of inmates. For example, a published study of prison religious programs analyzed groups of inmates participating in programs with groups of less than ten (Johnson, Larson, and Pitts, 1997). Comparison group sizes of less than 30 produce doubtful statistical comparisons while large groups of inmates increase our confidence in the reported rates.

For a recidivism rate to have any meaning, it must be compared to something. If a recidivism rate of 40 percent is reported, what does this mean? Is 40 percent good, or bad, surprising, or exactly what you would expect? Recidivism studies are often susceptible to the apples and oranges fallacy. For example, a sex offenders treatment program may report a recidivism rate that is considerably lower than the recidivism rate for the general prison population as evidence of its treatment effectiveness. This would not be a valid comparison as the recidivism rate of sex offenders is typically lower that of the entire offender population. An appropriate comparison group in this case would be sex offenders who received the treatment compared to sex offenders who did not receive the treatment. A true experimental design would include random assignment of offenders to treatment and nontreatment groups. However, in the field of correctional treatment, random assignment to treatment groups is almost never the case and this flaw is one of the reasons that there is so much debate about the effectiveness of treatment. A valid scientific test is hard to carry out in a correctional environment, and may be unethical as well, opening the way to a tangled wilderness of technical and inconclusive debate about what might constitute a valid comparison and what statistical methods might produce a meaningful test of significance. It may be unethical to randomly assign dangerous offenders to treatment and non-treatment groups and then release them, or to deny participation in available treatment to an inmate who wants it (Marshall and Pithers, 1994). Others believe that without random assignment, our conclusions will always be arguable (Miner, 1997; Quinsey, 1998).

Meta-analyses are one attempt to cope with this problem. If there is a large number of studies, all of which are flawed in some way (but not in the same way) and they all point in the same direction, or mostly in the same direction, that is, towards the same conclusion, our confidence in the results can be increased. This is known as having convergent validity. In a meta-analysis, a group of studies is reviewed. Ideally, the individual studies are scrutinized for appropriate methodology and those that are below standard are eliminated. An average recidivism rate across all of the retained studies is calculated. For example, Hanson and Bussiere (1998) published a meta-analysis of the recidivism of sexual offenders. They reviewed 61 individual studies and found that, on average, the sexual offender recidivism rate was 13.4 percent, though some subgroups of sexual offenders recidivated at higher rates (a detailed discussion of sexual offenders may be found in chapter seven). We can have more confidence in this result than in the results of a single flawed research study.

In considering recidivism in general, it also helps to look at a larger picture. The Bureau of Justice Statistics (BJS) released a report in 2002 on recidivism. The report stated: "Among 272,111 prisoners released in 15 states in 1994, 67.5 percent were rearrested within three years" (Langan and Levin, p. 1). This recidivism rate compares to a recidivism rate of 62.5 percent from a similar study released in 1983, indicating that the recidivism rate in the decade of the 1990s had increased slightly. The highest rearrest rates were for motor vehicle thieves (78.8 percent), and murderers had the lowest rearrest rate (40.7 percent). Property offenders (73.8 percent) had a higher rearrest rate than did violent offenders (61.7 percent). Men (68.4 percent) had a higher rearrest rate than women (57.6 percent). State and FBI criminal history databases were examined to identify recidivists. Langan and Levin also reported that these recidivism rates understated the true rate of recidivism because all arrests made by local authorities were not properly reported to state or federal agencies. The authors also reported data on reconviction, reimprisonment, and return to prison with or without a new prison sentence. Thus, we have a complete report including definitions of *recidivism*, how recidivists were identified, sample size, length of follow-up, and valid comparison.

The effect of prison or jail sentences on recidivism is an important issue to those concerned with public safety and the cost-effectiveness of incarceration. Opinions are divided between those advocating longer sentences in the interest of public safety, and those promoting shorter sentences with less cost to the public, under the assumption that longer prison terms will not reduce recidivism rates. In the BJS study cited above, the authors concluded there was no evidence that longer sentences *increased* recidivism and that "the evidence was mixed regarding whether serving more time reduced recidivism" (Langan and Levin, p. 2.). Thus, the debate will continue. But, for now, the reader is equipped with a more sophisticated view of reported recidivism rates, especially those which point towards treatment effectiveness, by paying close attention to the definition of recidivism, the method by which *recidivists* are identified, the size of the sample, the length of the follow-up, and the validity of the comparison.

In science, we endeavor to discover cause by employing the classical experimental design. In this design, subjects are selected that do not differ from each other in any way that would be important. The subjects are then randomly assigned to two different groups. One of the groups receives an intervention and the other group (the control group) does not. If, after the intervention, the two groups differ from each other on an important characteristic, this difference is directly attributable to the intervention. The intervention caused it. This is so because the random assignment of subjects to the two groups controlled all of the variation between them, except for the intervention. A major obstacle to discovering the cause of crime is the ironic ethical predicament that immediately presents itself when we attempt to use the classical experimental design to discover the causes of crime. It is ironic because the application of objective science is prevented by our moral standards, our subjective judgment of the wrongness of such an application in this case. For example, let's design an experiment to determine the cause of crime. First we select a group of perfectly normal adolescent boys. Next we randomly assign them to one of two groups. Then we expose the subjects in one of the two groups to negative criminal role models for an extended period of time. The other group does not receive this "intervention." We then follow up on the subjects for a significant length of time and discover (or not) that criminal offenses among the subjects in the intervention group is significantly higher than among the members of the second, or control, group. Of course, in the scientific course of things, further experimentation would be undertaken to replicate the experiment, to confirm the results, and to refine the findings. You might already be thinking of ways to refine the original experiment. For example, what would happen if you varied the length of the exposure to the criminal role models? But the point is that this series of experiments could be a definitive study on the cause of crime, except that it would be clearly unethical to conduct it! We could not agree to do anything to the subjects that might instigate or increase criminal behavior. But this is ironic since to apply objective scientific methods to determine the cause of immoral behavior is, we have decided, immoral! Thus, we are again warned that the explanation of crime is not entirely a scientific matter.

There are, however, ways around this dilemma which can provide useful information. One way to escape the dilemma is to start with a group of adolescents who have already engaged in criminal behavior. Then randomly assign them to two groups. Next, one of the groups receives an intervention which is designed to *reduce* criminal behavior. Let's say, for example, exposure to positive, prosocial role models. Then, after a follow-up period, any significant differences in criminal offenses between the two groups could be attributed to the intervention. We could then *infer* that role models and criminal behavior are related, even that role models have an effect on criminal behavior, but we have not found the *cause* of crime with the same confidence that we would have if we had conducted the unethical classical experiment described above. In fact, much of the research on the causes of crime is of this second type. Another type of research employed to circumvent the ethical dilemma is to compare groups of offenders with groups of nonoffenders and try to discover the differences between them. This type of research produces lists of variables, or characteristics, that are related, or associated, with criminal behavior, but this research does not demonstrate the cause of anything, not in the scientific sense. Since most of the research on criminal behavior is of these last two types, it is not hard to see why there is so much argument and disagreement about what the research has actually proven about the causes of crime or about the efficacy of particular interventions.

One. The Principal Issues

Criminologists inform us that the purposes of punishment are four:

1. Incapacitation: The individual offender cannot commit more crimes while he is incarcerated or otherwise incapacitated (such as medication, castration, and psychosurgery).

2. Retribution: The individual offender gets "what he deserves" and other people observe offenders receiving their "just deserts."

3. Deterrence: Individual deterrence means that the individual offender is deterred from committing more crimes by punishment. General deterrence means that other people are deterred from committing crimes by observing the punishment.

4. Rehabilitation: The rehabilitative ideal is that human behavior is the result of antecedent causes that may be known by objective analysis and that permit scientific control. The offender should be treated and not punished (S. Reid, 1994).

The first three purposes of punishment are very worthy subjects for analysis and discussion, but this book is about the last one, rehabilitation. How have we tried to rehabilitate prisoners in the past? How effective have these efforts been? Should we even be trying to rehabilitate criminal offenders? What is the future of corrections?

Chapter Two

Treatment and Punishment:
A Brief History of
the American Prison

*The degree of civilization in a society may be determined by enter-
ing its prisons.*
— Dostoevsky, *The House of the Dead*

The criminal justice system in the United States is permeated with
ambivalence about the purpose of imprisonment. Is imprisonment for punishment, for deterrence, for incapacitation, or for treatment and rehabilitation? There is also the irony that what was originally intended as the chief
means of reforming the offender, a period of solitary confinement in prison,
has now become the chief means of punishing him. This ambivalence about
punishment and treatment can also be seen, not only in the criminal justice system as a whole, but also in the structure and organization of any
individual prison, where both punishment and treatment regularly take
place, side by side. In the beginning, prison was for detaining the offender
while his punishment was decided upon, the punishment usually being corporal or financial. But, since the 16th century, we have had the suggestion
that imprisonment can be used to improve the person confined and thus
prevent further law breaking by that person. That idea was closely followed
by the proposition that imprisonment ought to replace corporal punishment entirely because such punishment is inhumane and not rehabilitative

of the offender. What eventually followed this 18th-century Enlightenment thinking was what the renowned social philosopher Michel Foucault has called "the great confinement," which took place in the 19th and 20th centuries and during which corporal punishment became carceral punishment (Foucault, 1975).

At the beginning of the 21st century, some analysts of our system profess the idea that incarceration is satisfactory for all purposes at once: it does punish the prisoner (though many would argue not enough), it does incapacitate the prisoner (though many would argue not for long enough), and it does include, or at least offer, some treatment (in most prisons). Others argue that treatment and punishment are incompatible and can't be done at the same time. Some have proposed that punishment is a type of treatment because its intent is to change the prisoner's behavior, and any such method having the purpose of changing the offender's behavior is a treatment. Others are adamant that the prisoner must be punished in any case, whether he is changed or not. Some argue that imprisonment as punishment is important and must be retained because of its deterrent effect on others; it serves as an example. Others will posit that some offenders should receive treatment, some should receive punishment, and some should be incapacitated because, whatever the cause of their behavior, they are dangerous to other people. In this way the argument about punishment and treatment can be reduced to an issue of classification. The purpose, and the efficacy, of imprisonment continues to be fiercely and divisively debated into the 21st century.

The first incarceration may have happened entirely by accident. Perhaps a large stone fell across the mouth of a cave, thus trapping some Neolithic felon inside. When the people of the clan noticed a beneficial effect from the fortuitous imprisonment of a troublesome tribal member, they decided to make it a deliberate action the next time. Or perhaps it was a sudden insight, like the invention of the wheel is supposed to have been, the invention of the jail cell. Or maybe it was the result of a long-running discussion in the tribal councils about what to do with offenders against the welfare of the tribe. It could have been simply evolutionary pressure: certain tribesmen had to be stopped so that the others could survive as a group. We may wonder if they worried, like we do today, about the conditions inside the cave and the ultimate effects of the confinement on the prisoner. Might they may have debated among themselves the purpose of their actions? Was it to protect the group from some antisocial scoundrel who was otherwise unstoppable, short of killing him? Or was it an example to the rest of the clan of what would happen to them if they offended the community? Or was it to make the miscreant suffer for his misdeeds? Or was it to facilitate a change of heart in the caveman offender by making him reflect upon his crimes in solitude? Or was it simply to buy time while the tribal elders decided what to do? We don't know and, in the absence of verifiable facts, we may have imagined too much altogether. Imprisonment, in any case, is most likely not prehistoric but is one of the products of civilization. We don't know who first had the idea of a prison, but we do know that the use of imprisonment is ancient. And the debate about its purpose and its proper conditions has been waged formally since at least the third century CE and remains unabated into our present century.

However they got started, prisons appear to be at least as old as human civilization. Ladislao Thot mentions that jails existed in ancient Babylon. They were deep, cisternlike structures and the most infamous one was known as "the lake of the lions" (cited in Drapkin, 1989). In the Book of Genesis, Joseph is thrown into prison, "a place where the king's prisoners are bound," by his master, Potiphar, somewhere around 1895 BCE. The scriptures say that Joseph impressed the "keeper of the prison," who put him in charge of the other prisoners, making Joseph one of the first *trusties* (a term used in the early part of the 20th century for an inmate trusted to run some part of the prison). Even that is an old idea!

The first Chinese imperial code from the fourth century BCE was called the Code of Li k'vei, and provided laws governing the use of prisons (Drapkin, 1989). Socrates was in prison in Athens in 399 BCE, where he was visited by his friends and later drank the hemlock. Barrabas, a criminal and "a notable prisoner," was released from jail in Jerusalem in a famous inmate exchange made by Pontius Pilate around 33 CE. Ulpian, who wrote on law and justice between 211 and 222 CE, and who was the most influential of the Roman jurists, declared: "Governors are in the habit of condemning men to be kept in prison or in chains, but they ought not to do this, for punishments of this type are forbidden. Prison indeed ought to be employed for confining men, not for punishing them" (cited in Peters, 1998, p. 20).

Ulpian's principle, that prison ought to be only for pretrial confinement, and not for the punishment itself, remained our dominant idea about imprisonment until the Enlightenment in the 18th century. Generally, prisons and jails were for pretrial confinement, for debtors, for prisoners of war, and for political prisoners, "the king's enemies." The punishment for crimes was either financial, such as fines or confiscation of property, or physical, such as branding, whipping, mutilation, or execution. By the 14th century in Europe, the most common penalty mentioned in the records was death (Korn and McCorkle, 1959). There were some exceptions, as confinement, forced labor while confined, and forced servitude were sometimes handed down as punishment, but this was not usually the case. In 1275, for example, in England's Statute of Westminster, there appears a prison sentence of two years for rape, but this sentence was notable for being exceptional (Eriksson, 1976).

In the 18th century, there appeared some eloquent arguments against the use of physical punishments. Cesare Beccaria became the most famous, but there were precursors to Beccaria, such as Anton Praetorius, a Calvinist theologian who published a book in 1613 protesting the torture of witches in Germany. This movement gained momentum and led reformers of the justice system in the direction of incarceration as the appropriate response to criminal offenses. Hudson writes:

> The 200 years from the middle of the eighteenth century (approximately) to the beginning of the third quarter of the twentieth century (approximately) is seen as a distinct period of penal modernism, a period characterized by two linked phenomena:
> 1. emergence of imprisonment as the main form of punishment for routine crimes;
> 2. a penal goal of bringing about change in the offender, and the use of the emergent human/social sciences to that end [Hudson, 2002, p. 235].

We could include in our brief history of prisons a list of the most notorious ones, many of which the reader will recognize. For example, there is the Tower of London, from which its first known prisoner, Bishop Flambard of Durham, escaped in 1100 CE. There is the Bridge of Sighs in Venice, built in the 16th century to connect the courts with the state prison. Convicted prisoners were marched from the Doge's palace directly to the dungeon over the "bridge of sighs." There is the Bastille, built near Paris as a fortress in the 14th century and used as a prison by the 17th century, and which held some famous prisoners, including Voltaire and the Marquis de Sade. There was Reading Gaol in England, made infamous by Oscar Wilde, and the Chateau d'If in France, the real setting for the fictional *The Count of Monte Cristo*. There were the infamous prison hulks, dismasted vessels lying in harbors and housing convicts, used by the English beginning in 1776 and still used well into the 19th century.

From more recent times, there were the Gulags, established in Russia in 1929 and made notorious by the novelist Alexander Solzhenitsyn. There is the famous American prison Alcatraz, an old military disciplinary barracks in the San Francisco Bay, which was turned into a federal prison from 1934 until 1963, and which held such renowned inmates as Al Capone and Robert Stroud, the Birdman of Alcatraz. There was Devil's Island in French Guyana, from which escaped the famous Papillon in the 1940s. There was Robben Island in South Africa, which held Nelson Mandela. We could also add the Lubyanka in Moscow and the "Hanoi Hilton" in North Vietnam. There is also Attica, famous for its riots in 1971, Sing Sing, which has been open in New York since 1828, and San Quentin, built in 1852 and today the oldest prison in California. There is Folsom Prison, which has housed inmates since 1880 and was made famous in part by the popular music of Johnny Cash. And now we may add the "supermax" prisons, like Marion in Illinois, Florence Federal Prison in Colorado, and Oak Park Heights in Minnesota, "state of the art" prisons of the last decade of the twentieth century. Most recently we may add the infamous prisons Abu Ghraib in Baghdad and Gitmo in Guantánamo Bay. This list is certainly not exhaustive, but it does give you a sense of how long and how widespread have been our use and misuse of prisons. Our cultural history is full of them.

The American prison is, of course, rooted in Europe. According to Eriksson (1976), the first early Enlightenment idea about punishment was that petty offenders and vagrants should be treated so that they would not become more serious offenders. This idea was gradually extended to the concept that serious offenders should be treated so that they would not commit more crimes. Under the influence of the Enlightenment, the purpose of the law became "amendment" as well as punishment.

The Treatment of Criminal Offenders

Among the most important European precursors of the American prison were the bridewells in England. The first known house of correction in London opened in 1555 in the old Bridewell Palace. It was established under the influence of Bishop Nicolas Ridley and was intended to keep vagrants, beggars, and harlots. The principal purpose of Bridewell was to address the rising problem of vagrancy and its attendant ills. Previously used physical punishments seemed not to be turning the tide of vagrancy and petty crime in England. Many of the penal reforms which became widespread in later centuries were suggested in the organization of Bridewell, which was based on the principles of discipline and hard work. There was a spinning mill where the women inmates worked and, for the men, a metalworking and carpentry shop, a flour mill, and a bakery. All the inmates were paid wages for their work and had to pay for room and board since Bridewell was self supporting. So successful was this effort that it was copied in other parts of England and such houses of correction became known generally as "bridewells." In 1576, Elizabeth I established a law in which every county in England had to have a house of correction; its main purpose was to put vagrants back to work. The general idea was that inmates would earn their living, they would be reformed through discipline and hard work, and they would set an example for other vagrants and petty offenders (Eriksson, 1976). "The distinctive purpose of these institutions was to reform as well as punish" (McGowen, 1995, p. 75). But by the middle of the 1770s these houses of correction had lost their reformatory character and returned to physical punishments. Originally intended for petty offenders, more serious offenders began to be sent to the bridewells and physical punishment reemerged, along with overcrowding.

The *rasphuis* (for men) and the *spinhuis* (for women) were houses of correction established by the Dutch at the end of the 16th century. In 1588, a judge and an Amsterdam court had refused to sentence a 16-year-old thief to death as the law required. The case was referred to the city council and an Amsterdam alderman named Jan Spiegel wrote a response to the situation in which he outlined how a *rasphuis* should work. Both Sellin (1944) and Eriksson (1976) consider this remarkable treatise to be one of the most important documents in the history of penology. Spiegel wrote that work would be the central feature of the institution, but that the treatment of the inmates should be, not to humiliate them, but to restore them to health, to teach them a trade, and to instill in them the fear of God. Spiegel's efforts eventually resulted in the first *rasphuis* being established at an old convent and opened for inmates in 1596. The rasphuis and the spinhuis were not merely for punishment but were also for the reform and correction of the inmates. As well as the work activities, there were also structured leisure activities, including competitions and games. These houses of correction lasted in Amsterdam until the 1890s. They were considered remarkable institutions and were visited by many foreigners, including the great English reformer John Howard. They were copied throughout Europe and were considered very successful (Eriksson, 1976).

The Benedictine monk Pater Jean Mabillon had written and published in 1724 a specific plan to apply the monastic life to criminal offenders. He proposed that the basic tenets of reforming the criminal offender were isolation, work, silence, and prayer. He also recommended that punishments be individualized. Even though most of his work was published posthumously and was not widely known until the 19th century, his general ideas about prisons appeared again and again in the writings of reformers (Sellin, 1944).

Penal reform in Europe in the 18th century was affected by the pressure of steadily increasing crime and the burgeoning number of prisoners, compounded by the presence of debtors in the prisons, along with pressure to reduce physical punishments and physical suffering (McGowen, 1995). Philosophers of the Enlightenment, including Montesquieu, Voltaire, and Beccaria, had set the stage for change in the justice system. Within this atmosphere of penal reform, the Ghent octagon was opened in 1775. It was new in both its physical design and in the idea of classifying prisoners by type. The Flemish provincial parliament declared that the prison ought to be able to separate various kinds of prisoners and to isolate each individual at night. The architect designed an octagonal structure surrounding a yard which allowed for the prisoners to be separated into eight different groups. The various sections of the Ghent octagon radiated out from a central yard. Impetus for this prison came from a Flemish politician, Vilain XIII, who wrote a "Memorandum on the means of correcting prisoners and idlers to their own advantage and of making them useful to society." The regimen of the prison was based on work as social rehabilitation and the teaching of trades to the inmates as the main activity. This type of prison was copied all over Europe and in the United States. Eriksson wrote that it "spread almost like an epidemic" (Eriksson, p. 22).

The prison at Ghent was influenced by Jeremy Bentham's Panopticon concept, introduced in 1791. Bentham proposed a prison in which the cells radiated outwards from a central point. From this central point, an "all-seeing" officer could supervise the prisoners. The Panopticon became famous as an object of discussion about the purpose of imprisonment, the treatment of prisoners, and prison architecture. Milbank Prison in England was modeled after Bentham's Panopticon, but it was severely criticized as too expensive and too ugly and was eventually abandoned. Though a Panopticon, as Bentham envisioned it, was never actually built, a number of prisons were strongly influenced by his ideas (see Eriksson, pp. 46–47; Burkhead, 2006).

John Howard was a wealthy man who had been appointed to the position of sheriff of Bedfordshire in England. He was also a pious man who was a friend of John Wesley. Upon taking up his post as sheriff, he toured his domain and was appalled at the conditions of the jails in Bedford. He subsequently proposed a list of reforms which impressed the local judiciary. They decided, however, that Howard must find precedents for his reforms in other counties. So he set off in 1773 on a long tour of prisons in England. He then decided to visit prisons throughout Europe. He collected his notes into a book called *The State of the Prisons in England and Wales, with preliminary Observations and an Account of some Foreign Prisons*, which he had printed in 1777 at his own expense. This work eventually resulted in important reforms of the penal system which made Howard famous in the history of prisons (see McGowen, 1995; Eriksson, 1976). Howard believed in the value of imprisonment as a way to reform offenders and that it was the appropriate response to criminal behavior, but he pointed out that prisons and jails in England were rife with abuses and that these institutions must be corrected and improved. He was tireless in his efforts to accomplish these reforms. It was Howard who coined the term *penitentiary*, meaning a place for moral reformation as well as confinement (Johnson and Wolfe, 2003). "No man did more to improve the treatment of prisoners than did John Howard" (Eriksson, 1976, p. 42).

Against this European background of Enlightenment penal reform, the American penitentiary system was initiated at the Walnut Street Jail in

Philadelphia in 1792, with an addition to the jail which was called "a penitentiary house." It consisted of sixteen single cells constructed in the yard of the jail. The driving force behind this development was a group of Quakers who had founded a prisoners aid society, the first of its kind in the world, and who were in contact with John Howard. Quaker reformers in the American colonies had battled against the British law, which they viewed as too harsh. They believed that the severity of the legal code was a part of the problem in stemming the tide of crime. The Americans also wanted to reduce the reliance of the justice system on executions to enforce the laws of the land. These considerations led to the acceptance of incarceration for long periods of time as the alternative to execution and other brutal physical punishments. Early American critics of the criminal justice system included Benjamin Rush and William Penn. Eriksson (1976) argues that the Philadelphia reformers had "merely copied European theory as well as practice" (p. 45), since England had already built three solitary confinement prisons, and since these ideas go back in Europe at least to Mabillon. The Quaker prisoner aid society published in 1788 a famous tract in which they announced the conclusion, after "much study of prisons," that solitary confinement to hard labor and total abstinence from alcohol was the most efficacious method of reforming offenders. In fact, according to Sellin (1953), not many prisoners were actually sentenced to solitary confinement and hard labor as most were allowed to mingle with others during the day and were confined in single cells only at night.

Nevertheless, this type of imprisonment became known as the solitary system, sometimes called the Pennsylvania system, and was much publicized and debated in the United States and throughout Europe. Increasing crime resulted in two more prisons in the Pennsylvania system, Western Penitentiary, near Pittsburgh, completed in 1826, and, three years later, Eastern Penitentiary, also called Cherry Hill. Western Penitentiary was built using many of Bentham's ideas in architecture. It was designed to keep the inmates in solitary confinement, and, even though the inmates found many ingenious ways of communicating, using pipes and walls, they nevertheless suffered in small dark cells for long periods of time. These prisons received wide publicity and many visitors including the Marquis de Lafayette, Charles Dickens, and Alexis de Tocqueville. Visitors were often critical of the severity of the confinement. They frequently noted that the regime of solitary confinement was not practicable and was not strictly followed. But these prisons had supporters as well as detractors.

Meanwhile, crime was growing in New York state, too, and new prisons were needed. The solitary system was considered a failure by many observers, so it was modified in 1821 to a new system that generally became known as the Auburn system (it would also be called the congregate system, the silent system, and the New York system). In the Auburn system, complete silence was observed and violations of this rule were punished by flogging. Inmates were required to keep their eyes downcast when walking and to walk in a measured coordinated gait known as "lockstep." They worked in small, well-supervised shops during the day and were locked in solitary cells at night. It was recommended that the prisoners be divided into three groups: hardened criminals held in solitary confinement all the time, a second group held in solitary confinement three days a week, and a third group consisting mainly of young prisoners held in solitary one day a week.

In 1825, Warden Elam Lynds left Auburn and went to Ossining, New York, to build and operate a new prison, which he built with convict labor and which was given its Indian name, Sing Sing, meaning "stone by stone." He took the Auburn, or "silent," system with him. The prisoners were kept in individual cells and silence reigned throughout the system. The guards wore moccasins to muffle their footsteps and to keep the silence. Demetz and Blouet, who visited the institutions in 1837, argued that the silent system was invariably unsuccessful in preventing the inmates entirely from communicating with each other. The rule of silence can never be totally enforced and cruel means are required to make it work at all including corporal punishment, flogging, and confinement in solitary on reduced rations (see Eriksson, 1976). They saw a number of prisons using the silent system. They also noted that the general public in America had protested the harsh conditions in these prisons, resulting in an amelioration of the conditions there.

Alexis de Tocqueville, who visited the prison, described the results of this system of penal practice:

> This experiment, of which such favorable results had been anticipated, proved fatal for the majority of the prisoners. It devours the victim

incessantly and unmercifully; it does not reform, it kills. The unfortunate prisoners submitted to this experiment wasted away so obviously that their guards were appalled. Their lives appeared to be in danger if they remained imprisoned under the same treatment; five of them had already died in one year; their spiritual condition was no less disturbing: one of them went out of his mind; another took advantage of a moment when a guard brought him something to hurl himself out of his cell, running an almost certain risk of a fatal fall" [quoted in Eriksson, p. 49].

In 1834, William Crawford had published a report surveying the two systems of prison discipline, the silent and the separate systems. Both systems emphasized work habits but the silent system at Auburn professed less enthusiasm and confidence in the possibility of reformation for the offender. In the separate system, there was more emphasis on reforming the prisoners. The separate system "isolated the convict for long hours in his own cell to commune with his conscience" (McGowen, p. 91). Architects and designers were busily employed creating prisons that would make it difficult for prisoners to communicate with each other and to prevent them any contact or even a glimpse of the outside world. Rothman writes: "In the 1820s and 1830s, when democratic principles were receiving their most enthusiastic endorsement, when the 'common people' were participating fully in politics and electing Andrew Jackson their president, incarceration became the central feature of criminal justice" (Rothman, 1995, p. 100). This is the beginning of Foucault's "great confinement."

The respective merits of the New York, or silent, system and the Pennsylvania, or separate, system were the subject of a fierce debate with critics and defenders, even though the two systems had much in common (Rothman, in Morris and Rothman, 1995). They both emphasized hard work, prison discipline, obedience, and isolation. They also shared the rehabilitative ideal that prisoners could be reformed, though the silent system was somewhat less enthusiastic on this point. In the end, the New York, or Auburn, system prevailed because it was more cost-effective. The workshops seemed to make prison labor more profitable. However, both systems went awry after the Civil War. "Prisons in the post Civil War era became modern, that is, characterized by overcrowding, brutality, and disorder" (Rothman, 1995, p. 112).

During this same period, there was what Eriksson calls one of the "most remarkable experiments in the history of penology" taking place in another part of the world (Eriksson, p. 81). This experiment is worth mentioning in a history of prisons because many of its ideas influence penology even today. Norfolk Island was a small island northeast of Sydney, Australia, which had been used as a prison colony since the end of the 18th century. In 1840, Alexander Maconochie arrived there as the new superintendent. Maconochie was a former naval captain who had made some experiments ameliorating the harsh discipline found on ships, such as, flogging and keelhauling, by reasoning with the men. On one commission, rather than canceling shore leave, which was a common practice while in North America, he made the continuation of shore leave dependent on no instances of desertion. This procedure worked quite well to prevent desertion. He called his procedure "collective responsibility." The Admiralty, however, was not entirely happy with his experiments and he was not encouraged to continue. After leaving the Navy, he became a geography professor.

While making a tour of Tasmania, his interest in penology was piqued by the large number of transportees there and the conditions under which they lived. He published a pamphlet on the subject which was widely read. He argued that the purpose of the punishment was to reform the individual if possible. Eventually, his request to be posted as superintendent of the Norfolk Island Prison was granted and he had the opportunity to test his theories. In a paper entitled "Secondary Punishment, the Mark System" and published in 1848, he wrote: "We should in every case seek primarily to reform the individual criminal" (cited in Eriksson, p. 83). He also wrote that convicts should be punished for the past and trained for the future. He argued for use of the indeterminate sentence. Sentences should not be for a fixed period of time, but should be in force until a task is completed. A convict should have to earn a particular number of marks, or credits, which could be earned through work and through good behavior. These are the same concepts as our modern rules for *good time* (time off a sentence for good behavior) and *gain time* (time off a sentence for work performed). The prisoner's sentence would be over when he had earned the specified number of marks. Thus, Maconochie argued that a prisoner should not be sentenced to three years or ten years or twenty years but should instead be sentenced to three thousand marks or five thousand marks, and so on. The prisoner should also be moved to positions of greater freedom as he accumulated marks. There were three stages in Maconochie's system. In the first stage, the prisoner cannot use his marks as he wishes, but in the second stage, he can. In the third stage, each member of a small group shared responsibility for the whole group. The convict should also be required to pay for his food and lodging. These ideas were not new and had been expressed by Howard as well as by Montesquieu, Beccaria, and Bentham, but Maconochie actually put them into practice. Norfolk Island was used for the most hardened criminals and was a brutal penal colony when Maconochie arrived there. His methods were very controversial and created heated debate and scathing criticism at home in England. He received high praise for his success in creating a safe, responsible, and non-brutal prison colony environment. The soldiers stationed on the island were not used during his tenure and the prisoners discharged under him had behaved very well; only a small number had relapsed into crime (Eriksson, p. 87). In 1844, he was removed from his position by the government after a firestorm of criticism. After leaving the island, he briefly held a position as superintendent in a prison in England, but mainly he campaigned tirelessly for prison reform. He died poor and mostly unappreciated in 1860. His life and work are chronicled in John Vincent Barry's biography, *Alexander Maconochie of Norfolk Island* (1958), and in Norval Morris's interesting historical novel and comments, entitled *Maconochie's Gentlemen* (2002).

Sir Walter Frederick Crofton was commissioned by the government to study the conditions of the Irish prisons. He was familiar with Maconochie's ideas and thought along the same lines. He made his study and instituted efficiently organized reforms in the Irish prisons beginning in 1855. He used a mark system, created an intermediate stage, and an open institution in which about 100 prisoners lived in an open barracks with minimal staff supervision. He was criticized but was a skillful defender of his views and methods. Crofton's system received a lot of attention from observers, even from different countries, and became "a minor mecca [sic] for penologists from all parts of the world" (Eriksson, p. 96). Ideas implemented by Maconochie and Crofton are still very much a part of our modern prison system.

Eriksson says that "national discussion on penal problems, as well as the international exchange of ideas, were very lively during the nineteenth century. A number of books and theses were published in the major world languages, and conferences, large and small, succeeded one another" (1976, p. 98). Within this atmosphere of debate and reform, Enoch Cobb Wines and Theodore Dwight were commissioned by the New York Prison Association to survey the prison system and to evaluate current penal practices. They submitted a massive report in 1867: *Report on the Prisons and Reformatories of the United Sates and Canada*. This report found much to disparage in the American prison system, from the physical facilities to overcrowding to the lack of oversight (Rotman, 1995). But "the critical finding was that not one of the state prisons in the United States was seeking reformation of its inmates as a primary goal or deploying efficient means to pursue reformation" (Rotman, p. 154). They outlined the shortcomings of the existing system and proposed many reforms including the abolition of corporal punishment, training for the guards, and programs to prepare prisoners for release by moving them progressively through stages of greater and greater freedom. Their reforms were inspired by the work of Maconochie and Crofton. "Their report heralded a new era in American penology, marked by the heavy emphasis placed on reform of the inmate..." (Johnson and Wolfe, 2003, p. 192).

Along with Wines and Dwight, Zebulon Brockway was one of the most outspoken and influential reformers. In 1876, Brockway was appointed as superintendent at Elmira in New York. He was given a free hand by the New York state legislature to implement his ideas about prisons. Brockway had previously espoused his ideas at a conference held by Wines in Cincinnati in 1870. Brockway believed in indeterminate sentencing with release based on participation in rehabilitative activities rather than on serving a specified length of time. He also felt that intellectual education must take a prominent place in the reform of prisoners. He implemented a period of conditional release before final release.

Brockway wanted to work with first offenders in the age range 16–30 years old, but, in reality, many of his prisoners were older recidivists and more serious offenders. He wanted a minimum sentence to be fixed by the institution and the main focus of the treatment to be to change the convicts' character. He believed that the basis of classification should be character rather than conduct. He kept the inmates occupied with strenuous labor and structured recreation. He borrowed ideas from Maconochie and Crofton. Inmates were paid for their work, including schoolwork. Vocational training was emphasized. Elmira eventually reached a population of 1,700 inmates and had 34 major trades represented (Eriksson, 1976). It inspired a reformatory movement and similar institutions were created in other parts of the country (Rotman, 1995). The reformatory received many visitors and was the subject of much debate. Its detractors complained that discipline was mild and reduced the deterrent effect of prison. They also argued that prisoners had good jobs while honest noncriminal people did not; it took bread from the mouths of honest workmen. Critics also pointed out correctly that Elmira supporters offered overly optimistic recidivism data since they counted only inmates who returned to Elmira and did not count inmates who were sent to other prisons and institutions. Thus, the claim that Elmira drastically reduced recidivism were not very accurate. It was not long before Elmira was badly overcrowded with older, more serious offenders. In later years, Brockway was distressed to see successors gradually dismantle his reformatory. He also became discouraged about reforming criminals, partly due to the influence of Cesare Lombroso, whose "criminal man" was not amenable to rehabilitation (Eriksson, 1976).

Evelyn Ruggles-Brise was one of the enthusiastic admirers of Elmira. He was Director of Prisons in England and had visited Elmira in 1897. He especially liked the aftercare and vocational training programs that he saw at Elmira. But he wanted to restrict the age group to 16–21. He succeeded in establishing such a youth prison in a jail in Kent in 1902, which was eventually named after the village of Borstal. His concept of a youth institution spread to continental Europe and became known as the Borstal system. Young inmates were sent to borstals where there was an emphasis on school and vocational training and relatively mild discipline. The Borstal concept, training prisoners through personal relations, trust, and responsibility, and organizing small institutions on this base, was considered very successful in the early part of the 19th century. The Borstal system faltered after 1945, but lasted until 1982 when it was formally abolished. Steep increases in crime and falling success rates contributed to doubts about the Borstal concept as gradually the public and corrections professionals lost confidence in it (McConville, 1995).

It was generally agreed upon by penal reformers of all persuasions that there should be separate reformatories for juvenile offenders and that a prison sentence should be avoided for them. Some of the best ideas and institutions included the Wehrli Institution, opened in Switzerland in 1810, where the teachers and supervisors were regarded as "older brothers" of the inmates. In Germany, the Rauhes Haus (the rough house) in Hamburg was begun in 1833 and the French reformatory, Mettray, opened in 1840. The Boston House of Reformation was in operation in 1826 and the George Junior Republic, started by William R. George, was initiated in 1895 in New York. The "Junior Republic" was for 14 to 21 year olds and operated with the principles of self-government. It was widely copied and eventually produced a National Association of Junior Republics. Some of them were functioning into the 1940s.

As the use of prison increased astronomically, ideas about probation began to emerge. Eriksson (1976) writes that probation was known as far back as the Middle Ages in Germany. At that time, it was referred to as *conditional release*. The execution of a sentence was postponed, but if the convict committed a new crime, the first sentence also went into effect. Peter Thacher, a judge in Boston from 1823 to 1843 used the method of "recognizance," in which a youthful offender was allowed to leave the court on his own recognizance provided some friends or family member vouched for his conduct and provided he committed no new crimes. John Augustus, also a citizen of Boston, became the world's first probation officer in 1841. Until his death in 1859, he had bailed and supervised nearly 2,000 probationers. He was especially interested in alcoholics but also worked with others, frequently housing them in his home. It was claimed that the majority of his probationers did not return to crime. By the turn of the century, six states had enacted laws providing for probation and probation officers. By about 1912, nearly all the states had laws which provided for juvenile courts and probation, though it took longer to extend probation to adult offenders (Eriksson, 1976).

Since the second century CE in Rome, there have been concerns about the criminal responsibility of the mentally ill and whether they should be punished the same as normal, nonmentally ill criminals. This issue is discussed in greater detail in chapter seven, The Treatment of Special Populations, but it is noted here that the first psychiatric prison was established in 1844 in England. Fisherton House, as it was called, housed 235 inmates. There followed similar institutions in Scotland and Ireland. There was a debate at the time about whether special institutions should be provided for insane criminals or whether there should be wards for mentally ill inmates within regular prisons. One of the most famous hospitals was established in 1863 in England, the Broadmoor Criminal Lunatic Asylum, which was made famous when Cesare Lombroso reported favorably on its methods (Eriksson, 1976). Efforts to treat criminals as patients were given a boost by the advent of psychoanalysis, which was enthusiastically applied to the treatment of criminal offenders. When psychoanalysis achieved virtually no results with criminals, it was followed by other types of psychological and psychiatric treatment in prisons. The therapeutic community movement, led by Maxwell Jones, also influenced the treatment of mentally disordered prison inmates. (The development of therapeutic communities is discussed in more detail in chapter four, The History of Psychologically Based Treatment.) It is useful to note that the debate about where mentally ill offenders should be kept, in a mental hospital or in a special unit inside a prison, is still today an issue of considerable disagreement.

The 20th century ushered in the era of the "big house." The big houses were large prisons that kept within their walls several thousand inmates each, such as Stateville in Illinois, Sing Sing in New York, and Jackson in Michigan. In 1929 in the United States, "there were two prisons with a population of more than 4,000 inmates each; there were four with more than 3,000 each; six with more than 2,000 each; and eighteen with more than 1,000 prisoners" (Rotman, 1998, p. 165). These huge institutions were expected to be operated by corrections professionals instead of political appointees and these professionals were to eliminate corporal punishment and prison labor, two practices that were so much abused in 19th-century prisons. A distinctive prison subculture emerged in these densely populated prisons and sociologists began to publish studies of inmate societies, with discussions of such topics as the convict code, gangs, snitches, rapos, and hacks (Clemmer, 1958; Sykes, 1958). Irwin and Cressey (1962) argued that the inmate culture was not created by the institutions but was imported into the prison from gangs and organized crime on the outside. Nearly every one came to view the big houses as failures. "The Big House exemplifies the superficiality of Progressive reforms in recreation, work, and assimilation with the open society. Indeed, in the world of granite, steel, and cement, the dominant features were stultifying routines, monotonous schedules, and isolation" (Rotman, 1995, p. 165).

The federal government decided to enter the business of prisons in 1892. A federal prison was begun at Leavenworth in 1897 and another one at Atlanta in 1902. The Federal Bureau of Prisons was created in 1929. One of its first efforts was to cope with the increase in crime and incarceration produced by Prohibition. The agency converted the military disciplinary barracks at Alcatraz into a federal prison in 1934 to hold those offenders "with no hope of rehabilitation." The Federal Bureau of Prisons now has over 170 correctional facilities nationwide and houses over 190,000 federal inmates (Federal Bureau of Prisons, 2006).

In the post–World War II period, low and declining crime rates and increased interest in psychological treatment led to the creation of some treatment-oriented correctional facilities, for example, the therapeutic community at Chino Prison in California in the early 1960s. This therapeutic community treatment approach to criminal offenders took place in small, decentralized units and made use of inmate counselors. Some reports claiming success for this approach were published (see Rotman, 1995). There was a wave of treatment optimism in the 1950s when the American Prison Association renamed itself the American Correctional Association and led an emphasis on the goal of rehabilitation and providing treatment to prisoners. While this enthusiasm for rehabilitation continued into the 1960s, in reality, incarceration on a very large scale continued to be the order of the day, as was lamented by *The President's Commission on Law Enforcement and Administration of Justice: Task Force Report on Corrections*, printed in 1967. In this report, it was pointed out that in 1965 more than 125,000 persons were received into the prisons and about one and one quarter million persons were under the jurisdiction of various correctional agencies and institutions. The foreword of the report stated that one cannot read the report without being struck by the fact that American correctional philosophy is a philosophy of institutionalization" (Rector, 1967). Rotman (1995) argues that the emphasis on the therapeutic model of rehabilitation led to abuses which caused a discrediting and general opposition in the 1970s to the abuse of intrusive therapies. From 1970 to 1980, the prison population in the United States doubled (Morris, 1998) and the great debate became suffused with a pessimism about rehabilitation known as the "nothing works" literature. From 1981 to 1995, the prison population doubled again. This development led to increased interest in alternatives to incarceration, such as electronic monitoring, drug courts, and intensive probation, as opposed to an overreliance on institutions. It was also coupled with a rethinking of the success of rehabilitative programs, collectively called the "what works" literature, which provides some cautious optimism for the successful treatment of criminal offenders. (The "nothing works" and the "what works" debate is discussed in detail in chapter six.)

Nevertheless, we have continued to incarcerate large numbers of offenders and our latest innovation for managing them is the supermax prison. There are now about 60 such prisons in the United States, including the United States Penitentiary Marion in Illinois, the Florence Federal Prison in Colorado, and the Minnesota Correctional Facility–Oak Park Heights. In supermax, the inmates are isolated 23 out of 24 hours every day. The one hour out of the cell is usually in a small enclosed area for exercise. The cells used at Oak Park are seven by ten feet and have reinforced concrete walls, floor, and ceiling. A cement slab with a thin mattress is the bed. The toilet is made of steel so it cannot be broken and there is no lid so it cannot be used as a weapon. There is little if any programming: "Offenders classified to this custody level are determined to be too dangerous to be out of their cells for any length of time, and, therefore, total control and solitary confinement is believed to be the sole solution.... The 'supermax' label identifies facilities housing the worst of the worst in total and complete isolation" (Bruton, 2004, pp. 37–8).

Over two-thirds of the states now house over 20,000 inmates in supermax correctional facilities. There is mounting criticism and dissatisfaction with the supermax concept due to the high cost of operating them and the perception that they are unconstitutional and inhumane. They also seem to have the unintended effect of increased inmate mental illness (Mears, 2006). This not surprising when we remember the history of the Pennsylvania, or separate, system in the early 19th century.

So we have come from the bridewell to the supermax. In summary, what happened was this:

(1) From Ulpian's declaration on the proper use of confinement to the reforms of the enlightenment in the 18th century CE to our present widespread use of imprisonment in the 21st century, penal systems moved from inflicting punishment on the body to punishments aimed at mentalities, at

changing the offender. We began with the use of physical punishment and fines, an eye for eye, a tooth for a tooth.

(2) Then there was the 18th-century Enlightenment reaction against the brutality of physical punishment combined with the observation that corporal punishment didn't seem to be working to reduce crime.

(3) There then gradually emerged the suggestion that the offender could be reformed with solitude, silence, religion, and hard work. These ideas began to be implemented with petty offenders and vagrants, then with youthful offenders, and finally with more serious offenders.

(4) By the post–Civil War period, these efforts were thought to have generally failed and there was a return to brutal and overcrowded prisons, but we did retain the idea that youthful offenders should be treated differently.

(5) In the latter part of the 19th century and early part of the 20th century, there emerged the idea that the criminal is sick and needs psychiatric and psychological treatment. This debate about whether or not a criminal can be "treated" continued on until the large crime wave resulting from Prohibition hit the United States. We began to incarcerate thousands of offenders in huge prisons we called "big houses."

(6) After World War II, with declining crime rates and increased optimism about psychological treatments, along with observations of the inhumanity of the big houses, we embarked once again on the road to rehabilitating prisoners with smaller, more humane, and more treatment-oriented "correctional facilities" instead of big houses.

(7) By the 1970s, with the prison population skyrocketing and the discouraging "nothing works" literature beginning to emerge, we built more and more prisons with harsher and harsher sentences.

(8) In the 1980s and 1990s, as the prison population continued to climb, there occurred a rethinking of rehabilitation, in the form of a "what works" literature, which supported the idea that some treatment works with some offenders. There was also increased interest in alternatives to incarceration, such as drug courts, intensive probation, and electronic monitoring, but we continued with a very heavy reliance on long-term incarceration as our response to criminal offenders and the supermax prison emerged.

(9) As the 21st century opens, we have a population of 2.2 million people in jail or prison. On June 30, 2005, about two-thirds of these were

in prison and about one-third in jail. One in every 136 residents of the United States is incarcerated. There has been a steady and substantial increase in the number of female inmates. We have an incarceration rate of 738 per 100,000 residents. As I write this, today's newspaper front-page headline is "Country's Prisons Bursting at Seams" (White, 2006).

Of course these phases gradually evolved, they were not completely distinct, and there was considerable overlap among them. There was also fierce debate at every period and in every country about the necessity of punishing criminal offenders. Though the crime rate has been declining in recent years, the prison population is very large. Norval Morris, one of our best penologists, has decried the "the cancerous growth of imprisonment" in the United States and wrote that:

> Wars on crime and wars on drugs are regularly declared in powerful rhetoric promising the enemy's surrender. But success never attends these efforts; there is no victory and no armistice. Instead, a new war is declared, as if the previous war had never taken place — and not even the rhetoric changes [998, p. 230].

One way to organize and summarize the history of prisons is to mark the publication of three massive commissioned reports on the prison sytem which were published close to 100 years apart. (All three were discussed in some detail earlier in this chapter.) First, there was John Howard's *The State of the Prisons in England and Wales, with preliminary Observations and an Account of Some Foreign Prisons*, printed in 1777; second, there was Enoch Cobb Wines and Theodore Dwight's *Report on the Prisons and Reformatories of the United States and Canada*, published in 1867; and, third, *The President's Commission on Law Enforcement and Administration of Justice: Task Force Report on Corrections*, published in 1967. All three reports concluded that the prison system was inefficient, costly, overly harsh, and not committed to rehabilitation. If we commissioned a fourth one today, it would fit the pattern perfectly.

Chapter Three

The History of
Biologically Based Treatment

*Prefrontal lobotomy seems destined to stay as a specialized thera-
peutic tool in the treatment of mental disorders.*
— Robert White, 1956

The implication of biological factors in criminal behavior can be traced
back at least as far as della Porte who, in 1586, published *The Human Physiognomy*, in which he suggested that criminals could be recognized by their
physical characteristics (cited in Jones, 1986). Associations between biological factors and crime were made prominent in the scientific study of crime
by Cesare Lombroso, who published *Criminal Man* in 1876. Since Dr. Lombroso's work in the 19th century, the study of biology and crime, taken as a
whole, has not helped us much in our efforts to treat and reduce criminal
behavior. Gottfredson and Hirschi write that the biological search for the
causes of crime "has produced little in the way of meaningful or interpretable
research. Instead, as we have seen, it has produced a series of 'findings' (i.e.,
physiognomy, feeblemindedness, XYY, inheritance of criminality) that survived only so long as was necessary to subject them to replication or to
straightforward critical analysis" (Gottfredson & Hirschi, 1990, pp. 61–62).

Nevertheless, the prospect of biological treatments for criminal, and
especially violent, behavior has intrigued us for many decades and continues to do so. Biological treatments for criminal behavior can be considered
in two general categories: psychosurgery and pharmacology.

43

Psychosurgery

Trepanning, also called trephining, is a procedure in which a small hole in the skull is made by scraping, cutting, or drilling. It is a very old idea. According to Parker (1995), trepanned skulls from the Neolithic Age are at least 7,000 years old and a trepanned skull found in Jericho is 4,000 years old. Trepanned skulls have been found in Europe, Asia, New Zealand, some Pacific islands, and North America, but the largest concentration of them have been found in Peru and Bolivia. The operation consisted of taking out a piece of the skull, thus exposing the dura mater, a membrane which covers the outside of the brain. If the dura mater is not punctured, the patient has a very good chance of surviving the operation. Most of the excavated trepanned skulls indicate that the patient survived because the bone shows signs of healing (Parker, 1995).

We can only speculate as to why the operation was done in ancient times. It may have been done for medical reasons to heal headaches, skull fractures, insanity, or convulsions. It may have been done to release evil spirits or, as some have suggested, it may have been done to acquire "rondelles," the pieces of the skull that were cut out, which were then used as amulets (Parker, 1995). In medieval times, it was used as a way of treating head ailments and/or to release demons (Millon, 2004). In more recent times, it was used as a method through which infectious matter could be drained or fluid pressure relieved.

In trepanning, there was no attempt by the primitive surgeons to alter the brain structures. In the modern era, psychosurgery has been used with the intent to change, or modify, the functioning of the brain itself and has been performed most frequently on patients with severe psychiatric disorders. Gottlieb Burckhardt, a 19th-century Swiss psychiatrist, removed portions of the cerebral cortex to eliminate fixed hallucinations in six patients. He reported success in reducing violent and hallucinatory behavior in five of the six patients, but it appears that no one continued his line of research (see Millon, 2004). Egas Moniz, a Portuguese neurologist, attended a neurological conference in London in 1935 at which there was presented a report on an operation called a prefrontal leukotomy. This operation had had a calming effect on chimpanzees who had been experimentally frustrated (Raine, 1993). It occurred to Moniz that mentally ill patients might benefit from this procedure. He invented a technique in which holes are drilled in the skull, through which an instrument, called a leukotome, could be inserted. This instrument could be swiveled to sever fiber tracts in the frontal lobes, disconnecting the frontal lobes from the rest of the brain. He reported success with this technique even though his postoperative assessment of the mental condition of the patient was cursory at best (Raine, 1993). Nevertheless, there was a rush to perform the procedure and other psychosurgical techniques were soon developed, including orbital undercutting, lobectomy, and lobotomy (Beaumont, 1983). Moniz received the Nobel Prize for his work in 1949. Ironically, he was shot and paralyzed by a former patient on whom he had operated (Quinsey, Harris, Rice, and Cormier, 2003).

Walter Freeman, an American neurologist, argued that this operation, which he called a prefrontal lobotomy, separated "the thinking brain" from "the feeling brain," by which he meant the frontal lobes and the thalamus, and thus removed the impact of psychosis. He began operating on patients in the early 1940s and eventually published a book that received widespread publicity. Even though Freeman believed that the operation should be considered as a last resort for severe and intractable cases of psychiatric disorders, he later altered his views on the appropriateness of the surgery and taught that earlier intervention, before the behavior became very severe, was preferable. He is credited personally with nearly 3,500 lobotomies (El-Hai, 2004). He eventually developed a new technique, called a transorbital lobotomy, in which he

> plunged a sharp pointed instrument, called an ice pick, directly into the underside of the frontal lobe through the orbital plate above the eye. The results were often melodramatic in two ways: the patients ceased their unmanageable behaviors forthwith, or became conscienceless, zombie like creatures with poor ethical judgment" [Bromberg, 1975, p. 307].

Freeman was a tireless promoter who believed that he had found the solution to mental illness and he traveled across the country to 55 hospitals in 23 states to demonstrate and promote his operation (El Hai, 2004).

From 1948 to 1952, tens of thousands of psychosurgical operations were performed. The operation became so well-known that a popular textbook of the period stated flatly: "Prefrontal lobotomy seems destined to stay as a specialized therapeutic tool in the treatment of mental disorders" (White, 1956, p. 481). However, in the mid–1950s the operations dwindled to an insignificant number, though they were continued for some violent chronic schizophrenics even into the early 1970s. Observers disagree about why the lobotomies declined.

> In the main, reactions to leukotomy, especially Freeman's crude surgery, were strong. Neurosurgeons in general were aghast at the technique employed, including the repeated electroshocks given to achieve anesthesia in Freeman's operation. As a consequence, lobotomy faded as a treatment of choice for schizophrenics" [Bromberg, 1975, p. 307].

However, others report that "by and large only a few isolated individuals complained" and that it was the advent of antipsychotic medication such as chlorpromazine (Thorazine) in the mid 1950s that ended the popularity of the prefrontal lobotomy (Quinsey et al., 2003, p. 11).

Psychosurgery which is more selective than lobotomy has been performed primarily in the United States and Japan, particularly with the amygdala. This surgery was thought initially to be successful in making aggressive patients more passive. Raine (1993) summarized four studies with a total of 185 cases and reported that the outcomes of amygdalectomy are variable, possibly because the amygdala, a small structure in the brain which is a part of the limbic system, is involved in both the excitement and inhibition of aggression; therefore, its total removal may affect aggressive behavior in individuals in different ways.

Psychosurgery has been primarily aimed at chronic and severe psychiatric disorders, but it has been suggested for violent and criminal behaviors as well (see Bromberg, 1975). O'Callaghan and Carroll (1982) reviewed 15,000 cases of psychosurgery and reported that 2.5 percent were performed for the control of antisocial behavior, but "outcome studies indicate that such surgery is relatively ineffective in controlling antisocial and criminal behavior" (Raine, 1993, pp. 122–3).

The history of psychosurgery in detail may be found in three excellent books: Elliot Valenstein, *Great and Desperate Cures: The Rise and Decline of Psychosurgery and Other Radical Treatments for Mental Illness* (1986); Jack Pressman, *Last Resort: Psychosurgery and the Limits of Medicine* (2002); and Jack El Hai, *The Lobotomist* (2004). "Valenstein's book is a cautionary tale of a technology wrongly conceived, hastily implemented, received with great enthusiasm, and widely applied, causing great and irreparable harm to tens of thousands of helpless people" (Quinsey et al., 2003, p. 9).

While psychosurgery is a large chapter in the history of mental illness, it is so far only a small episode in the treatment of antisocial and criminal behavior. Yet the suggestion remains that violent behavior may be controlled through surgical techniques. In the stereotaxic procedure, a small hole is made in the skull and then either insulated wire electrodes or hollow glass tubes may be inserted and affixed to specific sites in the brain. The wire electrodes allow for electrical stimulation of specific areas of the brain, while the hollow tubes permit chemical stimulation of specific sites. Some researchers believe there is great potential for the control of violence using these procedures (Bartol, 1999).

Surgery has also been used for sexual offenders. Organic approaches to sexual offending have included surgical castration and stereotactic brain surgery, which disconnects the sex drives (Schorsch et al., 1990). Today psychosurgery is a minimally invasive, highly selective treatment for a small number of patients with severe and otherwise untreatable affective or obsessive compulsive disorders (Feldman and Goodrich, 2001).

Freeman's well-known and disastrous foray into psychosurgery has tainted it with a layer of fear and disgust, still hampering legitimate efforts to understand brain functioning and to relieve debilitating and otherwise untreatable symptoms. It is also reminiscent of other episodes in the history of biological explanations for crime, for example, Lombroso's discovery of "criminal man" and the XYY chromosome affair, in which a mix of hubris and superoptimism, combined with a sincere but quixotic desire for a final solution, resulted in proclamations of momentous discoveries in the understanding of crime which turned out to be wrong. There are now enough historical examples of misguided biological explanations and treatments for crime to inculcate a healthy skepticism regarding them.

Pharmacology

Sexual Offending

Organic approaches for sexual offending today are mostly restricted to medications rather than surgery, particularly antiandrogens and antidepressants. Antiandrogens reduce testosterone, decrease erections and ejaculations, decrease sexual fantasies, and reduce sexual interest in general. The antidepressants, in this case, the SSRIs (serotonin reuptake inhibitors), have produced decreased paraphilic fantasies and urges. It is not known if this is because of their sexual side effects or because of increased control of anxiety, depression, and obsessionality (see Miner and Coleman, 2001).

> Pharmacological interventions seem to be at least as effective as behavioral methods in giving sexual offenders greater control over their urges. Bradford and Pawlak (1993) demonstrated that cyproterone acetate (an antiandrogen) specifically reduced arousal to deviant fantasies while enhancing arousal to appropriate stimuli. Federoff (1993) has reviewed the evidence on the value of serotonin reuptake inhibitors and concluded that they can be effective in bringing deviant urges under control" [Marshall, 2004, p. 156].

Raymond, Robinson, Kraft, and Rittberg (2001) review research which demonstrates that a number of medications have shown some efficacy for reducing sexual drive or the ability to perform sexually. Most of the studies are case reports, but there have been some placebo controlled studies that showed that antiandrogens were effective in decreasing sexual arousal and sexual interests, and the frequency of sexual behavior (Bradford and Pawlak, 1993; Cooper, 1981; Cooper et al., 1992). Raymond et al. (2001) cite other studies which were case reports or small series that support the efficacy of SSRIs, tricyclic antidepressants (TCAs), busiprone hydrochloride, lithium, desipramine, and clomipramine in treating paraphilia (Raymond et al., 2001, p. 81), but Saleh and Berlin argue, "More clinical trials are needed to substantiate the efficacy and tolerability of these psychoactive medications before membership in the pharmacopoeia of first line or even second line agents can be considered" (Saleh and Berlin, 2003, pp. 246–247).

Raymond et al. (2001) also report on the use of leuprolide acetate, which has fewer side effects as compared to other antiandrogens. Used in a single case presenting with pedophilia and multiple other comorbid psychiatric disorders, including bipolar disorder and substance dependence, the medication was effective in reducing pedophilic fantasies, urges, and behaviors. They conclude that "concurrent psychotherapy is always indicated in the treatment of these patients. No one is advocating that medication alone is effective in this population. Of note, psychotherapy for the patient's sexual offending was more productive once his unremitting/constant pedophilic fantasies and urges were better controlled" (Raymond et al., 2001, p. 86).

Some researchers report that the results of the SSRIs and the TCAs are promising in reducing symptoms of paraphilia (Saleh and Berlin in Geffner, Franey, & Falconer, 2003). Others suggest that "there is evidence that comprehensive cognitive behavioral programmes, and those that combine antiandrogens with psychological treatment, are associated with ecologically significant reductions in recidivism for treated sex offenders" (Ward, Hudson, and Keenan, 2004, p. 164).

Major Mental Disorders

"Mentally disordered offenders" is a phrase often encountered in the correctional treatment literature, but it has many different meanings. Diagnosable mental disorders, psychiatric disorders, major mental illness, and major affective disorders are also frequently encountered categories and often describe different populations of offenders. For example, "psychiatric disorders" may include substance abuse and dependence, anxiety, depression, personality disorders, as well as the major mental disorders, psychotic illness, brain damage, and the mentally handicapped. These different inclusions can make it difficult to compare data and results from various studies. It is useful to separate these out for discussion. Hodgins proposes that "the major mental disorders include schizophrenia, major depression, bipolar disorder, delusional disorder, and atypical psychoses" (Hodgins, 2004, p. 219). In this section, it is this population to which we are referring.

Pharmacological treatment for psychotic illness had a major breakthrough in the early 1950s. "In 1952, two French psychiatrists, Delay and Deniker, noted the antihistamine effect of Promethazine, from which Thorazine and kindred products evolved; the drugs reduced motor activity, slowed response to external stimuli, and improved the atmosphere of the hospital where treated psychotics were held" (Bromberg, 1975, p. 308). As Delay reported: "chlorpromazine acted like a 'chemical lobotomy'; within a matter of weeks, scores of patients were reported as being symptom free, no longer troubled by hallucinations and delusions, and markedly diminished in their hostile and manic behaviors" (Millon, 2004, p. 239). These drugs revolutionized the treatment of psychotic patients and over the next 25 years or so, phenothiazines, as this class of drugs was called, was taken by fifty million patients and more than ten thousand articles were written about them (Bromberg, 1975).

The treatment of mentally disordered offenders is a subject that will be covered in more detail in chapter seven, The Treatment of Special Populations, where we will consider the treatment of the mentally handicapped, sexual offenders, and substance abusers separately. While major mental disorders are biologically based, their causes are not well understood. Treatment generally consists of a combination of psychotropic medication, supportive psychotherapy, life skills training, case management, and a therapeutic milieu, which can be hard to achieve in a prison. Since the introduction of the first major tranquilizers, antipsychotic medications have steadily improved symptom reduction and have decreased side effects, but there is still no cure for these illnesses.

While it is important to consider the treatment of this group of offenders, they are a relatively small part of the criminal population. Persons in the mentally ill population are more likely than those in the general population to have engaged in criminal behavior, though most persons diagnosed with major mental illness do not commit crimes. (Hodgins, 2004). Because of the different ways in which offenders are grouped and counted, and the way in which the data is reported in different jurisdictions and in different research studies, it is difficult to accurately estimate how many offenders are diagnosed with major mental illness. One reliable report states that fewer than 10 percent of all prisoners are receiving psychotropic medication in state prisons (*Sourcebook of Criminal Justice Statistics*, 2003) and certainly not all of these are diagnosed with major mental disorders.

Personality Disorders

A personality disorder is a set of stable, enduring attributes and patterns of behavior that bring the person into conflict with the expectations of that individual's culture. Personality disorders are inferred from observations of a person's behavior when that person's behavior is consistently conflicted. There are ten specific personality disorders diagnosed by today's clinicians, including, for example, borderline personality disorder and obsessive compulsive personality disorder. None of them are well enough understood to have any consistently successful treatment for them. Antisocial personality disorder is one of the ten, the one that involves persistently criminal behavior. (Some observers continue to agree with Partridge [1930] that personality disorder is a garbage can category for a colorful assortment of mental and emotional disturbances which no one understands.)

The most recent version of the *Diagnostic and Statistical Manual (DSM-IV-TR)* of the American Psychiatric Association, published in 2000, lists the following criteria for a diagnosis of antisocial personality disorder:

A. There is a pervasive pattern of disregard for, and violation of, the rights of others occurring since age 15 years, as indicated by three (or more) of the following:

(1) *Failure to conform to social norms* with respect to lawful behaviors as indicated by repeatedly performing acts that are grounds for arrest

(2) *Deceitfulness*, as indicated by repeated lying, use of aliases, or conning others for personal profit or pleasure

(3) *Impulsivity* or failure to plan ahead

(4) *Irritability and aggressiveness*, as indicated by repeated physical fights or assaults

(5) *Reckless disregard* for the safety of self and others

(6) *Consistent irresponsibility*, as indicated by repeated failure to sustain consistent work behavior or honor financial obligations

(7) *Lack of remorse*, as indicated by being indifferent to or rationalizing having hurt, mistreated, or stolen from another

B. The individual is at least age 18 years.

C. There is evidence of Conduct Disorder (major age appropriate norms and values are persistently disregarded) with onset before age 15 years.

D. The occurrence of antisocial behavior is not exclusively during the course of Schizophrenia or a Manic Episode [2000, p. 706].

Notice particularly that, in this scheme, *violent behavior* is not a necessary characteristic and that the *absence* of recognized mental illness *is* a central criterion. Hare (1993) argues that these diagnostic criteria would qualify nearly every person in prison and that all people who have committed crimes are not psychopaths. Another way to make this point is to say that all psychopaths could be diagnosed with antisocial personality disorder, but not all persons diagnosed with antisocial personality disorder are psychopaths (in Hare's view). Some clinicians and researchers contend that the term *psychopath* should be reserved for the most extreme group of criminals, that is, extreme either in the number or pervasiveness of crimes committed and/or in the intensity or seriousness of the criminal behavior.

The confusion concerning this group of people persists into the present. The term *psychopath* is now most often used by clinicians to set apart and label a particular group of extreme criminals who repeatedly commit crimes. In its present and most precise usage, not all criminals are psychopaths and not all psychopaths have criminal records, though all psychopaths engage in antisocial behavior, whether they are caught or not. Some psychopaths are violent, but others are not. Psychopaths do not experience hallucinations, delusions, extreme anxiety, or loss of contact with reality. They are not considered mentally ill in the medical sense because they do not exhibit the symptoms of a known, diagnosable mental disorder of organic origin. Some researchers, Raine and Hare for instance, do argue that psychopathy *may be* a mental disorder of organic origin, but this has not been convincingly demonstrated yet and there is no medical treatment for psychopaths at present (Hare, 1993; Raine, 1993). Psychopaths are not mentally ill in the legal sense because they have "substantial capacity" to appreciate the wrongfulness of their conduct and to conform their behavior to the requirements of the law.

Burke and Hart report that a large amount of research conducted in different countries has consistently reported prevalence rates of 10–15 percent for personality disorders among populations of offenders and forensic patients. When offenders with a primary diagnosis of a major mental disorder and a secondary diagnosis of personality disorder are included, the prevalence rate jumps to 50 percent or more, 90 percent in some studies (Burke & Hart, 2000).

Knorring and Ekselius (1998) have argued that impulsivity is a principal component of personality disorders, including antisocial personality disorder. The trait of impulsivity could be targeted for treatment with drugs, especially since impulsive/sensation seeking is a major component of psychopathy and is prominent in a forensic psychiatric population. They argue that there are controlled studies demonstrating that major tranquilizers, carbamazepine, and lithium may have anti-impulsivity effects, but SSRIs are most effective. They quote Markovitz (1995): "SSRIs have proved the most successful in treating impulsivity and aggression.... The available studies are encouraging and suggest many areas for research" (p. 366).

McMurran (2004) warns that pharmacological treatments result in modest effects, are used for short periods of time, and should not be understood as a cure for personality disorder. They can, however, improve functioning (Soloff, 1998) and may improve an individual's capacity to benefit from other, psychosocial treatments.

> Reviews of pharmacological treatments permit the conclusions that symptoms of anger and impulsivity, leading to aggression and violence, can be successfully treated in a number of ways: antidepressants for those who are depressed and irritable, agitated, and impulsive; lithium or anticonvulsants for those with mood lability and impulsivity; low dose antipsychotic for anger and impulsivity related to cognitive-perceptual symptoms; and selective serotonin reuptake inhibitors for the highly anxious and impulsive" [McMurran in Hollin, 2004, pp. 245–246].

There has been some research that indicates that treatments for attention deficit hyperactivity disorder (ADHD) may improve symptoms of conduct disorder in children (Connor and Steingard, 1996; Riggs, 1998; Riggs et al., 1998; Hendren, 1999), but, as Yaralian and Raine observe, "given the numerous factors that influence antisocial behavior, the most effective treatment programs will undoubtedly rely on the integration of treatment from several different modalities, including social-environmental, prenatal, and psychopharmacological" (Yaralian and Raine, 2001, pp. 69–70).

Tiihonen (2000) reports that there are very few controlled studies of drug treatments with individuals classified with personality disorders, substance abuse, and habitual violent or criminal behavior and that, at present, there are none in which the outcome measure was the incidence of criminal offenses. This is because such studies are extremely hard to conduct, mainly due to the noncompliance and noncooperation of the treated individual subjects. Tiihonen writes that the pharmacological treatment of violent and criminal behavior can be achieved by treating the underlying mental disorder or by treating the violent behavior per se as a symptom. Personality disorder may be partly explained by poor impulse control; thus, poor impulse control is the main target when preventing violence with pharmacological agents. "Evidence from controlled trials indicates that the first choice of treatment for impulsive and aggressive behavior among patients with personality disorders is fluoxentine…," but "in all cases, patients should also receive counseling and, if possible, supportive or coping skills therapy" (Tiihonen, 2000, pp. 187–188). To the extent that alcohol abuse is a factor in violent and criminal behavior, naltrexone and acamprosate have been found to be effective in some cases. Mostly these trials have been with psychotic and mentally handicapped patients and much less so with personality disorders. Lithium, carbamazepine, SSRIs, and busiprone decrease impulsive and aggressive behavior in patients with various mental disorders (Tiihonen, 2000).

Conclusion

A number of biological factors have been associated with crime, particularly with violent offending (see Burkhead, 2006). Heart rate and EEG abnormalities have been extensively studied. Crime has also been associated with diet (refined carbohydrates high in criminals), lead (high levels in the body of criminals), cortisol (low levels in violent offenders), hypoglycemia (high in violent populations), and testosterone (high in violent offenders). Violent offenders are more likely to have experienced birth complications and to have had a head injury at some time in their lives. But, as Raine (1993) argues, many of these biological factors have strong social and environmental implications. For example, high levels of lead in a person are also associated with living in a socially disadvantaged home in an urban area with a high crime rate. Head injury may be the result of having adopted a violent lifestyle; thus, the frequency of head injury may be a *result*, not a *cause* of violent behavior.

Psychiatrist David Amen used brain imaging techniques to study 50 murderers and 200 other violent offenders. All, without exception, showed reduced activity in the prefrontal cortex, overactivity in the anterior cingulate gyrus, and abnormalities in the left temporal lobe. "If you have a left temporal lobe problem, you have dark, awful, violent thoughts. If you have a cingulate gyrus problem as well, you get stuck on the bad thoughts. And if you have a prefrontal cortex problem, you can't supervise the bad thoughts you get stuck on" (in Barovick, 1999). He suggests that violence and aggression can be treated with medication to compensate for the above listed abnormalities: an anticonvulsant to stabilize temporal lobe abnormalities, a serotonergic agent to decrease activity in the anterior cingulate gyrus, and a psychostimulant to activate prefrontal cortex activity (Amen, 1999). But are the abnormalities causative? These brain malfunctions may also be the *result* of other, outside factors that turn the capacity for violence into reality.

Hyman offers a caution about the whole subject of brain scanning: "with some notable exceptions, the community of scientists was excessively optimistic about how quickly imaging would have an impact on psychiatry. In their enthusiasm, people forgot that the human brain is the most complex object in the history of human inquiry, and it's not all that easy to see what's going wrong" (quoted in Carey, 2005, p. 2).

While we most certainly want to leave the door open for the discovery of specific medical treatments that can help certain impaired offenders, it is wise to remember what Hervey Cleckley wrote in his now classic work, *The Mask of Sanity*: "Many types of behavior formerly regarded as voluntary wrongdoing or the just results of sin are now classed as disease. This does not prove that eventually all wrongdoing will be plainly revealed as disease and all conduct necessarily evaluated at a level at which good or bad are nonexistent ... there are good reasons to believe that this tendency to classify wrongdoing as illness has in recent decades gone too far — perhaps in some instances to the point of absurdity" (Cleckley, 1988).

Chapter Four

The History of
Psychologically Based Treatment

*Despite these enthusiastic and at times embarrassing claims in
our behalf, our actual achievements should encourage profound
modesty.*
— Hervey Cleckley, 1941.

Although this chapter is a discussion of the history of psychological
treatments for criminal offenders, I have not attempted to cover every
instance of a treatment method or theoretically based program since such
an effort would require an encyclopedia. Instead, I have chosen to give the
reader a representative sample. So I have been necessarily selective, choosing some treatments and programs for discussion and omitting others,
though I have not omitted any important conclusion. The result is, I believe,
a fair and realistic picture of psychological treatment and criminal offending that is in a readable and digestible format.

Psychoanalysis

The theory of psychoanalysis had a widespread impact, not only in
psychiatry and psychology, but in Western culture as a whole. Psychoanalytic thought exerted a profound influence on art and literature, on our
understanding of sexuality and the family of origin, and on the treatment

of the mentally ill. It produced the first important method of psychotherapy. Its most familiar contributions to treatment include the concepts of unconscious motivation and catharsis, the id, the ego, and the superego, transference and countertransference, the defense mechanisms, dream analysis, and the technique of free association.

There was, inevitably, a phase of development in criminology when psychoanalytic theories and methods were applied to the problem of criminal behavior. Freud himself had almost nothing to say about criminals. The little that he did say, however, drew the sharp focus of some of his followers and was used by them enthusiastically for decades. Freud believed that everyone carries some Oedipal guilt from early childhood, from competition with the father over the attention of the mother, but that this guilt is largely unconscious. Freud observed that children will often be naughty in order to provoke punishment which, in turn, assuages their guilt. He wrote: "In many criminals, especially youthful ones, it is possible to detect a very powerful sense of guilt which existed before the crime, and is therefore not the result but its motive" (Freud, 1961, p. 52). This "criminality from a sense of guilt" was the idea seized by Freudian disciples wanting to explain criminal behavior. Alexander and Staub proclaim in 1931 that the reasons for crime are unconscious and the cure consists of making the unconscious known, to discover the reasons for committing crimes. Glover, writing in 1960, flatly states that this concept is "the key to all problems of delinquency."

Freud did not think that psychoanalysis was appropriate for criminals and juvenile delinquents because they had not developed the psychic structures and the particular attitude necessary for that form of treatment. He proposed that "something other than analysis" be used for this population (quoted in Yochelson and Samenow, 1976). This declaration did not, of course, prevent his followers from making the attempt. Alexander and Healy published a widely read book in 1935, *The Roots of Crime*, in which they asserted that antisocial behavior represents an unconscious effort to obtain punishment in order to alleviate feelings of guilt. They adopted the term *neurotic character* to label the psychopath and this began the use of the phrase, "character disorder." This term enjoyed a relatively brief popularity, but the problem of describing the difference between character and personality proved too difficult (describing the word *personality* is hard enough) and this term is no longer encountered in professional circles. The psychoanalytic point of view was popular for a while, but most clinicians and other interested observers concluded that the psychopath's lack of remorse was perfectly genuine and was not covering anything, a point well made by Cleckley in his classic work *The Mask of Sanity.* Cleckley's work laid the foundation for our present point of view on the theory of psychopathy (see Burkhead, 2006).

Nonetheless, psychoanalytical treatment of criminal persons still has its supporters (Meloy 1988; Kernberg, 1998; Lester and Van Voorhis, 2000). Reid Meloy (1988) has written a thick volume on the origin, dynamics, and treatment of the psychopath which is based on Freud's theory of psychoanalysis. Meloy supports long-term psychoanalytic psychotherapy for criminal behavior although it does "present major countertransference and resistance issues to the mental health professional." By these major issues, he means the well-known observations that psychopaths usually do not want to change and that psychotherapists think that they will not change. But, Meloy writes, "I am not going to propose a new model for treating the psychopath." Kernberg believes that psychoanalytic psychotherapy can be successful with antisocial personality disorders, but only under very specific conditions, conditions which rule out most criminals. Lester and Van Voorhis assert that psychoanalytic concepts, "valuable vestiges of psychoanalytic theory and practice," can help the correctional counselor to understand the criminal and to work with him more effectively (Lester and Van Voorhis, 2000, p. 125). Among these, they cite the defense mechanisms, issues of transference and countertransference, and the long-term effects of childhood trauma.

The influence of psychoanalysis waned as it became more and more apparent that a course of psychoanalysis for a single patient was so lengthy, so intensive, and consequently so expensive, that it could only be applied in practice to relatively few people. The practice of psychoanalysis required so much training that there were few qualified analysts available in any setting. Schoenfeld (1971) and others had noted that those patients who did seem to benefit from psychoanalysis were adults who were articulate, intelligent, and able to talk out their impulses rather than acting them out, in other words, people quite different from those engaged in criminal behavior, who are generally young, inarticulate, unintelligent, and have problems with self-control. In addition, a growing body of research strongly supported the finding that insight-oriented therapies were not sufficient to effect change in problem behaviors (Andrews et al., 1990; Lipsey, 1992).

The work of Sigmund Freud has had such a profound impact on our culture that virtually every textbook on criminal behavior and its treatment still includes a section on psychoanalysis, even though Freud never intended to address, explain, or treat the criminal, and even though psychoanalysis, after over a hundred years, has contributed little to the successful treatment of criminals. For now, let's leave the last word on psychoanalysis and crime to the intrepid Dr. Freud himself, who wrote in *Psychoanalysis and the Ascertaining of Truth in the Courts of Law* (1948, p. 21):

> With the neurotic, the secret is hidden from his own consciousness; with the criminal, it is hidden only from you.

Psychodrama

Jacob L. Moreno (1934, 1946) originated psychodrama. The basic principle of psychodrama is to stimulate the expression of feelings by spontaneous, unrehearsed playacting. The spontaneous playacting is similar to the psychoanalytic technique of free association and the early proponents of psychodrama argued that it was better than free association for eliciting deep emotions. The emotional expression that was elicited by psychodrama led to cartharsis and insight and presumably new behavior. Usually a theater setting is employed for the drama, but psychodramatic techniques, such as role reversal and empty chair, can be used in conventional group psychotherapy. From initial interviews and preliminary discussion with group members, the therapist selects the protagonist and the problem, or scene, to be worked on. Next, the protagonist, assisted by group members, while other group members comprise the audience, acts the scene. A past event may be reenacted or a future event may be anticipated. Then the group discusses what they saw and heard, their reactions to the play, and relate similar experiences to the protagonist. Moreno used psychodrama to treat marital problems and persons who seemed exceptionally inhibited and isolated. He also used it with some offenders.

There are a number of studies which report on the use of psychodrama with offenders, including sex offenders (Corsini, 1951; Bromberg and Franklin, 1952), addicts (Eliasoph, 1955), adolescent delinquents (Haskell, 1959), and medium security inmates (Schrumski, Feldman, Harvey, and Holiman, 1984). Most of these studies did not use a measure of recidivism but instead looked at general attitudinal measures or institutional behavior measures. One exception is Haskell and Weeks (1960), who gave offenders training in assuming new roles using psychodramatic techniques. Those offenders who showed improvement in role-taking skills had fewer parole violations during a three-month follow-up as compared to (1) offenders who received training but did not improve their skills or (2) offenders who received no training. According to some therapists, criminal offenders acting out antisocial impulses is contraindicated. Criminal offenders have not had difficulty in expressing their antisocial impulses; they don't need help in this area. Pithers (1997), who is critical of programs that use confrontational and emotional methods, describes a program which used such offensive methods of drama therapy that the participants requested an injunctive hearing through the assistance of the American Civil Liberties Union to prohibit use of that technique. Adams and Vetter (1981) used a follow-up of ten years and found reconviction rates to be higher in a group of young offenders treated by psychodrama than in an untreated control group. Whatever may be the efficacy of psychodrama with various emotional and psychological problems, it is fair to say that it is an unproven treatment for the reduction of recidivism among criminal offenders.

Transactional Analysis

Transactional analysis (TA) was an intellectual tour de force, created by the psychiatrist Eric Berne in 1961. TA was derived from psychoanalysis, but instead of id, ego, and superego, Berne proposed *ego states* which he called Child, Adult, and Parent. The Adult is an ego state which makes an objective appraisal of reality; the Parent is an ego state which resembles that of parental figures; and the Child is an ego state which was fixated in early childhood but is still active in the person. The goal of transactional analysis is to help people to achieve autonomy in their social lives. Autonomy is a combination of awareness, spontaneity, and intimacy.

Berne argued that in order to fulfill their needs, people engage in social intercourse. The basic unit of social intercourse is the transaction. In a transaction, one person (the agent) begins the transaction and another person (the respondent) responds to it. There are two basic kinds of transactions. In a complementary transaction, persons communicate with each other in complementary ego states, such as adult to adult, or parent to child. For example, in one type of complementary transaction, the agent communicates as one adult to another and the respondent replies as one adult to another. "What time is it?" (adult to adult). "It is 5 P.M." (adult to adult). Complementary transactions lead to unimpeded communication and ultimately to the fulfillment of needs. However, many transactions are crossed transactions. For example, the agent says, "What time is it?"(adult to adult). The respondent replies, "How the hell should I know? Am I your mother?" (angry child to parent). Transactions can also be simple or ulterior. Ulterior transactions involve the activity of more than two ego states simultaneously. In ulterior transactions, what is on the surface (the social level) is not the real transaction (the psychological level). For example, the agent says "What time is it?" and the respondent replies, "I could have a watch if I wanted one." This transaction appears to be adult to adult on the social level, but on the psychological level, it is critical parent to child and child to critical parent. The agent's ulterior motive is not to find out the time but is to point out the respondent's deficiencies (he doesn't have a watch). The respondent is hooked into this, hence his childish reply. The respondent's adult reply would have been, "I don't know."

Ulterior transactions are the basis for games. Games are ongoing series of transactions that have an ulterior motive and a payoff. One of the purposes of TA is to help people to recognize the games being played in their relationships. Because games interfere with intimacy, people are taught to replace with them with more fulfilling transactions. Berne is perhaps most famous for his book *Games People Play* (1964). In this book, he catalogues and describes numerous games with ulterior transactions. His analysis is very appealing and includes simple and colorful language, with such games as "Let's You and Him Fight," "Ain't It Awful," and "Now I've Got You, You Son of a Bitch." His game analysis contains considerable insight into human behavior.

TA became enormously popular. It was a system that appealed to common sense, it was explained in simple language, and it was easy for people to understand and apply to their own behavior. Analyzing transactions worked well in group settings, so TA made group counseling more common. So, of course, it was eventually applied to the treatment of criminal offenders. Berne had, in *Games People Play*, included some games which he called "underworld games" and which were applicable to offenders, such as "Cops and Robbers," "How Do You Get Out of Here," and "Let's Pull a Fast One on Joey." Transactional analysis became prominent enough in corrections that I received a course of TA as a part of my training as a probation/parole officer in North Carolina in 1979.

Lester (2000), in a review of transactional analysis with offenders, reported on six published studies conducted in the 1960s and 1970s. On the whole these studies reported an improvement in the behavior of the participants in the TA programs, but none of the studies provided meaningful recidivism data. TA has now waned in correctional circles as it fell prey to the failing of all the "insight" therapies: that insight alone is not sufficient to change behavior in general and criminal behavior in particular.

Reality Therapy

Reality therapy was developed by the psychiatrist William Glasser (1965). One of the forerunners of cognitive therapy, the basic principles were developed by Glasser at the Ventura School for Girls, an institution for seriously delinquent girls in California. The focus of reality therapy is to teach self-control and responsible behavior. It takes the perspective that offenders must face reality now.

Glasser asserts that everyone has two basic needs: the need to love and be loved and the need to feel worthwhile to ourselves and others. When attempts to fulfill these needs are unsuccessful, it is usually because people are denying the reality of the world. People must understand and accept the reality of the world and attempt to fulfill their needs within the framework of this reality. This requires involvement with at least one other person in a relationship of caring and respect.

The therapy is based on three procedures: involvement, rejection of irresponsible behavior, and teaching better ways to fulfill one's needs. The counselor concentrates on what the offender is doing, not on why he is doing it. Attitudes will change if behavior changes. The past is not a focus of attention and reality therapists show no interest in the offenders' past, concentrating instead on the here and now. The therapy is simple and straightforward and does not require training in psychiatry or psychology to deliver. Easy-to-understand procedures may be delivered by paraprofessionals trained specifically in reality therapy.

Glasser reported that his Ventura program was successful, with only 43 of 370 of the girls who were released on parole committing violations. However, there was no control group, no comparison group, and no long-term follow-up. Nevertheless, reality therapy was very popular in corrections and was taught across the country. Bartol (1999) reports that it was still widely used in corrections as late as 1999. It has also been used with drug addicts (Bratter, 1974). While correctional programs now are rarely classified as reality therapy, echoes of Glasser's perspective may be seen in state-of-the-art treatment programs today.

Person-Centered Therapy

Carl Rogers introduced a system of treatment in 1951 which he at first called "non-directive counseling." Later, his method was called client-centered therapy and it is now known as person-centered therapy. Rogers believed that the client should lead in the therapeutic process and that the therapist should not intervene by asking questions or by directing the conversation. The counselor uses only one active tool, *reflection*, which is the recognition, clarification, and acceptance of feeling. The counselor simply restates what the client just said, but he expresses the feeling side of it, not the content side of it. The counselor reflects back the feelings expressed by the client, thereby establishing an outflow of feelings. Then, according to Rogers, a predictable course follows: first the expression of negative feelings, then the expression of positive feelings, then the achievement of insight, then the client engages in positive actions, and then he begins to feel less and less of a need for the therapist until the therapy logically terminates. The counselor also offers to the client genuineness, empathic understanding, and "unconditional positive regard," which the client may never have experienced before. Rogers argued that most people are the recipients of "conditional positive regard," meaning that they are loved and respected only if they meet certain expectations. Unconditional positive regard, Rogers believes, is an essential ingredient of mental health.

Reflection is not as easy as it sounds. "At times, the counselor is almost amusingly evasive. He replies to the client's anxious queries by acknowledging that the client feels anxious, or he parries a request for advice by recognizing that the client would like someone to settle the question for him. But he sticks to his non-directive principles and the client soon learns that he himself must take all the initiative" (White, 1956, p. 316). Rogers thought that the greatest distortion of his work was the misunderstanding of the method of reflection, perhaps because of his own emphasis on the word *method*. It is more an attitude than a method (Rogers, 1986). Lester (2000) suggests that person-centered therapy is no longer a stand-alone treatment, but is a skill to be used by the counselor on those occasions when it facilitates therapeutic progress. Lester believes that it is a skill which every counselor ought to have in his repertoire.

The advantages of person-centered therapy are clarity and consistency and that it is not likely to do any harm to anyone. In addition, the therapist's feelings, interests, values, and goals are left out of the therapy. There were, however, immediate objections to the person-centered approach as it was originally presented by Rogers: that it was appropriate only for minor emotional problems (White, 1956), that it left out the important procedures of history taking and clinical assessment (Thorne, 1955), and that it would not work well with antisocial persons (Beier, 1952).

Person-centered therapy is just that type of treatment so roundly criticized by the "what works " researchers of the last 15 years in corrections. "Many programs are still operating on the basis of weakly formulated principles of group dynamics, often infused with a mish mash of Rogerian and existential notions of the underlying goodness of mankind (e.g., Rogers, 1961) which would become evident if only the person or group could experience trust, openness, and noncontingent valuing" (Andrews and Bonta, 1994, p. 200). They argue that a person-centered approach relies too much on the relationship principle and not enough on the contingency principle, especially when dealing with antisocial and criminal behavior.

Outcome studies of the person-centered approach with criminal offenders are few, even though Rogerian therapy is often included in courses for the training of correctional counselors (for example, Van Voorhis, Braswell, and Lester, 2000). There are some studies reporting on the efficacy of person-centered therapy with delinquent and antisocial populations (Corsini, 1947; Smith, Berlin and Bassin, 1960, 1965; Truax, Wargo, and Silber, 1966), but these studies do not report reductions in recidivism. The longevity and widespread popularity of person-centered therapy is an indication of its usefulness for certain types of problems, but, as with other insight therapies, such as psychoanalysis and TA, its efficacy with an offender population is not strongly supported.

Family Therapy

Family therapy is based on the assumption that the family should be viewed as a system and that, when there is a troubled family member, it is the system that is in need of help. Family systems therapies consider problem behaviors to be circular, reciprocal, and interrelated (Van Voorhis, Braswell, and Morrow, 2000). Factors within the family system can maintain problem behavior and changes in the way the family communicates and interacts can lead to improved behavior, and better outcomes, for all of the family members. Family therapy has been developing over the last three decades as a treatment for a variety of problems and includes the work of such notable family therapists as Virginia Satir (1967), Jay Haley (1976), and Murray Bowen (1978). There are many varieties of family therapy and all of them will not be reviewed here. Instead, family therapies which have been used specifically to prevent or change delinquent and antisocial behavior are covered.

One of the earliest was the work of Patterson and his colleagues at the Oregon Social Learning Center (Patterson, 1982). The goal of the center was to improve the parenting skills of children with conduct problems. The primary observation was that poor parenting skills led to antisocial behavior in boys. Patterson (1986) proposed that: (1) poor parenting led to antisocial behavior in the home and outside of the home, which led to (2) rejection by peers and failure at school, which led to (3) rejection by the parents, which led to (4) low self-esteem. The combination of low self-esteem, school failure, and rejection by parents and peers led to (5) academic drop out and a high risk for offending. Patterson conceived of poor parenting as "deficient interaction patterns." The four interaction themes are (1) monitoring, (2) discipline, (3) positive parenting, (4) problem solving and conflict (Snyder and Patterson, 1987). Risk factors for developing deficient interaction patterns are (1) low socioeconomic status with poor job skills, (2) unskilled parents, (3) a child with a difficult temperament, (4) major stressors in daily life, such as financial problems, medical conditions, and substance abuse. The solution is to teach parenting skills as well as to manage the use of resources to provide the parents more time for parenting and less stress in their daily lives. Parents of these at-risk children were taught negotiation skills and how to make rewards contingent on prosocial behavior.

Snyder and Patterson (1987), Bank et al. (1991) and Dishion and Andrews (1995) all report favorable results using Patterson's work, even with high-risk adolescents. In summarizing the research, Feldman states: "the general implication is that if all parents were highly skilled in child management there would be a dramatic drop in crime by their offspring" (Feldman, 1993, p. 195).

"Family treatment is one of the more frequently evaluated forms of prevention and correction in the criminological literature" (Andrews and Bonta, 1994, p. 146). Gordon, Hill, Andrews, and Kurkowsky (1992) found 27 studies of family treatment with offender populations that used a control or alternative treatment group and an objective measure of recidivism. These studies produced a meaningful, though small, reduction in recidivism with family treatment in comparison to alternative types of treatment and to no treatment conditions. But Swenson, Henggeler, and Schoenwald report that "the majority of family based treatments have received no empirical support" (2004, p. 79). They go on to argue that there are five methods of family therapy that have both received empirical support and have been utilized with youth who exhibit criminal activity or substance abuse. These five are *family preservation models* (Nelson, 1990), *functional family therapy* (Alexander and Parsons, 1982), *structural family therapy* (Minuchin and Fishmann, 1981; Kurtines and Szapocznik, 1996), *multidimensional family therapy* (Liddle, Dakof, and Diamond, 1991; Liddle, 1995), and *multi-*

systemic therapy (Henggeler and Bourdin, 1990). Swenson, Henggeler, and Schoenwald (2004) offer an excellent brief summary of these treatment models and the outcome research for each one. The following section draws on their review of the research.

Family preservation programs are models of service delivery to families which have been used extensively within the child welfare system and also have been used to some extent with juvenile offenders and their families (Nelson, 1990). Nelson identified three distinct practice models of family preservation: (1) crisis intervention, (2) home-based model, and (3) family treatment model. The services are intensive, usually are delivered in the home setting, and have the primary goal of preventing an out-of-home placement for the youth. Swenson, Henggeler, and Schoenwald (2004) report that the research on family preservation models consists mainly of evaluations and quasi-experimental designs. The one randomized trial study that was reported (Feldman, 1991) did not show that family preservation services were more effective for antisocial juveniles than other traditional services.

Functional family therapy (FFT) was introduced by Alexander and Parsons in 1982 and was one of the first family-based treatments to be used with antisocial juveniles. In FFT, the therapist uses conceptual, technical, and interpersonal skills to target problem behaviors within the family, to discern the functions that these problem behaviors serve, and then to offer alternative behaviors that will serve those functions more positively. The research on FFT, according to Swenson, Henggeler, and Schoenwald, indicates that it can be helpful with juveniles who have less serious antisocial behavior, such as status offenses rather than criminal offenses, or misdemeanor offenses rather than felony offenses, but the efficacy of FFT for juveniles with serious antisocial behavior is undemonstrated.

Structural family therapy (SFT) is a method of forming a therapeutic system with the family and the therapist in order to change the family's organization and structure so that it can better adapt to changes and stress (Minuchin, 1974; Minuchin and Fishman, 1981). It is an action-oriented and present-focused method. Individual problem behaviors are seen as an expression of the family's dysfunction and are addressed using the techniques of joining, diagnosing, and restructuring. Most of the reported research has been conducted by Szapocznik and his colleagues with drug-abusing adolescents from Hispanic families. Swenson, Henggeler, and Schoenwald state "scant results have supported the clinical effectiveness of SFT" and that additional research is needed to evaluate the effectiveness and generalizability of SFT (2004, p. 85).

Multidimensional family therapy (MDFT) is a multi-component intervention that was developed for adolescent substance abusers (Liddle, Dakof, and Diamond, 1991; Liddle, 1995). MDFT is "theme driven" in that it focuses on mutually agreed-upon themes or areas of work that have meaning to the parent and to the adolescent. Engagement of the whole family and all subsystems are viewed as critical to treatment success. Four domains are targeted: (1) the adolescent's intrapersonal and interpersonal functioning; (2) the parents' intrapersonal and interpersonal functioning; (3) the parent-child interactions; (4) the family's interactions with other sources of influence, such as schools. One controlled clinical trial (Liddle and Dakof, 1995) found MDFT to be more effective in reducing drug use, with a one-year follow-up, than were peer group therapy and family education. Swenson, Henggeler, and Schoenwald consider MDFT to be a promising intervention, which, when it has been more thoroughly evaluated, will be informative.

Multisystemic therapy (MST) was developed as a treatment for adolescent offenders by Henggeler and his colleagues at the Medical University of South Carolina. It is based on Bronfenbrenner's (1979) theory of social ecology and pragmatic family systems models. MST combines family therapy, individual therapy for an especially troubled family member, and other community services, such as child care and help with school. Nine treatment principles guide the conceptualization of the problem behavior and the implementation of individualized interventions. Specific techniques of child psychotherapy which have some empirical evidence for their efficacy are employed. MST seeks to be flexible and to recognize that each family system is a unique set of factors. Family system therapy, marital therapy, individual therapy, and community resources may all play a part in the overall treatment plan, with special attention to utilizing techniques and methods that have empirical support. The caseload of each therapist is small, averaging 4–6 families. The therapist works with parents to improve their parenting skills and with children to improve their interpersonal skills. Peer, school, and neighborhood systems are included and problems of alcohol and drug abuse are treated.

Swenson, Henggeler, and Schoenwald (2004) reported on several studies which compared MST with serious juvenile offenders using randomized control and comparison groups. For example, Henggeler et al. (1992) reported that adolescents participating in MST had significantly lower rearrest rates after a 2.4-year follow-up as compared to other intensive probation services. In another example, Borduin et al. (1995) randomly assigned the families (N = 176) of chronic adolescent offenders to either MST or individual therapy. At the completion of treatment, the MST group had significantly fewer behavior problems and the parents reported greater cohesion in family relations. At a four-year follow-up, the MST group had substantially reduced violent criminal activity, other criminal activity, and drug-related arrests. Summarizing the research on MST, Swenson, Henggeler, and Schoenwald state that "several randomized trials with youths presenting serious antisocial behavior have demonstrated the short-term capacity of MST to improve family relations and the long-term ability of MST to reduce rates of arrest and out of home placement" (Swenson et al., 2004, p. 89). MST is the only family treatment approach to show long-term reductions in recidivism in randomized clinical trials.

Scared Straight

Scared Straight is the title of a documentary film that won both Emmy and Oscar awards in 1978. The documentary was based on the efforts of the Lifers Group at the Rahway State Prison in New Jersey to convince young juveniles in trouble with the law to abandon their antisocial behavior or risk the miseries of prison. The format was a rap session with a group of juveniles and a group of inmates serving life sentences. It was dramatic, emotional, and highly confrontational. According to some observers, it amounted to "group intimidation akin to shock therapy" (Homant and Osowski, 1982). It could also be considered "an instance of negative modeling" (Feldman, 1993, p. 385). The program was instantly popular and was imitated across the United States and Canada, some of these programs claiming up to 90 percent success rates. Upon closer examination, these preliminary reports had not been carefully done and when controlled studies of Scared Straight programs began to be published, the results were far from impressive. One study reported no significant difference between a Scared Straight group and a control group (Homant and Osowski, 1982). Another reported that juveniles exposed to a Scared Straight program were *more* likely than controls to commit subsequent offenses and more serious offenses (Finkenaur, 1982). After the novelty wore off, Scared Straight programs predictably vanished from the correctional scene. It does serve the useful purpose of pointing out how fleeting and faddish correctional treatment programs can be and reminding us of how skeptical we should be of newly announced programs for offenders.

Therapeutic Communities

The therapeutic community (TC) concept was developed by Maxwell Jones and others as part of a shift in British psychiatric hospitals after World War II. This shift was towards a more collaborative and less authoritarian method of treatment in which the patients are more active participants in the treatment. In the TC, the "residents" interact with the staff and each other and continually examine these relationships, usually in daily intensive group therapy. There are frequent meetings in which the staff and the residents participate together in running the community. There may also be individual counseling, social activities, and work assignments. Honesty, sincerity, and compliance with the rules are valued. Veteran residents may act as peer counselors for new residents and may also lead groups. A TC may be built upon any number of treatment philosophies; there have been TCs based on reality therapy, transactional analysis, and psychodynamic therapies. Tom Main, who coined the term *therapeutic community* in 1946, wrote that it is not only the structure, but the culture of the community which is important for effecting change. The TC inculcates a culture of closely examining personal, interpersonal, and intersystem problems with concern and caring for each member of the group (Main, 1946).

Summarizing the research on TCs can be confusing since a great variety of programs may refer to themselves as TCs. As Dolan emphasizes, simply operating a treatment program within an institution is not the same as having a TC (Dolan, 1998). She also describes two types of TCs, the TC proper and the TC approach (Clark, 1965; De Leon, 1983). A TC proper is based on the four core principles of permissiveness, communalism, democratization, and reality confrontation. A TC approach is more hierarchical, more authoritarian, and more confrontational than the TC proper. The TC approach is often seen in the Unites States in TCs for addicts. The research on these has been generally favorable in treating substance abuse and dependence (Wexler, 1995). TCs have been operated in a variety of inpatient settings, such as psychiatric hospitals, day hospitals, and secure hospitals as well as in prisons. Treatment effectiveness in the hospital setting is often measured in terms of symptom reduction. There are also studies which report a beneficial effect of TCs on prison conduct (for example, Sandhu, 1970; Cooke, 1989), but these studies do not report effects on recidivism. For our purposes, we are interested in the research which measures the effect of TCs in prisons on criminal recidivism.

Guided group interaction (GGI) is a sociological modality designed specifically to utilize peer pressure to modify delinquent behavior and minimize institutional living problems (Bixby, 1951; McCorkle, Elias and Bixby, 1958). Lester (2000) cautions that GGI may actually be a label given to some applications of group therapy within a TC, but he adds that an adaptation of the principles of TCs and GGI, called positive peer cultures, has received one evaluation of a substantial reduction in recidivism of juvenile delinquents (Vorrath and Brentro, 1985). Other studies showing a significant effect of TCs on recidivism include Sewell and Clark (1982) and Wexler et al. (1999).

In a particularly interesting analysis, Cullen found "dosage effects" at the Grendon Underwood Prison in Britain. At Grendon the entire 200-inmate prison was operated as a TC. Cullen conducted a study indicating a 33 percent overall reconviction rate for Grendon inmates with a two-year follow-up (1993). When he matched inmates for sentence length, offense type, and previous convictions, he found that only 19 percent of those completing 18 months or more of the therapy were reconvicted, whereas 50 percent of those completing less than 18 months of therapy were reconvicted within two years (Cullen, 1994), indicating that the *length* of the treatment, the "dosage," was an important factor.

There are also a number of studies which found no significant effect of TCs on recidivism (Craft, Stephenson and Granger, 1964; Fink, Derby and Martin, 1969; Robertson and Gunn, 1987; McMurran, Egan, and

Ahmadi, 1998). One study, which is often quoted, showed that psychopaths had *increased* recidivism after treatment in a TC (Rice, Harris, and Cormier, 1992). The TC in this study was the Social Therapy Unit (STU), a program for mentally disordered offenders in Canada. The offenders in the study all had a history of violent criminality. Treated offenders were matched with untreated offenders on measures of age, criminal history, and index offense. The Psychopathy Checklist — Revised was used to delineate psychopathic from nonpsychopathic program participants. The outcome measures were criminal recidivism and violent recidivism and the average follow-up period was more than ten years.

This interesting evaluation had the following results: (1) the results showed no effect of the TC in reducing recidivism overall; (2) psychopathic offenders who received treatment in the TC exhibited *higher* rates of violent recidivism than did psychopathic subjects who did not receive treatment; (3) the opposite result was found for nonpsychopathic subjects. The authors speculate that the results may indicate that psychopathic individuals in a TC environment learn how to better manipulate others. Psychopathic offenders with antisocial, procriminal values may use newly learned and improved social skills to manipulate and exploit others. This leads to the conclusion that intensive TCs place psychopathic individuals where they can influence each other in antisocial ways (Quinsey, Harris, Rice, and Cormier, 2003).

Some have argued that the Social Therapy Unit was not really a TC and that radical and inappropriate treatment methods were used. Therefore, the conclusion that psychopathic offenders cannot be helped by TCs is not warranted (see Dolan, 1998).

We are reminded once again of the dangers of hubris in the treatment of criminal offenders by the intemperate statements made about the Social Therapy Unit prior to its evaluation for its effects on recidivism. In 1977, one review of the STU stated that "this is an exciting program which has the hallmark of being right as ... the final model of DNA molecule looked right to Watson and Crick" (Butler, Long, and Rowsell, 1977, p. 3). One program review by the government of Canada reported: "[The program designer has] developed the techniques that are the most fruitful of any in the universe at the present time" (quoted in Quinsey, Harris, Rice, and Cormier, 2003, p. 84). Apparently not.

It appears that the best that we can say about TCs and criminal recidivism so far is that TCs are variously designed and implemented and that comparisons are therefore difficult. There is contradictory evidence about their efficacy in reducing recidivism, especially with violent psychopathic individuals, but there has been some success when recovery from substance abuse and addiction are the focus of the TC.

Achievement Place

Achievement Place (Phillips, 1968) is notable because it was an early use of the behavioral technique of the token economy and because versions of the Achievement Place model were instituted in many places in the United States (Feldman, 1993). The program was organized into family-style group homes for delinquent boys aged 12 to 16. Each home housed six to eight boys and two teaching parents. The boys underwent a complex program based on the principles of a token economy as developed by Ayllon and Azrin (1968). The boys learned social and educational skills, had limited self-government, and met with the teaching parents in evening family conferences. Tokens were given out for achievements and desirable behaviors and these tokens could also be taken back for undesired behaviors. The teaching parents were active and attentive role models. This type of program eventually became known as the Teaching Family Model (TFM).

An early evaluation of TFM was positive, showing that the Achievement Place participants had a reconviction rate after two years of 19 percent as compared to the 50 percent reconviction rate of those placed on probation or placed into a conventional group home (Fixsen et al., 1972). Though this report was encouraging, subjects had not been randomly placed in treatment groups. Unfortunately, three subsequent evaluations, with follow-up periods of up to three years, all supported the conclusion that the TFM model did not result in significantly lower reconviction rates as compared to other types of group homes (Kirigin, Braukman, Attwater, and Wolf, 1982; Weinrott, Jones and Howard, 1982).

Conclusion

The earliest and most ambitious attempt relating criminal behavior, psychotherapy, and the family was the famous Cambridge-Somerville Youth Study carried out between 1937 and 1945 (Teuber and Powers, 1953). Two hundred and thirty-five preadolescent boys who were assessed as likely to become delinquents were matched and then randomly assigned to either (1) counselors who used either (a) a psychoanalytic approach or (b) a Rogerian approach or (2) no treatment. The treatment consisted of weekly sessions and lasted for two to eight years. At a three-year follow-up, the groups were nearly identical in terms of offending, demonstrating that the therapy had no effect on later criminal behavior. A 30-year follow-up by McCord (1978) included 90 percent of the original participants. No significant differences were found between the groups for either serious or minor crimes. McCord did find that six of seven "home atmosphere" factors were related to later offending. When socioeconomic status was controlled, maternal affection and parental supervision were the two most important factors. Father absence was the factor that was not related to future offending.

Denno and McClelland (1986) conducted a longitudinal evaluation of the Philadelphia Youth Services Center counseling program and found no long-term difference in delinquent behavior for those boys who received counseling and those who did not. After a review of available studies, Feldman concludes that psychotherapy has no preventive effect on criminal behavior. "By now it is clear that the potential degree of success of even the best planned and executed program for offenders is relatively limited" (1993, p. 409)

After another extensive review, Curt Bartol said it this way: "Each variant of the psychotherapies has been tried to some extent within the correctional system under wide variations in method and purpose and different degrees of commitment. Overall, they have been marginally successful or unsuccessful in reducing criminal behavior, depending on one's point of view" (1999, p. 400).

While there is little evidence that psychotherapy can affect recidivism, there is evidence that correctional programs with certain specific characteristics can reduce reoffending. Gendreau and Goggin (2000) point out that there now exists a very large body of correctional evaluation research and that overall this research indicates that 60 percent of the programs studied did reduce recidivism, with an average reduction of 10 percent (Lipsey, 1992; Losel, 1995; Gendreau, 1996). In addition, programs that share certain characteristics, called "appropriate interventions," can reduce recidivism by an average of 25 percent. These "appropriate interventions" will be discussed in more detail in chapter six, The Principles of Effective Intervention. One of the major characteristics of appropriate interventions is that the treatment is based on behavioral strategies, such as radical behaviorism, social learning, or cognitive behavioral methods (Gendreau and Goggin, 2000).

In another review of the relevant literature, Hollin writes: "The message emerging from these studies was that treatment with offenders can have a small but significant effect in terms of reducing re-offending," especially if using a cognitive behavioral perspective (2004, pp. 8–9). In chapter five, we will focus on cognitive behavioral intervention, the most promising of the psychological interventions so far.

Chapter Five

The State of the Science:
Cognitive Behavioral Intervention

A man's life is what his thoughts make it.
— Marcus Aurelius

For criminal offenders, cognitive behavioral intervention, called CBI, is the treatment method which has accumulated the strongest research support so far. CBI is a cognitive intervention because it focuses on thinking and it is behavioral because it employs behavioral principles and techniques to effect change in the offender's behavior. These behavioral techniques include, among others, role-playing, contingency management, modeling, goal setting, token economies, and problem solving. Cognitions, as well as behaviors, are learned and the principles of behavioral conditioning apply to them. CBI is based on the assumption that thinking precedes behavior and that changes in thinking can change behavior, as illustrated at the top of page 78.

The principles of behaviorism were first put forward by the great Russian psychologist Ivan Pavlov. Pavlov demonstrated learning in which a stimulus comes to evoke a response that it did not previously evoke. For example, if a dog is given food at the same time that a bell rings, then, after a number of such pairings, eventually the sound of the bell alone will cause the dog to salivate. This type of learning is called classical conditioning, in which the food is the unconditioned stimulus and the salivation is the unconditioned response. The bell is the conditioned stimulus, which is

Figure 2: The Thinking Cycle.

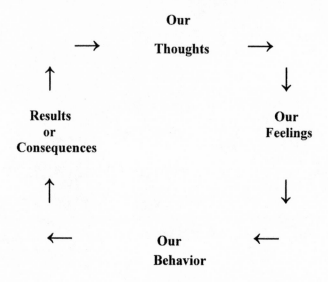

paired with the unconditioned stimulus (in this case, the food) until a conditioned response is produced (salivation to the bell alone).

A second type of conditioning was observed and described by Tolman, Guthrie, and Thorndike. They demonstrated in a series of experiments that, if a particular behavior was consistently followed by a reward, then that behavior was more likely to occur again. This type of learning is called operant conditioning. B. F. Skinner elaborated on this principle by defining different types of reinforcers according to whether they increased or decreased the frequency of a particular behavior. *Positive reinforcement* increases the likelihood of a behavior because that behavior is followed by a desirable consequence, a reward. In *negative reinforcement*, an undesirable consequence (such as anxiety, someone complaining) is avoided by a particular behavior. In *punishment*, the frequency of a behavior is decreased because it is followed by an undesirable consequence. In *extinction*, the likelihood of a behavior is decreased because nothing happens after a particular behavior is performed.

One of the most famous experiments in psychology was conducted by the American behaviorist John B. Watson (Watson and Raynor, 1920) shortly after World War I. Though it was not intended to explain crime, its results did lead to attempts to explain criminal behavior and to suggest how that behavior might be changed. Little Albert was a boy, aged 11 months, who was the subject of the experiment. Watson conditioned a fear of white rats in Little Albert, who previously liked white rats and often played with them. Watson did this by pairing a loud, upsetting noise with the presentation of the white rats. Every time Little Albert reached out towards the rats, Watson would hit a metal bar with a hammer. The noise caused Albert to whimper, cry, and withdraw. (This experiment would not meet ethical standards of research today, which is one of the problems in learning about criminal behavior from scientific experiments.) After a few such pairings, Little Albert would cry and try to crawl away every time the rats were introduced even without the loud noise. This conditioned fear reaction to the white rats persisted over a long time and even generalized to other furry objects such as rabbits and teddy bears. This phenomenon is called stimulus generalization. Watson's experiment resulted in an explosion of research on human learning.

Hans Eysenck (1977) took the findings of this body of theory and research on human learning and applied it to the problem of crime. He reasoned that when we ask why people commit crimes and other antisocial acts that we are putting the cart before the horse. It is our natural inclination to act selfishly and to take what one needs or wants. Babies and young children act this way and so do animals. Therefore, the crucial question, argues Eysenck, is why people do *not* commit crimes. What is it that stops us from acting with selfish aggression and total disregard for others?

Eysenck believes that it is conscience which prevents most people from acting in antisocial ways and that conscience is a conditioned emotional response acquired in childhood, just like Little Albert's fear of white rats. Because his parents or caretakers punished antisocial behavior, after which stimulus generalization occurred, the child came to experience anxiety, fear, tension, "unpleasure" towards antisocial activities of many kinds. Some people are autonomically prone to this kind of conditioning, argued Eysenck, while others are not.

If conscience is acquired in this way, and it is conscience which prevents antisocial behavior, what has happened when conscience is absent or defective? There are three possibilities: (1) lax parenting in which the necessary conditioning experiences do not happen; (2) the wrong experiences are reinforced; (3) low cortical arousal makes certain individuals extremely hard to condition. Cortical arousal is a state of the organism in which the brain is wide awake, concentrating, focusing, attentive, working at maximum capacity. Low arousal is like sleepiness, lack of attention, or lack of interest. Low arousal can lead to the sensation seeking that we often find in psychopaths. Low arousal also makes learning by Pavlovian principles extremely hard. Psychopaths condition slowly and therefore, in contrast to normals, are able to acquire the values and inhibitions of their social group only to a minimal degree. Eysenck writes that these observations about conscience explain a great deal of the known facts about antisocial conduct and have strong experimental support (Eysenck, 1977). He presented research to support this which he regarded as strong, but which other scientists have regarded as weak support for his contentions. Nevertheless, Eysenck's work is an integral part of the chain of research which led from classical and operant conditioning to cognitive behavioral intervention for criminal behavior. Eysenck and his colleagues did apply conditioning principles to clinical problems with some success.

Researchers and clinicians continued to develop techniques based on conditioning principles. Therapies with significantly successful outcomes included Wolpe's (1958) systematic desensitization, Cautela's (1967) covert sensitization, Ayllon and Azrin's (1968) token economy, Birk's behavioral medicine and biofeedback (1973), and Bandura's (1977) participant modeling. In systematic desensitization, a patient is taught a relaxation procedure and then, guided by the therapist, progresses through a step-by-step graded hierarchy of the feared situation while maintaining the relaxation. In vivo situations were used at first, but then imagined situations proved also to have beneficial therapeutic effects. In covert sensitization, unwanted behavior is imagined as paired with unpleasant stimuli, for example, exposure or arrest. In a token economy, residents are given tokens for desired behavior and may then exchange the tokens for a selected reward. In biofeedback, patients learn to control their physiological responses by receiving instant information about changes in their physiological system.

While these behavioral therapies had some success, the limitations of a strict adherence to behavioral principles became evident, and was critiqued by clinicians such as Lazarus (1971) as being too "mechanistic." They began to add cognitive components to therapeutic techniques. Lang (1970) had laid the foundation for a merger of cognitive and behavioral principles with his notion that the human organism has three response systems: behavioral, cognitive/affective, and physiological. Lang's three systems did not turn out to be the most useful way to conceptualize it, but his idea did offer an alternative to a single, unitary concept of psychological problems which was now seen as too simplistic.

Bandura demonstrated in a series of famous experiments the importance of observational learning in forming behavior patterns. His work focused attention on cognitive factors in therapy (Bandura, 1977). Meichenbaum (1975) proposed a model of self-instructional training in which he suggested that change can be brought about by helping patients to change the "instructions" (called self-talk), that patients give themselves. Patients are taught to dissipate destructive, maladaptive, and negative thoughts and to focus on positive and adaptive thinking.

Another precursor of CBT is rational emotive therapy (R.E.T.) created by Albert Ellis in 1955 (Ellis, 1962, 1973). R.E.T. has a long and successful history and has been applied to many mental health problems. In R.E.T., the patient is taught that negative emotional states are the result of irrational beliefs rather than activating events and he is taught to dispute these irrational beliefs. Rational beliefs increase positive feelings and happiness and decrease pain and anxiety. Ellis proposed the ABC model in which an activating event (A) is followed by an irrational belief (B), which has as a consequence (C), a negative emotional state. Thus, a typical sequence could be that a person fails at a task (A), believes that he is worthless and doomed to failure (B), which results in depression, anger, and self-pity. It may also be seen that, in the language of conditioning, (A) is the activating stimulus and (C) is the conditioned response with (B) intervening between the two. Thus, changing (B) changes (C) even though (A) remains unchanged. The therapy then consists of disputing the patient's irrational beliefs (B) and replacing them with rational ones, which will result in a better consequence, a positive emotional state. Ellis now calls his system R.E.B.T., rational emotive behavior therapy, to acknowledge that the goal is changed behavior: one must put one's thoughts into action. Research on R.E.B.T. with criminal offenders is scant, and Ellis believed that it is not likely to be successful with many psychopaths (Ellis, 1962).

Maultsby (1975) did report on extensive use of R.E.T. with probationers with some modest success. Ellis' work is important in the treatment of criminal offenders even though R.E.B.T. is not often used with that population because many of the current state-of-the-art treatments are very similar to R.E.B.T. and are indebted to its development over the last 50 years.

Another major figure in the development of CBI is Aaron Beck (1970, 1976). Beck was first concerned with the treatment of depression but later extended his model to a wide range of emotional disorders. Beck proposed that negative thinking was not merely a symptom of depression but played an important role in the maintenance of depression. Depression originates in childhood where attitudes and assumptions are formed based on experience. Some of these attitudes and assumptions, or beliefs, are helpful, but some of them are distorted and pathological. Beck quotes Abraham Maslow who wrote, "The neurotic is not only emotionally sick — he is cognitively wrong" (1976, p. 76).

Beck offers the following example of such a cognitive distortion. A patient who was a novelist reported that he had a chain of thoughts whenever someone complimented him on his work: "People won't be honest with me. They know I'm mediocre. They just won't accept me as I really am. They keep giving me phony compliments." Beck commented that since the novelist irrationally evaluated his own work as inferior, he considered compliments to be insincere. The novelist then concluded this chain of ideas with yet another irrational belief, that he couldn't have a genuine relationship with other people. These irrational beliefs made him feel even more lonely and isolated, leading to a deepening depression. The work of a cognitive therapist would be to point this out to the patient, to dispute the irrational beliefs, and to lead the patient to discard those distorted beliefs and replace them with more rational ones (1976, p. 27). The effect of this work, sometimes called cognitive restructuring, would lead to a change in mood. Moods are governed by what Beck called "the cognitive triad": thoughts about self, current experience, and the future. These thoughts govern mood and can be changed. Beck observed that patients often had "automatic thoughts," thoughts which emerged automatically and very rapidly. Patients have to be instructed to focus on the thoughts which preceded a negative emotional state. Thus, patients are taught to focus on negative automatic thoughts and cognitive distortions and to replace them with positive and rational thoughts. This replacement, or cognitive restructuring, leads to positive emotional states, which leads to changed behavior.

Both Beck and Ellis are fond of quoting the Greek philosopher Epictetus, who wrote, "Men are not disturbed by events but by their perception of events." So Epictetus might be considered the great progenitor of CBI. Ellis, Beck, and the other behavioral and cognitive precursors of CBI were not specifically focused on criminal offenders, but their groundbreaking work did lead to treatments specifically for the offender population.

The Case of James V.

One of my few triumphs as a therapist in prison was a case of agoraphobia. The phobias are one of the most treatable of the mental disorders, but they are not a common problem within a prison population since phobic disorders do not typically lead to criminal behavior. Agoraphobia is an overwhelming anxiety about having panic attacks in a variety of situations where escape is difficult or help is not available. Such situations include being outside of the home alone, being in a crowd or standing in a line, being on a bridge, or traveling in a bus, train, or car.

Each Tuesday I held an outpatient mental health clinic at the Clark Prison Unit. The morning session was nearly over and I had only reached the fourth name on my outpatient clinic list of 15 inmates. I had started with an inmate who wanted a transfer to another prison and thought that he "would go crazy" if he didn't get the transfer, so he had signed up to see the psychologist about that transfer.

"Ain't it your job to keep me from going crazy?"

Next I had seen a paranoid schizophrenic who showed up for his regular monitoring visit with his shirt on backwards and a small piece of aluminum foil tucked behind each ear.

"Calvin, have you stopped taking your medicine?"

He was followed by a sex offender who had been court ordered for psychological assessment. He related to me that he thought it was best that his 13-year-old daughter should learn about sexual intercourse from him since he was her father and really cared about her. Those teenage boys she was seeing weren't really going to care about her. He was only trying to do what was best for her just like any father would do and didn't I agree? He said that he simply had no clue as to why his wife filed charges against him.

"She must have been mad about something."

The fourth patient of the day was a slightly overweight African American man who appeared to be in his early forties. He had a passive, hesitant manner about him. He sat down carefully and appeared nervous.

"You are?" I asked.

"James V.," he answered.

"Well, Mr. V., how can I help you?" I had his prison record in front of me. Convicted of second-degree murder. Life sentence. Average IQ. Sixth-grade reading level. Completed the substance abuse treatment program. A regular participant in Alcoholics Anonymous. Unit psychiatrist has him on a mild anti-anxiety medication. In minimum custody. Over 18 years in prison. No prison rule violations in the last 10 years.

"I'm afraid to go out the gate," he said.

I asked him to describe what he felt like as he approached the sliding electronic gate which led out of the prison.

"I feel scared, like something bad is going to happen to me."

"Does your heartbeat speed up?"

"Yeah."

"Do you feel a tightness in your chest?"

"Uh-huh."

"How about sweating? Do you break into a sweat?"

"Sometimes. I think so. Yeah."

"Do you ever feel like you're choking?"

"No. I never felt like that."

"Do you feel like you can't breathe, like having shortness of breath?'

"Yeah. It's like I'm breathing real fast and can't catch my breath."

"Do you feel dizzy or nauseated like you might throw up?'

"No, I never felt like I was goin' to throw up."

"Do you start trembling or shaking?"

"Sometimes, if I don't leave and go back in the yard."

"Do you feel like this couldn't be real? Couldn't be happening to you?"

"Yeah, it's like I'm thinking that I'm going crazy."

"Do you think about this problem a lot?"

"I thinks about it every day. Every time I sees the gate."

"Do you want to get over this problem?"

"I got to get over it or I will never get out of the penitentiary. It never bothered me when I was at Central or when I was in brown clothes. I wasn't allowed out the gate. But ever since I been in honor grade, I been scared and nervous."

"How long have you been in honor grade?'

"About six months. My caseworker says I can have a job now. If I go on work release, after that, I can make parole. But I'm afraid I'll never make it. I ain't been outside in 18 years."

This was an uncommon experience for me. Here was a prison inmate politely seeking out treatment on his own for a genuine emotional problem that was treatable. I hoped that I didn't appear as surprised as I felt. In my effort to dissemble, I overdid it and with barely concealed excitement I spoke in a near whisper. "James, it is possible to overcome this problem."

We made a treatment contract between us. I would teach him breathing exercises and deep muscle relaxation exercises and he would agree to practice them faithfully. Next we would construct a hierarchy of panic- and anxiety-producing situations from least threatening to most threatening. We began with walking past the gate but not stopping, then going up to the gate and standing, going through the gate, walking down to the bus stop, waiting for the bus, getting on the bus, riding the bus, getting off at the right stop, walking to the job site, until at last he was walking onto his job site and reporting to his work supervisor.

Next we would conduct practice sessions in which he would use breathing and muscle relaxation exercises to feel "calm and in control" and then he would imagine going through the hierarchy of threatening situations, from least threatening to most threatening. He would practice until he could imagine each one without a feeling of panic or undue anxiety.

After mastering the situation in imagination, we would next practice the real situations, one at a time, from least threatening to most threatening, not progressing to the next step until the previous step could be taken with a "feeling of being calm and in control." We agreed that he could continue taking the mild anti-anxiety medication that he was receiving from the psychiatrist, but that it would be one of our goals to reach a point where he could engage these situations without medication.

Over the next weeks, we held our sessions and practiced. James attended all of the sessions, reported practicing between sessions, and appeared to be improving. I offered to accompany him on his first real trial at the gate, but he declined, perhaps because he thought it might be embarrassing to be seen at the gate with the prison psychologist, or maybe because he really didn't think he needed that much support. In any case, he succeeded. I arranged with the custody staff to allow him to pass through the gate, walk down to the bus stop, remain there for a while, and then return through the gate at any time during the day. Of course, the custody staff regarded this procedure as clearly lunatic as well as contrary to policy, but I prevailed because I had good rapport with the prison superintendent whom I had known for years and because I asserted that it was necessary for treatment reasons. Otherwise, this modest treatment procedure would have met an insurmountable obstacle, which is often what happens in the practice of psychology in prison.

Over the next several weeks James reported that the most difficult step for him turned out to be waiting at the bus stop.

"The first time, I couldn't take it for long and I left and went back to the prison. But then I thought about how I would never get out of prison if I couldn't do this. So I practiced my breathing like you said and I went back."

After three months of working together, James had been approved for work release, was able to go all the way to his job site and return to the prison via the bus without incapacitating panic, and had discontinued his anti-anxiety medication.

One early morning, James stopped me as I was walking across the prison yard towards the medical office. "I've been at work for four weeks now," he said. "I wanted to thank you for helping me. I'm not afraid no more. I practice my breathing just like you taught me." He offered to shake hands and then he walked off towards the gate and the "street world" outside.

This sequence of events doesn't happen very often in prison and I felt an unaccustomed pleasure and satisfaction. Obstacles to treatment prevail in prison and many prison psychologists eventually restrict themselves to assessment and crisis intervention, knowing from experience the limitations and the opposition that they will face in attempting treatment. It must be said, however, that some of the greatest obstacles to treatment are the inmates themselves. They generally do not show up for treatment unless someone else is requiring it of them and they usually see nothing wrong with their behavior. They point to the behavior of other people as the cause of the problems they are facing. In this case, James was self-motivated to solve a genuine problem and undoubtedly this fact was the major contributor to his success.

This case is an example of using a behavioral treatment successfully with an offender, but the treatment did not address his criminality, nor did it address a problem believed to be directly related to his criminality, such as substance abuse. One of the things that we learned in chapter four was that applying psychotherapeutic methods that are not intended to reduce crime is generally not successful in reducing crime though it may be successful in addressing other problems. Since we are mainly interested in reducing recidivism, what about cognitive behavioral treatments that are directed specifically at this goal?

The Treatment of the Criminal Personality

One of the earliest cognitive treatments designed specifically for criminal offenders was the work of Samuel Yochelson and Stanton Samenow (1976, 1977). According to Yochelson and Samenow, crime resides within the person and is "caused" by the way he thinks, not by his environment. They prefer the term *criminal personality* because it avoids the confusion that is usually raised with terms like *psychopath, sociopath, antisocial personality disorder,* and *dyssocial offender.* They also prefer to avoid what they regard as the "usual euphemisms" for a criminal, such as *offender, client, violator, resident, delinquent,* or *inmate.* Samenow believes that using the word *criminal* focuses us on what we are really concerned about, that is, the person who commits crimes, and on the behavior that we wish to change, that is, criminal behavior.

Samenow, a psychologist who is now in private practice in Alexandria, Virginia, worked for 15 years at St. Elizabeth's Hospital in Washington, D.C. He, together with the psychiatrist, Samuel Yochelson, began treating patients who had been committed to the hospital by the courts as not guilty by reason of insanity. Their project, the Program for the Investigation of

Criminal Behavior, was carried out in the 1960s and 1970s. Their original group consisted of 255 males. Gradually, over the years, they expanded their efforts to include offenders of all types. Together they published the results of their work in *The Criminal Personality*, which eventually became three volumes and nearly 1,500 pages (Yochelson and Samenow, 1976, 1977, 1986). Dr. Yochelson died of a heart attack in 1976 while, ironically, on his first out-of-town speaking trip. Samenow has continued work on the criminal personality until the present time, lecturing tirelessly across the United States and publishing additional books and articles (Samenow, 1984, 2004).

Samenow began with an examination of the historical and current theories of the cause of crime and found all of them inadequate. "When I first began this work, I believed that criminal behavior was a symptom of buried conflicts that had resulted from early traumas and deprivations of one sort or another. I thought that people who turned to crime were victims of a psychological disorder, an oppressive social environment, or both" (2004, p. xxi). But he writes that, as he became experienced with criminals in treatment and as he searched through the literature on the causes of crime and the treatment of criminals, he and his colleague became "reluctant converts" to a new point of view. They concluded that sociological explanations were too simplistic. If these theories were accurate, that social conditions cause crime, then there should be many more criminals then there are. Criminals cause crime, not bad neighborhoods, inadequate parents, television, schools, drugs, or unemployment. They saw criminals not as victims but as victimizers who had freely chosen their way of life. They concluded that focusing on forces outside of the individual is futile for understanding the criminal and for engaging him in a change process. So they abandoned the search for causes and launched their treatment program, based on the proposition that, for unknown reasons, hard-core criminals simply choose, from childhood, to engage in antisocial behavior.

Samenow and Yochelson propose that a criminal is a person whose patterns of thinking have led to arrestable behavior. Their approach to the understanding of the criminal is "phenomenological," by which they mean "thinking about thinking." Like Pinel and Cleckley (1988) before them, they are astute observers of human behavior who carefully document their observations. Their intensive work, including hundreds of interviews, led them to describe the criminal as a person who reveals himself when the thinking by which he supports his actions is uncovered. Samenow and Yochelson describe what they call "thinking errors" which exist in the criminal's mind and which inevitably lead to criminal actions. The concept of thinking errors is not an original contribution; it is an idea that can be traced throughout the development of cognitive psychology. It can be found in the rational emotive therapy of Albert Ellis and in the cognitive therapy of Aaron Beck, among others. But no one has applied this idea to the criminal person so specifically and with such deliberation and thoroughness as have Yochelson and Samenow.

For example, one of the thinking errors is called the "victim stance." The criminal constantly attempts to blame others or anything at all except himself for his crimes. In this mode of thinking, the criminal attempts to convince others that he is really the victim and not responsible for what he has done. This is a common trait among criminals. It might be said that self-justification is a common human characteristic and not confined to criminals alone. But with the criminal, this trait, or thinking error, is extreme, both in the frequency with which he exhibits it, applying it to virtually every behavior, and in degree, in the lengths to which he will carry it. One example of this extremity is the inmate that I interviewed who had shot to death a convenience store clerk during a robbery. His explanation of his behavior was that he had been fired from his job and had no money. Therefore, he had no choice but to rob. When the store clerk reached for a weapon from behind the counter, he had no choice but to shoot. "Really," my inmate explains, "if he hadn't done that, he would be alive today. He killed himself by doing that. I had no choice." The clerk killed himself! Therefore, my inmate had concluded that it was *his employer's fault* that my inmate had no job, it was *society's fault* that he had no money, and it was *the clerk's own fault* that he was killed. What a tidy explanation for armed robbery and felony murder! Furthermore, the inmate feels that *he* is the victim now because he is forced to serve life in prison just for "being in the wrong place at the wrong time." This type of extreme thinking, extreme both in frequency and in degree, is what Samenow calls a "thinking error"; it is clearly beyond the common human tendency for self-justification. Other examples of thinking errors include "the I can't attitude," "lack of a concept of injury to others," lack of empathy, "superoptimism," and "sentimentality." Samenow and Yochelson identify and describe in detail a total of 52 thinking errors, a study which is both exhaustive and exhausting to read. Nevertheless, professionals who are very experienced with criminals find these personality descriptions to be very accurate.

Another helpful contribution made by Samenow and Yochelson is *The Continuum of Criminality* (1976, pp. 252–253). In developing the continuum of criminality, they emphasize the thinking processes in the individual which inevitably lead to irresponsible behavior. The irresponsible but nonarrestable person, the petty thief, the professional criminal, the white-collar criminal, and the illiterate bank robber all have thought patterns in common, though they differ in degree, in intensity, in pervasiveness, and in the consequences that their behavior incurs. On the one end of our continuum, we have the basically responsible person. The responsible person has a lifestyle of hard work, fulfillment of obligations, and consideration for others. He derives self-respect and the respect of others through his achievements. Desires to violate the law do occur in such a person, but they usually disappear quickly and without much effort. The responsible person does have moments of anger, of vindictiveness, of deceit, but even these moments do not result in serious injury to the person or to the rights of others.

Some people do not violate the law, but they can be considered irresponsible. These are the people who are chronically late, perform poorly at work, and fail to fulfill their obligations. They do not consider other people or the effects that their behavior has on other people. They are frequently untruthful. However, they cannot be arrested for these shortcomings and we do not call them criminals. Yet they are defaulters, liars, excuse givers, and are generally unreliable and very self-centered in their personal relationships. People referred to as arrestable criminals have all the thinking patterns and irresponsible behavior of the hard-core criminals, but their crimes are less extreme and less serious in terms of the injuries that are inflicted on others. They are minor violators. People in this category have strong recurrent desires to violate the law, but they can be deterred from committing serious crimes.

Finally, at the opposite end of our continuum from the basically responsible person is the extreme criminal. He is the one that we refer to as a *criminal personality*. His criminal thought processes are operative at an early age. Although he is member of a relatively small group of offenders, he poses the greatest problems in terms of the heavy injuries that he inflicts. He violates the rights of others as a permanent lifestyle. He commits literally hundreds of violations of the law and is convicted for only a small portion of what he has done. He thinks constantly of crimes and is totally inconsiderate of others. He is deceitful in the extreme and is almost completely devoid of empathy. Lying is a way of life to him. His life goals are excitement and power over others. He has a chessboard view of life in which everyone is his opponent. One wins by making calculated moves which are as deceitful as possible and which result in the elimination of threats to his position. We are not calling "criminal" anyone who has ever told a lie or been irresponsible or violated the law. All of us have behaved irresponsibly at some time or been deceitful at some time, perhaps in order to avoid some difficult situation. But the extreme criminal is really different in the intensity and the frequency of his criminal thinking patterns. He appears, as Samenow asserts, "morally retarded." His style of life, his attitude towards others, and his choices are different from those of responsible persons. He has freely chosen an irresponsible lifestyle and he supports this lifestyle with thought processes that justify these choices. He is not a victim; he is a victimizer; he is the one who has victims. If this extreme criminal also chooses to abuse drugs and alcohol, he becomes even more extreme in his thinking and behavior (Samenow and Yochelson, 1986).

Figure 3: <u>The Continuum of Responsibility</u>.

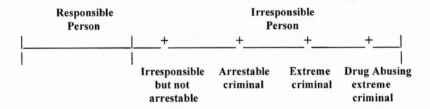

Samenow writes, "the essence of this approach is that criminals choose to commit crimes" (1984, p. xiv). The plain language categories and resistance to the temptation so common in psychology to invent obscure, tongue-tying terminology is attractive. The continuum of criminality is a helpful way to think about offenders, to see their errors in thinking as different in degree and intensity from the average person's errors in thinking. The detailed descriptions of the criminal personality and the errors in thinking that characterize them lead to a deeper understanding of the criminal's actions and decisions. This approach to understanding the criminal person results in a specific and practical treatment method that can be applied to all levels of offenders, from minor violators to extreme criminals.

The treatment consists of a group process, led by a therapist with a firm and directive stance, in which the criminal is led through patient and repetitive corrections of his errors in thinking. The goal of the treatment is to move him along the continuum towards being a more responsible person, both in word and in deed. Samenow argues that successful treatment requires two conditions. The first is a "lever." The lever is usually the threat of incarceration. The criminals in their program were mostly on probation or parole or incarcerated with the hope of early release for participating in treatment. Typically the criminal's motivation span is short. It is one of his traits to be enthusiastic about a quick success but to be very impatient with any activity that requires endurance and steady application. Consequently, treatment requires that the treatment agent have a lever to encourage participation over a significant period of time.

The second condition is vulnerability. Though the criminal is not, in Samenow's view, mentally ill, he does have periods of depression and discouragement. It is characteristic of the criminal to alternate between periods of exaggerated self-esteem and periods of intense discouragement and feelings of worthlessness. Samenow refers to these low periods as "the zero state," which comes from the criminal's self-description: "I feel like a zero, a nothing." This is the time when he is most vulnerable and also most treatable.

The treatment program requires a four-year commitment, though some participants may spend less time in it and others may spend more, depending on the severity and intensity of their criminality. However, it is never over. It is like Alcoholics Anonymous in that a person may need less of it over time but will always need some of it. The program begins with a series of intensive interviews conducted by the change agent. Yochelson and Samenow prefer the term *agent of change* rather than *therapist* or *clinician*. This is because they view the change agent as primarily a teacher rather than a therapist and because training in psychiatry or psychology is not required, only training in this treatment method is required. The interviews are designed to assess the person's criminal career, to push him to drop the victim stance, that is, to begin to accept personal responsibility, and to enhance his sense of self-disgust. This last phrase, "to enhance his sense of self-disgust" is not meant sarcastically, but is intended to refer to the correction of the criminal's lack of empathy with the people that he has harmed. This process is begun in the initial interviews.

After this series of interviews the criminal is placed in a group. The group is composed of the change agent and five or six criminals who are at different stages of the change process. The group method is preferred because it is efficient and because the group members eventually act as correctives to each other. The group meets three hours a day, five times a week, for one year. The group has three purposes:

(1) to teach phenomenologic reporting;
(2) to correct the thinking errors;
(3) to conduct an examination of conscience.

Phenomenologic reporting means "thinking about thinking." The criminal has to be taught to do this as he is not a naturally reflective person. The group participants are taught to report their thoughts over the last 24 hours at each group meeting. They are taught to make notes and present to the group in a logical and coherent manner what their thinking was. The group then points out the thinking errors and their correction. It is, of course, characteristic of the criminal to be self-serving and a great liar, so what value is this procedure if you don't get genuine and truthful reports? There are several checks on the criminal's genuineness and truthfulness. The change agent is in constant communication with significant others in the criminal's life: employer, probation/parole officer, spouse, girlfriend, and family members. The change agent uses this information as a check on the criminal's reporting. The other members of the group, who are themselves intimately familiar with tactics used by criminals to obstruct effective treatment, challenge the individual to be authentic. Finally, it is not particularly significant if the criminal gets away with some untruthfulness. The main point is the criminal's thought processes in general and this will eventually come out. The change agent does not need to become a detective who attempts to cross-check every detail. Perfect veracity really doesn't matter because enough material about the basic thought processes will emerge even without complete honesty.

The second thing to be done in the group is to point out the thinking errors and offer ways to correct them. For example, attempts to take the victim stance are not accepted and a focus on what the criminal himself did, the choices that he made, is insisted upon. There are five levels of deterrence, that is, deterring criminal thoughts, which can be taught to the group members. These include aborting a crisis, disposing of a criminal thought by reasoning, preempting criminal thinking, taking a moral inventory, and automatic deterrence.

The third thing that is taught in the group is an examination of conscience. This examination of conscience is similar to the searching moral inventory of Alcoholics Anonymous. Criminals are not very good at this and have to be taught how to do it. It is most effective when the criminal is vulnerable, that is, in his zero state.

After at least one year in the group, contacts are reduced to a group meeting once a week. After about two years, contact is reduced to a rate that is determined by the criminal himself. This works out in practice to be frequent at some times and infrequent during other periods. However, the change agent maintains contact with significant others as a check on how the criminal is doing.

The program can be started while the criminal is incarcerated, but at some point he must be released in order to test his functioning in the real world. It is a stringent requirement of the program that a released participant maintain a regular eight-hour-a-day job, that he not be arrested, and that he demonstrate responsibility in his personal relationships. Noncompliance results in reincarceration.

Free will is a basic premise of the program. Samenow believes that a person has the capacity to make choices and can choose responsible over irresponsible behavior. A total "180 degree change" is demanded in the criminal's thinking pattern to produce an about-face in his behavior patterns. This is "habilitation," not rehabilitation, because the criminal is not returning to the way that he was, but instead he is learning responsibility for the first time, to act in ways which he never has before.

Has this treatment approach proved effective? Samenow and Yochelson report data indicating that they were successful (as defined by no rearrests) with one out of three. Some of the men in the original treatment group of 255 were followed up for as long as twelve years (Yochelson & Samenow, 1976, pp. 44–54). Considering that they were working with the most extreme criminals, a success rate of approximately 33 percent is very good. However, a definitive evaluation of this method of treatment has not been conducted, even three decades after Samenow and Yochelson began to publish their ideas (Samenow, personal communication, 2005). Part of the reason for this is that to replicate the program in all of its components would be a very expensive and lengthy project. Samenow's work has been criticized as an immense effort for a small amount of people and for the fact that he has "abandoned the search for causes" and, hence, this approach to the treatment of criminals offers no understanding of how criminals come to be the way that they are.

Nevertheless, this perspective has influenced the training and practice of many corrections professionals and the thinking errors in particular have been included as a part of many cognitive behavioral corrections programs. It is useful to know that not all trained and experienced scientists and clinicians are settled on a deterministic point of view towards criminals, including even serious repeat offenders, and that at least some careful observers in the field of crime are not hesitant to assert that their understanding of the criminal is "unapologetically moralistic."

A Menu of CBI Programs for Offenders

A number of CBI programs for offenders have now been developed and implemented with criminal offenders. One of the earliest (and best) of these is the work of Arnold Goldstein and his colleagues. Goldstein's *Aggression Replacement Training* (Goldstein and Glick, 1987) is designed to teach adolescents to understand and replace aggression and antisocial behavior with positive alternatives. The three-part training approach focuses on (1) teaching prosocial skills, called *skill streaming,* (2) anger control, based on earlier work by Novaco (1979), and (3) moral reasoning, based on work by Kohlberg (1976). In an expanded and updated version of this classic intervention program, Goldstein, Glick, and Gibbs (1998) describe a wide range of program applications and settings. They also summarize a number of outcome-evaluation studies that demonstrate the effectiveness of the program. Appendices include over 100 pages of guidelines, checklists, moral reasoning problem situations, and more. Goldstein's *Prepare Curriculum* (1988) is an extensive inventory of teaching prosocial skills to youth. Many of Goldstein's ideas show up in later cognitive behavioral programs.

The EQUIP program added together Aggression Replacement Training (ART) and Positive Peer Culture (PPC). PPC (Vorrath and Brentro, 1985) uses group meetings to motivate young offenders to help each other and to behave responsibly. The EQUIP program has achieved some favorable results (Gibbs and Goldstein, 1995).

Moral Reconation Therapy (MRT) is presently in use in over 40 states and in several foreign countries, including Canada and Bermuda. MRT was developed by Little and Robinson from their work with drug abuse programs in Memphis in 1985–1987. The term *reconation* is derived from the word *conation* and is intended to mean reevaluating decisions. MRT is based also on the moral judgment theory of Kohlberg. The purpose of MRT is to raise the participant's level of moral reasoning which, it is assumed, will improve his social behavior, including reducing offending.

The adult offender workbook for MRT was first published in 1986. The workbook currently in use, *How to Escape Your Prison*, was refined through trial and error, inmate input, and research (Little, 2000). MRT is a process group in which homework is presented. Each participant works through each module in the workbook with feedback from the group participants. Faulty beliefs are addressed and alternatives are provided. The groups are open-ended, ongoing groups with 5–20 or more clients in a group. The groups typically meet twice a week for 1.5 hours, but may meet from once a month (probation groups, for example) to five times a week (therapeutic communities, for example). MRT may be used to enhance other treatment programs or as a stand-alone treatment method.

Little (2001) reported on 75 published studies of MRT. These studies reported on various aspects of the program, such as treatment completion, program attrition, personality characteristics, changes in moral reasoning, and prison conduct. For our purposes, we are mainly interested in changes in recidivism. Little stated that seven of these 75 studies reported recidivism rates of MRT–treated offender groups as compared to nontreated controls with a one-year follow-up after release. However, Little notes that these studies did not randomly assign subjects to treatment and control groups and thus only "quasi randomization was achieved." One study did not show any reduction in recidivism. The others did report reductions in recidivism after one year. In a meta analysis, Little concludes that MRT results in a 23 percent recidivism rate as compared to the expected 30–50 percent expected recidivism rate from his nonrandom controls. (A meta analysis is an alternative to a narrative literature review. In a meta analysis, a statistical measure of the association between program intervention and reduced recidivism across multiple studies is calculated and reported.) Thus, he concludes, MRT cuts the expected recidivism rate in half, which is certainly an overly optimistic interpretation of the data since a 30–50 percent expected recidivism is a rather large range. And why assume the 50 percent for comparison rather than the 30 percent? In which case, the reduction is 7 percent rather than "half," remembering also that this result is based on data from studies with "quasi randomization." To be fair, evaluation research with true experimental designs are relatively rare in the field of offender treatment. This is one of the reasons that we know so little about the effectiveness of programs and why there is so much debate about them.

Little, Robinson, and Burnette (1993) reported in another study that MRT–treated felony offenders had a 37.1 percent recidivism rate as compared to a recidivism rate of 54.9 percent for a nontreated control group. In a more recent experimental study, 256 youth offenders held in a jail in Maryland were randomly assigned to MRT and to a control group. There were no statistically significant differences in the risk of recidivism between the randomized control group and the treatment group. A "high implementation group," which received at least 30 days of treatment and was compared to the control group, again showed no significant differences in the risk of recidivism (Armstrong, 2003).

The Reasoning and Rehabilitation Program (R & R), also known as Cognitive Skills Training, was originally developed and presented by Ross and Fabiano (1985) and further developed and tested by Ross, Fabiano, and Ewles (1988). The program has been implemented widely in the United States and Canada and also in a number of other countries including England, Germany, and Australia. The R & R model is based on the observation that many offenders did not acquire the necessary cognitive skills for prosocial adjustment in the course of their child and adolescent social-ization. The absence of appropriate adult role models and/or the presence of poor parenting practices resulted in skill deficits. The R & R approach is based on the assumption that the necessary skills can be acquired through structured interventions. The R & R model does pose to the clients a choice: in one pocket are the old skills and ways of adapting and in another pocket are new skills and methods of adapting acquired through the R & R pro-gram. You may choose which pocket to draw from in adapting to the real-ity of your life from here on. (Robinson and Porporino, 2004).

R & R consists of 36 two-hour sessions delivered by intensively trained paraprofessionals who are considered "coaches" or "trainers." The groups are composed of 6–12 offenders and the group sessions combine the teach-ing of cognitive skills with individual and group skill practice. Target skills include problem solving, perspective taking, self-control, critical reason-ing, cognitive style, and values. Exercises include role-playing, dilemma games, cognitive puzzles, and board games. Many of the social skills are based on the work of Goldstein (discussed above). The program empha-sizes teaching participants to become more reflective and less reactive.

The published research on R & R has produced mixed results. For example, Ross et al. (1988) compared the postprogram outcomes of pro-bationers randomly assigned to one of three groups: (1) a group receiving the R & R program; (2) a group receiving life skills training; and (3) a group of regular probationers. During the follow-up period, none of the R & R group were incarcerated, while 11 percent of the life skills group and 30 per-cent of the regular probation group were incarcerated. This result was very encouraging, though the numbers (n = 62) were small. On the other hand, some reports have not produced positive results on recidivism for R & R participants (for example, Mitchell & Palmer, 2005; Wilkinson, 2005).

The preponderance of the evidence so far supports some positive effects from the R & R program. Robinson and Porporino (2004) write that the available body of research on this specific approach to the rehabilitation of criminal offenders suggests that the program can produce beneficial effects for many types of offenders, including high-risk adult offenders, substance-abusing offenders, and juvenile offenders. "Ideally, the programme is suited to offenders who are at medium to high risk of recidivism and exhibit deficits in the various cognitive skills that are included in the programme"

(2004, p. 75). There is considerable ongoing research involving the R & R program and we should have a clearer picture of its effectiveness in various settings in the near future.

This discussion does not exhaust the range of cognitive behavioral programs but merely describes some of the more well-known ones. There are others as well, such as *Direct Decision Therapy* (Greenwald, 1973), *Cognitive Self Change* (Bush & Bilodeau, 1993) which is an adaptation of Yochelson and Samenow's work on thinking errors, and *Thinking for a Change* (Glick, Bush, and Taymans, 2001), developed for the National Institute of Corrections and widely used by corrections agencies.

The research is generally supportive of cognitive behavioral approaches (Hollin, 2004), but claims of superiority of one particular version over another do not appear well founded, and sometimes these claims have a commercial rather than a scientific flavor about them. It seems that program proponents sometimes exaggerate the significance of positive results and ignore negative results, an affliction which Andrews and Bonta have called "theoreticism" (Andrews and Bonta, 1994). So there is all the more reason to seek studies by authors other than the program developers themselves, though there is nothing wrong with program developers pointing out to potential consumers the results of available studies. It is up to the consumer to make a judgment about the quality of the evaluation and what the results mean (see chapter one on recidivism). Successful correctional programs have a number of important elements, of which a cognitive behavioral perspective is only one, and these elements must be combined for success. These principles of effective intervention are the subject of the next chapter.

Chapter Six

The Principles of
Effective Intervention

[T]he evidence is persuasive that specific styles of service delivery can reduce offenders' criminal behavior to a degree that has profound policy implications.

— Paul Gendreau, 1996

"Nothing Works"

The publication in 1974 of Robert Martinson's paper, "What Works? Questions and Answers About Prison Reform," signaled a retreat by criminal justice professionals from the rehabilitative ideal in the management of criminal offenders. Such a desertion suited the political temper of the times (Cullen and Gendreau, 1989). Martinson's analysis offered scientific support, eagerly received by some, for the abandonment of rehabilitative efforts in the correctional system. The criminological pendulum was swinging towards deterrence, due process, just deserts, and "punishment with dignity." Clive Hollin called Martinson's paper "a gunshot precipitating an avalanche" (Hollin, 2004, p. 7).

In his paper, Martinson reviewed 231 studies of prison rehabilitation programs and concluded: "With few and isolated exceptions, the rehabilitative efforts that have been reported so far have had no appreciable effect on recidivism" (1974, p. 25). Rebuttals were immediately forthcoming, but these opposing arguments were much less known outside of scholarly circles than was Martinson's overall conclusion and his catchy slogan, "nothing works."

Ted Palmer published a critique of Martinson's work the next year (Palmer, 1975). He pointed out that 48 percent of the programs reviewed by Martinson demonstrated at least some success with some offenders, which was an important result. He argued that Martinson was prone to dismiss partial successes because he was focused on finding a "cure-all" treatment that worked with every offender all of the time, an unrealistic objective. Palmer's criticisms infuriated Martinson, who responded with an ill-considered diatribe in which he asserted that "a partially positive" result is like a "partially pregnant girlfriend," and he went on to dismiss all correctional treatment as "nine tenths pageantry, rumination, and rubbish ... [with it] and thirty cents you can buy a cup of coffee in New York" (Martinson, 1976). This was not the kind of dialogue one would expect from objective scientists in a principled search for the truth. Martinson wrote that he never cared about recidivism anyway and that there was no evidence that treatment affected aggregate crime rates. This assertion was true, but no one engaged in this debate, including Palmer and Martinson himself (Andrews and Bonta, 1994). Martinson had suddenly inserted a different issue.

After a storm of criticism and correction from the research community, Martinson recanted many of his conclusions in a 1979 paper, but this was largely ignored in the rush to abandon the rehabilitative ideal. At that time, the political left was suspicious of any government intervention, especially if it sounded like indoctrination or brainwashing, and the political right was suspicious of correctional management that didn't sound like punishment. It was not the reasoned rebuttals nor Martinson's retractions that the professional and public audience remembered. It was the "nothing works" that stuck. (A few years after taking his unpopular stand, Martinson had become so alienated and isolated, that he killed himself [Farabee, 2005]).

What Works?: The Continuing Debate

There were some studies which seemed to support Martinson's declaration of ineffective treatment. Garrett in 1985 did a meta analysis of 111 studies with a total of 13,000 participants and found there was no significant difference in outcome for treated and untreated subjects in the 60 percent of studies that he judged to be rigorous work. Research reports on various forms of psychotherapy in institutional settings found no significant effects (Feldman, 1977; Romig, 1978; Quay, 1987). In summing up the research since Martinson, Feldman wrote: "Subsequent reviews have not been as nihilistic, but none has achieved more than mild optimism" (1993, p. 381). More recently, Hollin has concluded that "sustained documented success in reducing offending is remarkably thin on the ground" (2004, p. 269).

There was, however, a contradictory stream of research that supported treatment effects for criminal offenders. Martinson was criticized on several general grounds. Halleck and Witte (1977) pointed out that Martinson's work consisted of studies conducted from 1945 to 1967. During this period, the research methodology was relatively primitive. Studies since 1967 have better research designs and show better treatment results.

Quay (1987) argued that evaluations of correctional treatment programs often did not concentrate on the integrity of the programs being evaluated. Issues like the quality of treatment delivery, the qualifications of the treatment providers, and the stated goals of the program were not investigated. Programs with very little integrity would be expected to fail and really proved nothing about the efficacy of treatment programs with high program integrity. What much of the "nothing works" research really meant was that programs which are poorly conceived and poorly implemented usually fail to reduce recidivism, which is not a stunning result at all. Unfortunately, programs initiated in a prison environment often were (and are) of low integrity.

There is also the issue of generalizability. Is there a treatment that has beneficial effects for all types of offenders or are there specialized treatments that are appropriate for specific types of offenders? This issue is sometimes called matching, and is sometimes expressed in the research literature as Type of Treatment by Type of Offender interactions. Many of Martinson's critics argued that the research produced plenty of Type of Offender by Type of Treatment interactions, though a single program that was effective with any or all offenders had never been found. For example, a specialized treatment program for sex offenders may be quite effective with sex offenders (or with certain types of sex offenders), even though a generalized offender program may be entirely ineffective in reducing recidivism for any offenders at all, including sex offenders.

Gendreau and Ross (1979) surveyed 95 studies that were published between 1973 and 1978. They found that 86 percent of them achieved reductions in recidivism with treatment. In 1987, they repeated their survey with studies published between 1981 and 1987 and reached the same conclusion (Gendreau and Ross, 1987). Mark Lipsey (1992) studied 443 programs and found that 64 percent of the studies reported reductions in recidivism and the average reduction was 10 percent. Most importantly, he found that some types of treatment were substantially better than others, with some treatment programs achieving reductions in recidivism of 30 percent.

Palmer (1996) examined 9 meta analyses and 23 literature reviews which covered studies from 1955 to 1996. Palmer divided the studies into 20 different categories of interventions, such as group counseling, diversion, confrontation, vocational training, and life skills. He found that effective program interventions were those that had a behavioral or cognitive behavioral orientation, taught life skills or were skills oriented, involved family intervention, and were multimodal. By multimodal, he meant programs which included more than one approach, such as job placement plus individual counseling plus remedial education. He considered these multimodal, or combination, programs to be most promising and recommended a research program for investigating which combinations work best with which group of offenders. This effort came to be known as the "what works" literature. Ineffective programs cited by Palmer were group or individual counseling alone, confrontational methods, intensive probation supervision, and areawide strategies of delinquency prevention. He also found that a number of the categories had mixed or inconclusive results, including probation and parole enhancement, diversion, restitution, and physical challenge programs, such as Outward Bound and Vision Quest.

Andrews and Bonta (1994, 1998) reported that "it was now clear that, on average, 'treatment' reduced recidivism, at least to a mild degree"; that is, certain types of treatment with certain types of offenders did impact recidivism. They asserted that we can't know the cause of crime because true experimental designs are not possible with crimes and criminals, but we can know the correlates of crime, and we can know the effects of certain types of interventions with criminal offenders. Their summary of the research led them to what they call "the big four": antisocial attitudes, antisocial associates, behavioral history, and personality. Their strategy was to choose for causal variables the strongest of the correlates and these four are the strongest of the correlates. This strategy makes for the most empirically defensible theory. They relied on summaries of the research, some conducted by themselves and some by other notable researchers including Paul Gendreau, Bob Ross, and Mark Lipsey. These summaries represented literally thousands of individual research studies. Andrews and Bonta concluded that the research as a whole supports reasonably well the following correlates of criminal behavior:

1. Antisocial/procriminal attitudes
2. Antisocial/procriminal associates and peers
3. Personality factors such as impulsivity, aggression, below-average verbal intelligence, egocentrism, sensation seeking, and psychopathy
4. History of antisocial behavior evident from a young age
5. Family factors such as criminality, poor parenting, neglect, abuse, and low levels of affection
6. Low levels of education and employment

A history of antisocial behavior cannot be changed and so is called a *static risk factor. Risk* means that it is a correlate of criminal behavior and *static* means that it cannot be changed. Andrews and Bonta suggest that our efforts to reduce crime at the individual level should be focused on *dynamic* risk factors, that is, risk factors that could be changed, such as antisocial attitudes and antisocial/procriminal associates and peers. Thus, we reach the appealing shorthand formula for reducing criminal behavior: *antisocial attitudes and antisocial associates.* They argue that this conception of criminal behavior is more empirically derived than other concepts of crime causation and that it more clearly points to specific interventions that could reduce crime. It also corrects some commonly held misconceptions about the correlates of crime. For example, they point out that low self-esteem and personal distress are not on the list of empirically derived correlates of crime.

Andrews and Bonta argue for the application of the *risk/needs princi-*

ple in our efforts to reduce crime: (1) criminal behavior can be predicted; (2) there are, as we saw above, two types of risk factors, dynamic and static; (3) there should be a match between offender risk and intensity of treatment, with the more intensive level of treatment for the highest risk offenders; (4) dynamic risk factors, also called "criminogenic needs," should be targeted for intervention and this is what will reduce crime.

By 1999, 25 years after Martinson's "nothing works" paper, Bartol reported that "the concept of rehabilitation has yet to regain a comfortable foothold within the correctional system," though it is a viable alternative within the scholarly community (1999, p. 389). It is a viable alternative in the scholarly community because a very large amount of research has now accumulated that shows that certain types of treatment with certain types of offenders can produce modest reductions in recidivism (about 10 percent) and that some especially well-designed, exemplary programs have produced large reductions in recidivism (20–80 percent). Nevertheless, the harsh era of shock probation, boot camps, three strikes, scared straight, and punishing smarter is still the dominant mood in corrections. Funding and support is still more likely for these types of programs. The accumulated research on "what works" in rehabilitation has had some impact, however, as can be seen in the requirement of many agencies and government sponsored programs for "evidence-based practice" in correctional treatment, even though the implementation and proliferation of such evidence-based programs is not yet generally perceived as our best course of action.

The authors of these numerous studies and meta analyses have made a valuable contribution to the understanding of crime. They have helped us to see how much research has been done and to what it does, and does not, point. They have made a rational, empirical case for specific crime-reducing interventions. These interventions are best understood as the "principles of effective intervention with offenders," described by Paul Gendreau.

The Principles of Effective Intervention with Offenders

Modern research has demonstrated that practical and effective correctional programming is possible and that certain types of programs have a good probability of success. There is extensive research which concludes that correctional programs with certain essential characteristics are effective in reducing recidivism. These essential characteristics, supported by many research studies of functioning treatment programs, have been summarized by Paul Gendreau (Gendreau, 1996; Gendreau and Goggin, 2000).

The following are those principles of effective intervention which have been identified by systematic and well-designed research:

(1) The treatment provided is based on behavioral strategies, including especially cognitive behavioral therapies. Successful behavioral strategies include token economies, problem solving, and modeling. Positive reinforcers are under the control of the program therapists and program contingencies are enforced in a firm but fair manner.

(2) The treatment is offered in the offenders' natural environment, that is to say that community-based programs have demonstrated better success at reducing recidivism than institution-based programs.

(3) The treatment is multimodal. Programs provide matching between the offender, the therapist, and the specific program. The program offers a range or variety of services and targets the criminogenic needs of high-risk offenders.

(4) The program offers *intensive* treatment, defined as at least 100 hours of direct service over a period of 3–4 months. Treatment lengths of over one year may lead to diminishing returns.

(5) Treatment is individualized as much as possible and offers positive rewards for prosocial behavior.

(6) The behaviors that are targeted for change are dynamic risk factors, primarily antisocial attitudes and antisocial associates, as discussed above. This aspect of successful programming makes actuarial assessments to identify high verses low risk offenders a priority. One of the best assessment tools for criminogenic needs and risk is the Level of Supervision Inventory-Revised (LSI-R). This type of assessment permits the program to identify and target high-risk offenders. Targeting low-risk offenders does not reduce recidivism.

(7) Programs employ the *responsivity principle*. This principle suggests matching offender characteristics and learning styles with therapist characteristics and program features which will facilitate the learning of proso-

cial behavior. Treatment programs are delivered in a style and mode that is consistent with the ability and learning style of the individual offender, accounting for such characteristics as his level of anxiety, amenability to treatment, verbal intelligence, and cognitive abilities.

(8) Continuity of treatment through aftercare services is a vital component of recidivism-reducing programs, especially with chronic problems such as sexual offenses and substance abuse. Relapse prevention models are highly effective. Relapse prevention models include monitoring and anticipating problem situations, planning and rehearsing alternative prosocial behaviors, training "significant others," such as family and friends to monitor and reward prosocial behavior, and providing "booster sessions."

(9) Several system factors must be in place for effective service delivery. There is a high level of advocacy or brokerage in the community for community-based services. Quality of program implementation, the qualifications of the staff delivering the services, the participation of the staff in program decision making, and the efforts taken to monitor changes in the program participants' behavior are all important ingredients of correctional treatment programs that succeed in reducing recidivism.

Correctional treatment programs designed and operated according to these principles have produced reductions in recidivism of 20–80 percent, with an average reduction of 50 percent (Andrews et al., 1990). These types of programs have been implemented with juveniles and adults, with males and females, and with both incarcerated and community-based populations. Designing and operating treatment programs for offenders utilizing these principles results in the best probability of reducing recidivism.

Gendreau and Andrews (1994) have developed an instrument for assessing the degree to which a treatment program for offenders is consistent with the principles of effective intervention as identified by empirical research. The inventory indicates whether or not a program is likely to be successful in reducing recidivism. Called the Correctional Program Assessment Inventory (CPAI), it provides measurements for several dozen items in six separate dimensions: program implementation, client preservice assessment, program characteristics, staff characteristics and practices, evaluation, and an "other" category. It also provides an overall percentage score of program quality. Overall scores are then placed in one of three categories: 70+ percent, very satisfactory, 50–69 percent, satisfactory, and <50 percent, unsatisfactory.

The first 101 offender programs to which the CPAI was applied produced a mean score of 25 percent. Less than 10 percent of the programs scored very satisfactory or satisfactory. These scores indicate low program integrity and remind us of the lack of therapeutic integrity in the programs that made up much of the initial "nothing works" research. These results also underscored the need for qualified personnel and for improvements in the education and training of therapists who deliver programs to an offender population. The CPAI has now been applied to well over two hundred correctional treatment programs (Gendreau and Goggin, 2000). Two studies have recently showed that CPAI scores are highly predictive of recidivism among program participants (Nesovic, 2003; Lowenkamp, 2004).

The work that revealed the principles of effective intervention with offenders also uncovered the principles of *ineffective intervention*. These include traditional psychodynamic approaches or "talking cures" and medical model approaches using diet, drugs, or surgery. Labeling approaches, based on the sociological theory that it is the social stigmatization of offenders which leads to criminal behavior and, therefore, offenders should be diverted from the criminal justice system, have not been effective. Programs that target low-risk offenders and programs that target anxiety and depression, which are weak correlates of criminal behavior, have not been supported by empirical research so far. Neither have "punishing smarter" approaches, such as shock incarceration, boot camps, and electronic monitoring, which have attempted to make punishment more effective in preventing recidivism.

Though punishing smarter is still the dominant ideology in corrections at the present time, it does seem that the more scientific and practical attitude of "what works?" has replaced the unscientific and political attitude that "nothing works." Increasing insistence on evidence-based practice is also a sign of a shifting direction in correctional treatment. Clive Hollin sums it up this way:

> Now it would be wrong to assume that the case for treatment is proven: it is evident that a great deal more work needs to be carried out on the

effectiveness of treatment. In particular, the outcome research from current treatment programmes configured according to "what works" principles will prove critical over the coming years [2004, p. 9].

We will be wise to keep in mind that the research findings on recidivism are not the only considerations to be made in determining correctional policy and priorities. Morality, justice, proportionality in sentencing, economics, victim issues, and "a myriad other organizational and bureaucratic goals" are important contributing factors to the direction we should take (see, for example, Petersilia, 1996). Whether or not a correctional treatment program should or should not be continued is not based solely on scientific judgments.

Nor should reducing recidivism be taken for granted as the purpose of it all. Judge Bazelon wrote that rehabilitation "should never have been sold on the promise that it would reduce crime. Recidivism rates cannot be the only measure of what is valuable in corrections. Simple decency must count, too. It is amoral, if not immoral, to make cost-benefit equations a lodestar in corrections" (1977, p. 3). Here we are reminded again that the study of crime is a crossroads where science and morality meet and mingle.

Chapter Seven

The Treatment of Special Populations

The perceived willfulness of criminal behavior is clearly an obstacle to viewing crime as a disorder.
— Adrian Raine, 1993

The purpose of this chapter is to focus on the treatment of special populations within the correctional system, including substance-abusing offenders, mentally disordered offenders, mentally handicapped offenders, sex offenders, and female offenders.

Substance-Abusing Offenders

The diagnosis of substance dependence is based on (1) a developed tolerance for the substance, (2) withdrawal symptoms, (3) unsuccessful efforts to stop using, and (4) interference with other normal social and occupational activities due to use of the substance. Substance abuse is characterized by (1) failure to fulfill major obligations due to use of the substance, (2) persistent use even when it is physically hazardous, such as driving under the influence, (3) persistent and recurrent interpersonal problems due to use of the substance, and (4) recurrent legal problems resulting from use. These basic criteria hold for any type of potentially addictive substance, whether it is alcohol or any other legal or illegal drug (DSM IV-TR, 2000).

Most people in our culture have used mood-altering substances. "At some time in their lives, as many as 90 percent of adults in the United States have had some experience with alcohol. A substantial number, 60 percent for males and 30 percent for females, have had one or more alcohol related adverse life events (e.g., driving after consuming too much alcohol, missing school or work due to a hangover)" (DSM-IV TR, 2000, p. 212). For other substances, estimating prevalence is more problematic since the data for prevalence rates is often from self-report surveys and many of the substances of interest are illegal; merely to possess them is a crime, so many people may not readily admit to using them. A 1996 survey found that 10 percent of the population had tried cocaine at some time, with 2 percent reporting use in the last year, and .8 percent reporting use in the last month (DSM-IV TR, 2000, p. 248).

The Bureau of Justice Statistics reports that in 1997, 60 percent of mentally ill inmates and 51 percent of other inmates stated that they were under the influence of alcohol or other drugs at the time of their current offense. The Arrestee Drug Abuse Monitoring Program (ADAM) collects data on adult arrestees in 38 sites across the country. Alcohol and drug addiction affect at least 70 percent of all incarcerated offenders (Wanberg and Milkman, 1998). In 2000, ADAM reported that 64 percent of male arrestees and 63 percent of female arrestees tested positive for at least one drug. At most sites, a half or more of all arrestees tested positive for at least one drug. In 2002, about one-quarter of convicted property offenders had committed their offenses to get money for drugs (U.S. Department of Justice, 2006). By any measure, substance abuse is a major characteristic of the offender population.

The treatment of substance abuse is not fundamentally different for offenders than it is for nonoffenders. For incarcerated offenders, there is less access to alcohol and drugs, which facilitates treatment in the early stages, but, at some point, the person receiving treatment must face the access to drugs and the temptations of the "real world" in order to claim that treatment has been successful. It is difficult to say with certainty that an incarcerated person is a treatment success while he or she is still confined. Some programs that are designed for nonincarcerated offenders include drug courts, drug testing, and day treatment. Treatment for substance abuse is usually in one of three modalities: (1) twelve-step programs, (2) cognitive behavioral programs, (3) behavioral programs. In twelve-step programs, total abstinence is the goal and they are operated by former addicts. In the other two modalities, total abstinence may or may not be the goal and they are often operated by mental health professionals. There are also "harm reduction" programs such as methadone maintenance and needle exchange programs (Stimson, 1998).

A continuum of treatment, with different levels of treatment based on an accurate and careful assessment of the problem, is recommended, whether in or out of prison.

Levels of Substance-Abuse Treatment

1. *Assessment*: by a qualified professional. There are several standard assessment instruments that can be used. The assessment includes a personal interview (at least one, sometimes two). It should also include collateral contacts (information gathered from other people who know the person well) and an official record check. The assessment should result in a recommendation for level of treatment.

2. *Alcohol/Drug Education*: an education class which typically meets once a week for 4–12 weeks in a classroom or small-group format. Extensive information about alcohol and drug abuse is disseminated.

3. *Regular Outpatient Treatment*: usually takes place in a small group format, though it may be individual. The program usually runs for 2–3 hours per week for 30–50 weeks. It is sometimes called "ROPT."

4. *Intensive Outpatient Treatment*: usually includes both a group and an individual format for a total of 10 hours per week for 8–52 weeks. The program usually has several phases which gradually reduce the number of hours per week. Aftercare is an important part of this treatment. It is sometimes referred to as "IOPT."

5. *Detoxification*: usually consists of 3–5 days in a hospital setting and is usually followed by residential treatment. It is sometimes called "detox."

6. *Residential Treatment*: usually continues 24 hours a day for 7–30 days. It usually includes alcohol and drug education, individual and group counseling, 12-step groups, and family conferences. Aftercare is a very important part of residential treatment. It is often called a "28 day program."

7. *Therapeutic Community*: usually goes on 24 hours a day for 6–24 months. It typically includes the same items as the residential program but lasts longer. It also usually includes some provision for work assignments or jobs outside of the community. These programs are often spiritually based (though not always) and often operated by former addicts (though not always). Aftercare is a crucial component of the program.

Effective substance-abuse programs which are "state of the art" have the following characteristics:

1. The treatment providers have appropriate qualifications and experience, including experience with offenders.
2. A thorough assessment is conducted for each program participant.
3. There is a plan of referral for each level of treatment.
4. There is a continuum of treatment with appropriate levels of treatment (as outlined above).
5. The program has a "track record" in the local area.
6. There are aftercare plans, including relapse-prevention planning, in place.
7. Records are kept and reports provided.
8. The treatment providers can explain and justify the treatment modality employed.
9. There is an awareness of local concerns/problems.
10. The cost of the program is within reasonable expectations for the local area.

The research suggests that some treatment is better than no treatment (Prendergast, Anglin, and Wellisch, 1995), but there is no single treatment that is effective for everyone (Palmer, 1992; Van Voorhis and Hurst, 2000). Project MATCH compared three treatment approaches: Alcoholics Anonymous, cognitive behavioral therapy, and motivational enhancement. All three achieved client improvements (Project MATCH Research Group, 1997). There is some research to support behavioral and cognitive behavioral approaches to substance abuse (Miller et al., 1995; Wexler and Lipton, 1993). And Van Voorhis and Hurst report: "With offender populations, therapeutic communities have a long standing history of success" (Van Voorhis and Hurst, 2000, p. 285).

Research on 12-step programs is limited. There is some reluctance to evaluate 12-step programs because there is some ambiguity about whether such programs are spiritual, faith-based programs not amenable to scientific evaluation, because the program providers are usually nonprofessionals who are untrained and/or uninterested in research, and because of their tradition of anonymity. One important contribution to our understanding could be more controlled evaluations of 12-step programs with offenders. In a nationwide survey, Strasser (cited in Bartol, 1999) found that two-thirds of American respondents thought the sale and use of drugs was the key cause of crime. While this percentage would likely decrease if the same survey were done today, it would still be large enough to emphasize the drug use → criminal activity link in the minds of many. There is evidence for a drug use → criminal activity link (for example, Hough, 1996) and there is evidence against it (for example, Bacchus, Strang, and Watson, 2000). Preble and Casey (1969) in a now classic New York study found that the activity and lifestyle of the drug user was just as attractive as taking the drug itself. South summarizes a review: "studies are by no means unanimous in their conclusions about the impact of treatment upon drug related crime behavior" (2000, p. 932). And Bartol, after a good review of research, concludes: "Individuals who are chronic, persistent criminals often are polydrug users, but it is unlikely that the drugs they ingest directly cause them to engage in criminal activity. It is more likely that they were criminally prone prior to and independent of polydrug use" (1999, p. 383).

Nurco et al. suggest that "the long and continuing controversy over whether narcotic addicts commit crimes primarily to support their habits or whether addiction is merely one more manifestation of a deviant and criminal lifestyle seems pointless in view of the fact that addicts cannot be regarded as a homogenous group" (1985, p. 101). That addicts are a heterogeneous group is a point well taken, but it does matter in which group they fall. This is because their substance-abuse treatment would be the same in either case (which was Nurco et al.'s point), but if the criminality preceded the drug abuse, then you are not finished with substance-abuse treatment alone. You must treat the substance abuse first, but then you must treat the criminality which preceded it.

In my own practice, I referred to these as Type A substance abusers and Type B substance abusers. A Type A substance abuser is a person who led a conventional lifestyle until his use of a mood-altering substance began to substantially interfere with his life, including eventually criminal offenses related directly to his or her use of the substance (such as DWI, possession, larceny to get money for drugs, assault while under influence, etc.). When treated for substance abuse, this Type A person will return to what he or she was before the substance abuse began: a responsible person with a law-abiding, conventional lifestyle.

A Type B substance abuser is a different person. This person was engaged in criminal activity before the alcohol and/or drug abuse began. If you treat him for substance abuse, he also will return to what he was before the substance abuse, which was, in his case, a criminal with an irre-sponsible and deviant lifestyle. After successful substance abuse treatment, you have now what Stanton Samenow (1986) liked to call "a sober thief." You must now treat the criminality. The biggest danger here is to assume that once you have treated the substance abuse, you now have a responsi-ble, honest, conventional person — not unless that is what he was previous to the substance abuse. In the case of the Type B substance abuser, you have only completed the first part of the treatment. The key to avoiding mistakes here is a good initial assessment, especially in understanding the offender's history before the substance abuse began in earnest (beyond sim-ple experimentation).

In any case, however one may decide to categorize the offender pop-ulation, substance-abuse treatment is a necessary and vital component of the correctional system. Research which helps us to understand what meth-ods of treatment are efficacious with which groups of offenders will be a major contribution to our understanding.

Recently, the National Institute on Drug Abuse published *The Prin-ciples of Drug Abuse Treatment for Criminal Justice Populations* (Fletcher and Chandler, 2006). It lists the principles of treatment that have been distilled from over four decades of treatment for offenders with substance abuse problems. The authors point out that treatment offers the best alternative for interrupting the well-known cycle of crime and drugs. The thirteen principles which emerge from both basic and applied research supported by NIDA are listed below.

(1) Drug addiction is a brain disease that affects behavior.

(2) Recovery from drug addiction requires effective treatment, followed by management of the problem over time.

(3) Treatment must last long enough to produce stable behavioral changes (at least, three months).

(4) Assessment is the first step in treatment.

(5) Tailoring services to fit the needs of the individual is an important part of effective drug abuse treatment for criminal justice populations.

(6) Drug use during treatment should be carefully monitored.

(7) Treatment should target factors that are associated with criminal behavior (especially criminal thinking and attitudes).

(8) Criminal justice supervision should incorporate treatment planning for drug abusing offenders, and treatment providers should be aware of correctional supervision requirements.

(9) Continuity of care is essential for drug abusers re-entering the community.

(10) A balance of rewards and sanctions encourages prosocial behavior and treatment participation.

(11) Offenders with co-occurring drug abuse and mental heath problems often require an integrated treatment approach.

(12) Medications are an important part of treatment for many drug abusing offenders.

(13) Treatment planning for drug abusing offenders who are living in or re-entering the community should include strategies to prevent and treat serious, chronic medical conditions, such as HIV/AIDS, hepatitis B and C, and tuberculosis.

Mentally Disordered Offenders

Punishment or treatment for the mentally ill who commit crimes is a very old issue. In the 2nd century CE the co-regents of the Roman Empire, Marcus Aurelius and Commodus, replied to a letter regarding the case of Aelius Priscus, who had murdered his mother.

> If you have clearly ascertained that Aelius Priscus is in such a state of insanity that he is permanently out of his mind and so entirely incapable

of reasoning, and no suspicion is left that he was simulating insanity when he killed his mother, you need not concern yourself with the question how he should be punished, as his insanity itself is punishment enough. At the same time he must be closely confined, and, if you think it advisable, even kept in chains; this need not be done by way of punishment so much as for his own protection and the security of his neighbors. If, however, as is very often the case, he has intervals of sounder mind, you must carefully investigate the question whether he may not have committed the crime on one of these occasions, and so have no claim to mercy on the ground of mental infirmity; and, if you should find that anything of this kind is the fact you must refer the case to us, so that we may consider, supposing he committed the act at a moment when he could be held to know what he was doing, whether he ought not to be visited with punishment corresponding to the enormity of his crime. But when we learn by a letter from you that his position in respect of place and treatment is such that he is in the hands of friends, even if confined to his own house, your proper course will be, in our opinion to summon the persons who had charge of him at the time and ascertain how they came to be remiss, and then pronounce upon the case of each separately, according as you see anything to excuse or aggravate his negligence. The object of providing keepers for lunatics is to keep them not merely from doing harm to themselves, but from bringing destruction upon others... [quoted in Eriksson, 1976, pp. 198–199].

This interesting letter, eighteen centuries old, includes all the issues debated today about the responsibility of the mentally ill for their criminal behavior.

Attitudes towards the mentally ill changed during the Middle Ages and they were viewed as possessed by evil spirits and were often treated brutally. Such inhumane treatment began to change with the efforts of the great French reformer Philippe Pinel in the 18th century. Pinel helped to revive the old Roman attitude towards the culpability of the mentally ill. He was a mental health reformer who got the opportunity to be chief of the hospital at Bicêtre and later at Salpêtrière as a result of the French Revolution. He had a rare compassion for the mentally ill and an intense motivation to try to understand them. "The mentally sick far from being guilty people deserving of punishment, are sick people whose miserable state deserves all the consideration that is due to suffering humanity. One should try with the simplest methods to restore their reason." He released the mentally ill patients from chains and physical torment. Pinel's work eventually inspired reform throughout the Western world.

Another step in that same direction occurred as the result of a criminal case in England in the 19th century. Daniel M'Naughten had killed the prime minister's secretary by accident; he had meant to kill the prime minister himself. He was acquitted on the grounds of insanity, but this verdict caused such a public outcry that the judges in the case were required to explain their decision. They formally presented their reasoning in 1843:

> it must be clearly proven that, at the time of committing the act, the party accused was laboring under such defect of reason, from disease of the mind, as not to know the nature and quality of the act he was doing, or, if he did know it, that he did not know that what he was doing was wrong [quoted in Eriksson, 1976, p. 201].

These judicial guidelines became known as "the M'Naughten rules" and they influenced criminal law significantly. A second development regarding mentally disordered offenders and the law was *Parsons v. State* in 1886. This case added the "irresistible impulse test" to the concept behind the M'Naughten rules. In order to be criminal, an act must be both knowing and voluntary (Johnson and Wolfe, 2003). The third legal development was *Durham v. United States* in 1954. This case introduced a criterion which became known as the Durham rule: an accused is not legally responsible if his unlawful act was the product of mental disease or mental defect. This rule was eventually abandoned by the courts due to the difficulty of defining mental disease and determining its causal influence on the crime (a problem we still have today). Finally, the American Law Institute adopted the following in 1961 as a section of the Model Penal Code. An offender may be excused by reason of insanity if, "as a result of mental disease or defect he lacks substantial capacity either to appreciate the criminality of his act or to conform his conduct to the requirements of the law" (quoted in Johnson and Wolfe, 2003, p. 197).

A great deal has been written about this special population of offenders even though it is a very heterogeneous and variously defined group (Halleck, 1988; Howells and Hollin, 1993; Hodgins and Muller-Isberner, 2000). The term *mentally disordered offender* has been applied to many different types of offenders, including offenders who have been judged incompetent to stand trial, offenders judged to be guilty but mentally ill, and offenders found not guilty by reason of insanity. It also refers to mentally disordered sex offenders and mentally ill inmates in prison. Muller-Isberner and Hodgins (2000) proposed that mentally disordered offenders are persons with a history of offending and/or violence who fall into one of the following groups: brain damaged, personality disorders, schizophrenia, psychopathy, and major affective disorders (primarily bipolar disorder and major depression). These offenders "present multiple problems, which include rather severe affective and cognitive deficits and poor life skills and social skills. Many of them, in addition, present a long history of substance abuse, a lifestyle conducive to deviant behavior, and a high risk of re-offending" (2000, p. 13). Sometimes, the personality disorders are excluded from this group and only offenders suffering from a major mental disorder are considered to be mentally disordered offenders. The "major mental disorders" include schizophrenia, bipolar disorder, major depression, and atypical psychoses.

Monahan and Steadman (1983) reported that, as a group, mentally disordered offenders were responsible for a only a small fraction of crimes in society. They found that 6.6 percent of all offenders detained in the United States were officially designated as mentally disordered. Within this group, they reported that 8 percent were insanity acquittees, 32 percent were incompetent to stand trial, 6 percent were mentally disordered sex offenders, and the majority of 54 percent were convicted prisoners who had been sent to mental health facilities. In state correctional facilities in the United States in 2003, 12.8 percent of prisoners were receiving counseling or therapy and 9.7 percent were receiving psychotropic medication (U.S. Department of Justice, 2003, p. 531).

However, if you include substance-abuse disorders and antisocial personality disorders, one study found only 5 percent of prison inmates *without* a mental disorder (Hodgins and Cote, 1990). Although this surprising prevalence rate has been found to be lower in other jurisdictions and although many would argue that antisocial personality disorder is not a major mental disorder, "it is clear that many prisoners meet the criteria for some mental disorder" (Quinsey et al., 2003, p. 76).

Quinsey and his colleagues summarized several studies of violent recidivism and found a range of violent recidivism from 16 percent for

120

schizophrenic offenders up to 77 percent for treated psychopathic offenders. This last finding resulted in their now well-known caution that treatment may actually make severe psychopaths worse. They found that the best predictors of violent recidivism are criminal history, antisocial personality disorder or psychopathy, early antisocial behavior, and alcohol abuse.

Quinsey et al. proposed that to reduce the risk of violent recidivism, "clinical problems" should be addressed by the methods shown by research to be most efficacious for that particular problem. Clinical problems to be addressed include criminal propensity, aggression, anger, substance abuse, life skills deficits, active psychotic symptoms, social withdrawal, and family problems. They readily admit that this treatment procedure has not been shown to be effective by convincing research with mentally disordered offenders, but that it is the best that we can do at present. It is the current state of the science.

Eaves, Tien, and Wilson (2000) report that there is a reliable though modest relationship between mood disorders (affective disorders) and criminality. They also report that it is not sufficient to treat the underlying mood disorder alone but that a multifaceted approach addressing all of the assessed factors is necessary. Other researchers agree: "Treatment must include multiple components which target the different problems presented by the mentally disordered offender, it must be planned and organized in a long term perspective, it must be intense and involve outreach ... and include close supervision" (Muller-Isberner and Hodgins, 2000, p. 13).

In regards to psychotropic medication for mentally disordered offenders, Tiihonen reports that "the results of controlled clinical studies have shown that lithium, carbamazepine, SSRI's, beta blockers, and busiprone decrease impulsive and aggressive behavior in patients with various mental disorders," but there is less evidence for efficacy in personality disorders (2000, p.187). He recommends that "in all cases," the offenders receive coping skills and supportive therapy in addition to medication. Other researchers are even more cautious:

> The efficacy of psychotropic medication in controlling violent behavior is difficult to measure. The literature is replete with uncontrolled case reports advocating the use of one agent or another. Few controlled double blind studies exist. Overall, the information available on the efficacy of pharmacological treatments in preventing violence among persons

with psychotic disorders is limited. Caution must be exercised before extrapolating from the studies on aggressivity in patients with other diagnoses, such as mental retardation, dementia, or post traumatic stress disorder. These results may not be generalizable to patients with schizophrenia or other psychotic disorders [Citrome and Volavka, 2000, p. 154].

Comorbid substance abuse disorder and comorbid antisocial personality disorder, which both increase the risk of violent behavior, must be a part of the assessment and treatment of mentally disordered offenders.

Penrose (1939) studied prison and mental health populations in several European countries and noted a strong negative correlation between them which became known as Penrose's law: "As the size of the prison population goes up, the size of the mental hospital population goes down proportionately, and vice versa, presumably because people move from one system to the other" (Quinsey et al., 2003, p. 77). Quinsey and his coworkers note that the evidence for Penrose's law in North America has been mixed, but there is no doubt that there is considerable overlap among the two populations. Toch (1982) referred to this situation as bus therapy because, in some jurisdictions, there were such rapid cycles between the prison and the mental hospital that the bus ride must be the only therapy taking place. (This was facilitated in Raleigh, North Carolina, when I worked there by having the maximum security prison and the state mental hospital across the street from each other.) The recent deinstitutionalization of the public mental hospitals has resulted in prison correctional facilities becoming de facto mental hospitals.

Hodgins concludes that "an empirical foundation for the treatment of mentally disordered offenders is in its infancy" (2000, p. 217). She argues that the construction of a knowledge base for mentally disordered offenders must include the special needs of mentally retarded offenders, female offenders, and substance-abusing offenders. She also points to one often neglected factor which is the influence of the living environment on the risk of offending/violent behavior. "Yet there are many hints in the literature that the living environment has a powerful effect on offending and aggressive behavior" (Hodgins, 2004, p. 227). Treatment recommendations for mentally disordered offenders now consist mainly of taking treatments that have been effective with other groups of patients and adapting them for use with mentally disordered offenders. For example, treatment which has been effective with bipolar patients is adapted to offenders diagnosed with bipolar disorder. This approach is not empirically supported and can be a difficult approach to implement. For example, incarcerated mentally disordered offenders cannot "practice new living skills in a realistic environment."

Quinsey and his colleagues, who have contributed excellent work in this field, including the development of the Violence Risk Appraisal Guide, conclude:

> The relationship between various clinical problems and the dangerousness of individuals is sometimes direct (e.g., assaultiveness), sometimes indirect (e.g., suspiciousness), and sometimes unknown (e.g., life skills deficits). What is evident from the foregoing discussion is that the relationship between response to any particular form of treatment and subsequent dangerousness is largely uncharted empirically. Like other clinicians, we regard the improvement of patients' conditions and behaviors as desirable in themselves. Moreover, the relationship between therapeutic interventions and subsequent behaviors cannot be established until the interventions are appropriate, implemented properly, and guided by plausible theory. Progress will not be made unless coherent treatment programs can be developed, delivered, and evaluated [Quinsey et al., 2003, p. 207].

As we saw in chapter six, program integrity and theoretical underpinnings, often weak points in correctional treatment programs, turn out to be crucial components of "what works" for criminal offenders of all types.

The Mentally Handicapped

Since at least the 13th century in Europe, offenders who were considered "idiots" were "not to blame" for their crimes and were referred to the king for the disposition of their cases (Walker and McCabe, 1973). In the 17th century, there were people who were acquitted of crimes on the basis of their cognitive disabilities (Lindsay, Taylor, and Sturmey, 2004). In the late 19th and early 20th century, "feeblemindedness" was thought to be the cause of *most* crime. The English physician Charles Goring, in his famed refutation of Lombroso's theory of crime in 1913, reported a strong correlation between intelligence and criminality. Goring found that, of the factors he studied, level of intelligence most clearly differentiated the criminals from the general community (Driver, 1973).

In the next year, Harry Goddard, an American physician and administrator of the New Jersey School for the Feeble-Minded, presented his data and his conclusions on criminality and intelligence. He had studied the intellectual capacities of inmates in 16 reformatories. "Every investigation of the mentality of criminals, misdemeanants, delinquents and other antisocial groups has proven beyond the possibility of contradiction that nearly all persons in these classes, and in some cases all, are of low mentality ... it is no longer to be denied that the greatest single cause of delinquency and crime is low grade mentality, much of it within the limits of feeblemindedness" (1920, pp. 73–74). Goddard's claim is overwrought, not because of the observation that there is a strong relationship between below-average intelligence and incarceration in training schools and prisons, a finding which has generally held up, but because of the prideful leap which declares that we now know the single greatest cause of delinquency and crime. Goddard goes on: "The hereditary criminal passes out with the advent of feeble mindedness into the problem. The criminal is not born; he is made. The so called criminal type is merely a type of feeblemindedness, a type misunderstood and mistreated, driven into criminality for which he is well fitted by nature" (quoted in Jacoby, 1994, pp. 140–141). Goddard offered data which seemed to show that 50 percent of all criminals are mentally defective. He pointed out that whether the "feebleminded" person actually becomes a criminal depends on the interaction of his temperament and his environment against the backdrop of his mental deficiencies. "The first special institution for defective delinquents was opened in Napanoch, New York in 1921" (Rotman, 1995, p. 160), though there was at the time no uniform definition of "defective delinquent."

There was opposition to this line of thought. The U.S. Army began to administer IQ tests to draftees during World War I. Zeleny (1933) reported that these tests indicated that one-third of army draftees would be classified as feebleminded. This was a startling result and cast doubt on the work of Goddard and others who had found so much "feeble mindedness" in reformatories and prisons. Carl Murchison of Clark University published his book *Criminal Intelligence* in 1926 in which he reported a comparison of prison inmates and army draftees. He found *higher* intelligence among prison inmates at Fort Leavenworth than among enlisted men in World War I.

Sutherland reported in 1931 on 350 studies of mentality and crime and concluded that the relationship between crime and feeblemindedness is "comparatively slight. Certainly intelligence is not as closely related to crime as is age or sex." The majority of prison inmates are not mentally handicapped and the mentally handicapped, as a group, are not especially inclined to committing crimes. However, both of the above observations could be true without leading necessarily to the conclusion that there is no relationship of importance between IQ and crime. Sutherland's determined attack on the link between crime and IQ, and his prestige in criminology, effectively silenced the debate for several decades. As Wilson and Herrnstein wrote in 1985, Sutherland correctly observed that, as the methods of testing improved, the apparent intellectual deficits shrank, but this did not warrant the conclusion that there were no intellectual deficits at all among the offender population.

The debate reopened in the 1970s. Marvin Wolfgang's landmark Philadelphia cohort research in 1972 reported that, among nearly 9,000 males in the study, the chronic offenders in the group had consistently lower IQ scores than did those without police records. This result held even within social classes. In 1977, Hirschi and Hindelang determined that a low IQ is a good predictor of "official" juvenile delinquency, but an even better predictor of self-reported delinquency. (However, this result has a possible interpretation which is somewhat humorous: high–IQ delinquents are smart enough not to self-report illegal acts!) Wilson and Hernnstein reviewed the research in 1985 in *Crime and Human Nature* and wrote that there "is a clear and consistent link between criminality and low intelligence," and they criticized criminology textbook writers for ignoring the research in this area. As estimated by Wilson and Hernnstein, the extent of the IQ deficit in delinquents was 10 IQ points.

Farrington published a study in 1989 as a part of the Cambridge Study of Delinquent Development, which showed that IQ at age 8 predicted both self-reported delinquent behavior and official measures of violence at age 32. In 1995, David Lykken, of the University of Minnesota, writes that:

"It is now well established that offenders, whether juvenile delinquents or adult prison inmates, have lower IQ's than nonffenders, a mean IQ of about 92 compared to the general population value of 100, or to the estimated mean for nonoffenders of about 102.... The relationship between IQ and crime is curvilinear, peaking in the borderline range of 70–80 and decreasing in both directions" (1995, p. 106). The Canadian psychologists Don Andrews and James Bonta agreed in their 1994 comprehensive study of the factors influencing crime: "The data are clear: delinquents tend to score lower on standardized measures of intelligence than nondelinquents" (p. 133).

William Healy was an American psychologist and influential expert on delinquency who published, along with Franz Alexander, a book called *The Roots of Crime* in 1935. This book was widely read at the time. Healy's data convinced him that the delinquent male is five to ten times more likely than a normal boy to be mentally deficient.

Another suggestion is found in the fact that IQ has been found to be related to type of crime. Such crimes as bribery, forgery, and embezzlement are associated with higher IQs than is average for the offender population. Assaults, homicide, and rape are associated with lower IQs. In the middle, or average range of intelligence for offenders, are property offenders, burglars, auto thieves, and alcohol and drug offenders. Low test scores are associated with impulsive crimes. This impulsiveness, or lack of self-control, led Gottfredson and Hirschi (1990) to develop a general theory of crime based on the factor of self-control.

Another line of thought is that IQ does not directly affect delinquency, but that low IQ hinders academic performance which then affects other factors which are critical for criminal behavior, such as peer associations and employment opportunities. Other important attitudes and skills are also affected by IQ, especially verbal IQ, such as goal setting, problem solving, delay of gratification, and moral reasoning. Hirschi wrote that "hundreds" of studies showed the relationship between academic competence and criminal behavior and that the lack of relationship between school achievement and delinquency as posited by many criminologists "must be considered one of the wonders of social science" (1969, p. 111).

It has been best stated by Wilson and Herrnstein:

A child who chronically loses standing in the competition of the classroom may feel justified in settling the score outside, by violence, theft, and other forms of defiant illegality. School failure enhances the rewards for crime by engendering feelings of unfairness. In addition, failure in school predicts, to a substantial degree, failure in the marketplace. For someone who stands to gain little from legitimate work, the rewards of noncrime are relatively weak. Failure in school therefore not only enhances the rewards for crime, but it predicts weak rewards for noncrime" [1985, p. 171].

The relationship between IQ and delinquency remains robust, but three qualifications apply (Lindsay, Taylor, and Sturmey, 2004):

(1) The relationship is much less strong if other factors such as socioeconomic status are controlled.

(2) Many studies have focused on the IQ range of 80–120 so the relationship to intellectual disability can only be inferred. Only a few studies have focused on extending the range of IQs below 80 and these showed that there is no simple linear relationship between IQ and delinquency.

(3) No studies investigated severe and profound disability and criminal behavior.

In determining the prevalence of developmental disability in the offender population, there are three problems:

(1) The definition of developmental disability varies over time and from place to place. While the relationship between below-average intelligence and delinquency has held up, with developmental disability, we are speaking of IQs below 70 with accompanying social skill deficits and adjustment problems and with indications that the deficits appeared in the developmental years. However, sometimes persons with IQs in the borderline range and persons with learning and attention deficit disorders are included in this group, confusing the issues.

(2) The criminal justice system often keeps data indicative of developmental disability in a very haphazard and unverifiable manner and methods of determining developmental disability vary across jurisdictions.

(3) There is the problem of comorbidity in the offender population,

that is, developmental disability coexisting with another disorder needing treatment, such as substance abuse, major mental illness, or personality disorder. Some researchers propose that the assessment of psychopathy can be useful with developmentally disabled offenders because knowledge of personality disorder in this group is just as important as with any other population. The assessment of risk is now usually linked with the assessment of psychopathy in an individual and such an assessment is just as useful for the developmentally disabled offenders as it is with other offenders [Reid et al., 2004].

There have been many studies of the prevalence of developmental disability in prison (Holland, 2004). These studies have shown between 1.5 percent and 5.6 percent of sentenced prisoners have developmental disabilities, though some estimates of mental retardation in the prison population have been as high as 10 percent (Smith et al., 1990). The variation in the figures is by geography (more developmental disability in prison in the United States than in Europe) and by method of determining developmental disability. This is certainly not a large percentage of the criminal population, but, as Holland writes, "there is understandable concern about the vulnerability of this group of people when in prison, and the potential harm and long term effects of, for example, assault in prison (Holland, 2004, p. 30). Noble and Conley (1992) conclude: "there is little point in trying to nail down to the nearest decimal point the percentage of people with mental retardation and other mental disabilities who reside in the nation's prisons. We know that the number is significant and that many inmates with mental retardation are not receiving appropriate services" (cited in Lindsay et al., p. 169).

Winter, Holland, and Collins (1997) found that people with developmental disability who offend also have substance abuse disorders, a family history of offending, homelessness, psychosocial disadvantage, and other mental health problems. Holland writes that: "It cannot be overstressed that people with developmental disabilities are not committing large amounts of crime — or at least if they are, it is not leading to arrest and conviction. In addition, there are certain crimes, such as fraud, motor offences, and white collar crime which people with developmental disabilities do not commit" (2004, p. 32).

For sex offenders, there must be a range of treatment and management options since the etiology of sexual offenses committed by people with developmental disabilities is varied and includes some offenders who have poor knowledge of sexual matters and appropriate behavior in public; some who are sexually and socially curious but do not know what is appropriate behavior; some offenders who seem to be starved for intimacy and touch; some who were sexually molested by a trusted adult and told that this was normal behavior; and finally some who are predatory and have sexually deviant tendencies (Lindsay et al., 2004).

Lindsay et al. also report that the three most common treatments reported for sex offenders with developmental disabilities are behavioral treatment, cognitive interventions, and pharmacological treatments. These treatments are discussed in detail in the section on sex offenders treatment. Taylor, et al. (2004) report the same methods for anger and aggression treatment for offenders with developmental disabilities, though they state that medication has not been shown to be very effective in this regard and that some of the purely cognitive components are too difficult for this population (cognitive behavioral treatment is discussed in detail in chapter five). Relaxation and behavioral skills training appear to be the parts which are most effective. While some treatment and management approaches appear promising, treatment of less than one year is "of little value" (Lindsay et al., 2004).

Sex Offenders

Our culture is curiously ambivalent about many forms of sexual behavior. Consequently, there have been, and continue to be, many revisions of the criminal sexual codes. Fornication, cohabitation, incest, adultery, sodomy, crime against nature, homosexual acts, and prostitution have all been crimes in some places at some times and not in others. Our attitudes and values, as reflected in the law, and in our enforcement of the law, change, evolve, and often recirculate.

An especially poignant example may be found in an excellent biography by Andrew Hodges (2000) in which he describes the life of Alan Turing, the father of modern computer science. Turing was a brilliant mathematician who theorized a working computer in the 1930s and who participated significantly in breaking the German Enigma code during World War II. Turing was arrested in England in 1952 for engaging in a homosexual relationship. He declared that he had done nothing wrong, but homosexual acts were against the law at the time. In the climate of the Cold War, homosexuals were considered special security risks. He was offered a choice between imprisonment and taking estrogen treatments to weaken his libido, an early example of sex offender treatment. He accepted the treatment. He was denied a security clearance by the government that he had served so well and he continued to be monitored, searched, and harassed. In 1954, he committed suicide. The laws under which he had been convicted, homosexual acts between consenting adults, were changed in the UK in the 1960s, but that was no help for the brilliant and patriotic Turing.

In considering sexual offenses as crimes, and sexual offenders as criminals, we will choose to circumvent large (and important) areas of social debate on sexual and moral behavior by focusing on a single aspect of sexual behavior: the issue of consent. Whatever may be moral or immoral, acceptable or not acceptable, it is the issue of consent which is the *criminal* issue. "All nonconsenting sexual encounters are assaults," writes Nicholas Groth (1979, p. 3). He proposes that there are three ways to gain sexual access to another person: (1) consent, or negotiation; (2) pressure, or exploitation; and (3) force, or intimidation. The defining factor for force is the risk of physical injury or bodily harm for refusal to participate in the encounter. We may add to Groth's position that children cannot give consent in any legal, or moral, sense and therefore all sexual acts with children are nonconsensual and are assaults. Marshall writes that a sexual assault is "any unwanted direct sexual contact" (2004, p. 147). In the evolution of our thinking about *criminal* sexual behavior, conceptualizing varying degrees of sexual assault, from unwanted touching to forced intercourse, has generally replaced our earlier, narrow focus on rape. Nonconsenting men and women, and children (who are always nonconsenting in the legal sense), are the victims of sexual assault.

Prevalence

We simply do not know the accurate numbers of sexual offenses, but "it is clear that sexual offending occurs at high rates, is usually not reported to agencies ... and few of the offenders are actually prosecuted" (Geffner, Franey, and Falconer, 2003, p. 3). For example, Koss, Gidyez, and Wisniewski (1987) found that more than half their national sample of women in the United States had been sexually victimized sometime after 14 years of age. Marshall and Barrett (1990) found that every seven minutes a Canadian woman is the victim of a rape or an attempted rape. Data from European countries indicate similar rates (van Dijk and Mayhew, 1992). Finkelhor and his colleagues surveyed 2,626 American men and women and found that 16 percent of the men and 27 percent of the women reported a history of sexual abuse (Finkelhor, Hotaling, Lewis, and Smith, 1990). Furby, Weinrott, and Blackshaw (1989) calculated from victimization data that a woman has a one in five chance of being raped in her lifetime. In 1995, persons 12 and older reported 260,300 attempted or completed rapes and 91 percent of the victims were female (Greenfeld, 1997).

The recent scandals involving sexual abuse of boys by Catholic priests in the United States indicates that the abuse of young boys may be more widespread and more underreported than previously acknowledged. Robinson and Rezendes (2003) estimated that as many as 1,000 children were abused by priests over several decades in only one state. Data on child sexual abuse are difficult to obtain but "a variety of retrospective surveys of the general population indicate that from a quarter to a third of all females and a tenth or more of all males were molested during childhood" (Bartol, 1999, p. 295).

Kilpatrick and his colleagues (1988) surveyed the general population and found that subjects who had been raped identified their husbands as the assailants in 24 percent of the cases and male friends in 17 percent of the cases. In other words, over 40 percent of the rapes were marital or acquaintance (date) rapes. About seven in ten female rape or sexual assault victims stated the offender was an intimate, other relative, a friend, or an acquaintance (Greenfeld, 1997). Tjaden and Thoennes (2000) found that 4.5 percent of women stated that they had been forcibly raped by a current or former intimate partner.

Most sexual assaults are never reported to the police. Victims are affected by feelings of shame, humiliation, suppressed anger, and self-blaming and often do not report a sexual assault. Russell (1984) found that 44 percent of women in a California sample had been sexually assaulted as adults but only 8 percent had reported it to the police. Abel and his colleagues estimated that only 3 percent of sexual offenses find their way into court (Abel et al., 1987). In 1994 and 1995, 32 percent of the victims of rape and sexual assault reported the crime to a law enforcement agency; in other words, more than two-thirds did not (Greenfeld, 1997).

Many sex offenders have a high rate of incidence, that is, they commit a large number of offenses per offender. Abel, Mittleman, and Becker (1985) interviewed 411 sex offenders who reported 218,900 sex crimes, or an average of 533 sex crimes per offender. The average number of victims was 366. The research points to a sex offender usually in his 30s and likely to be white and likely to know the victim. Sex offenders were substantially more likely to report having experienced physical or sexual abuse while growing up (Greenfeld, 1997).

By "sexual offending" we mean a range of behaviors, from unwanted touching to forced intercourse, with a nonconsenting partner. Is this behavior a symptom of a mental disorder? Some argue that diagnoses of mental disorders for sexual offenders are not appropriate; it's the sexual behavior itself, not mental illness or psychological dysfunction which should be the focus of attention (Doren, 2002; Green, 2002). Rapists, for example, do not display the psychopathology that might be expected in such offenders. Only about 5–8 percent of rapists have a psychotic disorder, serious brain dysfunction, or are mentally handicapped (Abel, Rouleau, and Cunningham-Rather, 1986; Seghorn, Prentky, and Boucher, 1987). Other researchers argue that sex offenders are not "specialists" and that they typically engage in nonsexual criminal behaviors as well as sexual offenses. Perhaps the factors which influence criminality in general are just as important as the factors which influence specific sexual offending (see Andrews and Bonta, 1994, pp. 220–226).

The American Psychiatric Association includes a section on sexual deviations in its diagnostic manual. The manual describes a *paraphilia* as a recurrent, intensely sexually arousing fantasy, sexual urge, or behavior generally involving (1) nonhuman objects, (2) the suffering or humiliation of oneself or one's partner, or (3) children or other nonconsenting persons that occurs over a period of six months or more. People may experience sexual arousal to a wide variety of persons, situations, and nonhuman objects, but such arousal is paraphilic, or diagnosable, only when the fantasies, behaviors or objects lead to "clinically significant distress or impairment," which means that they are obligatory for sexual arousal, result in sexual dysfunction, require participation of nonconsenting partners, lead to legal complications, or interfere with social relationships" (DSM-IV-TR, 2000, p. 568). In the context of this discussion, sexual offenses are those which require the participation of nonconsenting partners and lead "to legal complications," which is perhaps too delicately stated, as we are referring to behavior which is against the law and very harmful to the victims. Miner and Coleman write that "A paraphilia is a condition of compulsive response to, or dependence upon, an unusual and unacceptable stimulus in the imagery of fantasy, for optimal initiation and fantasy during solo masturbation, or sexual activity with a partner" (2001, p. 116). Here also, the unacceptable stimulus is that it requires a nonconsenting partner and the behavior is against the law. There have been over forty paraphilias identified and discussed in the research literature (Money, 1986). The most common include exhibitionism (exposing one's genitals to a stranger), voyeurism (observing an unsuspecting person), frotteurism (rubbing or touching), fetishism (using inert objects), pedophilia (involving children 13 or younger), sexual masochism (suffering pain), and sexual sadism (inflicting pain).

Typologies

The observation that sex offenders are a heterogeneous group of offenders has led to the development of various typologies of sexual offenders, who are usually divided at first into two groups: (1) offenders who assault adult women and (2) offenders who assault children. (Offenders who sexually assault adult men are a rarely studied group.) Sex offenders who assault children are usually given a diagnosis of pedophilia. There are numerous typologies specifying subtypes of rapists and child molesters (also called pedophiles). Groth introduced a typology of rapists in 1979 that is still popular among clinicians and law-enforcement personnel due to its simplicity and ease of use. His typology of rapists includes three major subgroups: (1) *the anger rapist*, for whom the sexual offense is means of discharging pent up feelings of anger and rage; its defining characteristic is physical brutality beyond what would be necessary to achieve sexual penetration; (2) *the power rapist*, who seeks to express mastery and control over his victim as compensation for feelings of inadequacy; he uses only the degree of force needed to gain compliance form the victim and his intimidation or physical force is directed toward achieving sexual submission; (3) *the sadistic rapist*, in which both power and anger have been eroticized and the aggression itself is sexual; the rapist achieves sexual pleasure directly from the victim's pain and distress. Often there are bizarre and ritualistic aspects of the rape including bondage, torture, and mutilation. Usually the victims are strangers to the rapist and are often prostitutes, or women that the offender views as promiscuous.

Bartol (1999) proposes two main groups of rapists, those who use *instrumental sexual aggression* and those who use *expressive sexual aggression*. Rapists who employ instrumental sexual aggression use only enough force to gain submission from the victim whereas those who employ expressive sexual aggression intend to harm the victim physically and psychologically and that harm is their primary objective.

There are other typologies of rapists offering greater degrees of complexity. The Massachusetts Treatment Center Rapist Typology Version 3 (MTC:R3) includes nine types of rapists, including categories of rapists who are opportunistic, vindictive, and sadistic, with or without a well-rehearsed fantasy, and combined with different levels of social competence or assertiveness (Knight et al., 1998). It is important that such complex subtypes be linked to prevention, risk assessment, or treatment, or they really do not increase our understanding of the rapist to any appreciable degree.

Pedophilia is diagnosed by the American Psychiatric Association if there are "over a period of at least six months, recurrent, intense sexually arousing fantasies, sexual urges, or behaviors involving sexual activity with a prepubescent child (age thirteen years or younger)" (DSM-IV-TR, 2000, p. 572). Pedophiles are also classified as to whether they are sexually attracted to males, females, or both, and if they are attracted to children exclusively or to both children and adults. One of the best-known typologies of child molesters is the model of Groth (1978). The two main categories are *situational* pedophiles and *preferential* pedophiles. The preferential pedophile confines himself to children of a certain age range, but the situational pedophile will stalk almost any vulnerable victim. The preferential pedophiles are, in turn, composed of two subtypes: (1) the seductive pedophile, who slowly courts or seduces, sometimes called "grooming," his victims, who are almost always boys; and (2) the sadistic pedophile who stalks his victims, uses force, prefers anal sex, and harms his victims, sometimes killing them. Within the group of situational pedophiles, there are three subtypes: (1) the regressed pedophile, who prefers female victims and who will attempt to seduce any vulnerable victim, child or adult, and may surf the Internet looking for victims; (2) the indiscriminate pedophile, who is often a charming, sociable character who looks for victims through other people, like seeking referrals, sometimes from previous victims; and (3) the immature pedophile, who usually stalks victims in his own neighborhood and sometimes is content to fondle his victims with no particular attempt to achieve intercourse.

Theory

Rape occurs in all societies, both primitive and sophisticated, and some evolutionists claim that rape was a common practice in the beginning of our history as a species (Thornhill and Thornhill, 1987). They argue that rape was a reproductive strategy employed by males who were not successful in attracting a mate. But many aspects of rape do not fit this framework. For example, rape often consists of oral or anal sex which has no chance of reproductive success; a substantial number of rapists have some kind of sexual dysfunction, such as lack of erection or premature ejaculation; and a significant proportion of rapists have high social status, or are married and have children, and therefore don't need rape as a reproductive strategy (see Raine, 1993, pp. 41–43).

What we do know about sexual offenders is that they tend to be young men, with a history of antisocial behavior, including both sex and non-sex offenses, and they are quite likely to be repeat offenders (Greenfeld, 1997). Generally our thinking about the causes of sexual offending has included lack of social skills, masturbatory conditioning, excessive anger and hostility toward women, central nervous system dysfunction, and a history of victimization. But no specific theory of sexual assault has taken center stage.

"No generally accepted theory of sex offender behavior exists at this point" (Quackenbush, 2003, p. 77).

A number of studies have pointed to inadequate social skills among sex offenders, such as being relatively low in assertiveness, in capacity for intimacy, in empathy, and in self-esteem. But the research as a whole is not unequivocal since some sex offenders appear socially competent and sex offenders as a group are as socially competent as non–sex offenders, both groups being less socially competent than a community sample of men who are not offenders (Stermac and Quinsey, 1985; Marshall, 2004). Such findings have led some researchers to suggest that factors which influence criminality in general may be as important as sex-specific factors in understanding sex offenders (Andrews and Bonta, 1994).

Researchers have suggested that cognitive distortions are at least a part of sexual offending. Cognitive distortions are beliefs and attitudes which distort reality. In the case of the sex offender, cognitive distortions which tend to promote and justify sexual offending are apparent. For example, "When a woman says no, she really means yes" and "Sometimes having sex with a child can be a way of showing love for the child" are cognitive distortions that facilitate and support sexual offending. Cognitive distortions have been shown to play an important role in many types of problem behavior including depression, obsessive compulsive disorder, and antisocial personality disorder. As we will discuss under treatment, identifying and correcting cognitive distortions has become an integral part of most treatment programs for sexual offenders as well as for non-sex offenders.

Masturbatory conditioning has been shown to have a powerful reinforcing role in clinical studies of sexual offenses (Marshall, 1988). Identifying sexually arousing fantasies are an important part of the assessment and treatment of sex offenders. One possible explanation of pedophilia is that during masturbation the pedophile has concentrated on especially satisfying childhood experiences, and in the absence of satisfactory adult sexual experiences, he has become conditioned to children as sexual partners. It reinforces his attraction to children.

Many workers in the field of sexual offenses have considered a history of victimization as a crucial variable in the development of sexual aggression and violence. If a person was sexually abused as a child, he is likely to abuse others as an adult. However, research has failed to show that a history of sexual victimization is a necessary and sufficient cause of adult sexual offending (Davis and Leitenburg, 1987). In addition, it seems hard to explain how sexual trauma in childhood, which is aversive, would become translated into pleasure as an adult (Bartol, 1999).

An excess of testosterone, abnormality in the limbic-hypothalamic-pituitary-gonadal axis, which is thought to regulate both rage and sexual behavior, and chromosomal abnormalities, such as Klinefelter's syndrome, have been tentatively linked with increased likelihood of paraphilic behavior, suggesting the possibility of a genetic predisposition to sexual deviancy (Saleh and Berlin, 2003). Drugs used in the treatment of paraphilias include the testosterone-lowering medications and the serotonergic antidepressants, which have been shown to reduce sexually inappropriate thoughts and urges. Double-blind studies have not been conducted generally and the pharmacological treatment is almost always combined with a psychological treatment such as cognitive behavioral therapy so that the efficacy of the medications alone has not been demonstrated. As is so often the case with the study of biological factors and crime, the suggestion is there, but there is no convincing evidence of a causal relationship.

Finkelhor and Araji (1986) divided theories of pedophilia into four general categories: (1) emotional congruence theories; (2) sexual arousal theories; (3) blockage theories; and (4) disinhibition theories. Emotional congruence theories are based on the idea that the pedophile's emotional needs fit with the characteristics of the child, a kind of "arrested psychological development." Sexual arousal theories are based on the assumption that, for some people, sexual play as a child was more satisfying than any adult sexual experience has been. Hence, the pedophile seeks to repeat the pleasurable experiences of his childhood. Blockage theories are based on the idea that satisfying adult relationships are blocked by factors such as excessive shyness and lack of social skills so that the pedophile seeks the company of children for emotional and sexual gratification. Disinhibition theories emphasize circumstances which break down normal control of unacceptable sexual behavior such as poor impulse control, stress, and use of alcohol and drugs.

Marshall and Barbaree (1990) have proposed an Integrated Theory of Sexual Deviancy which incorporates hormonal influences, the effects of poor parenting, sociocultural attitudes, and limited environmental influences. They recommend that all of these variables be considered when planning treatment for sex offenders.

Yates (2003) explains the important point that research shows that deviant sexual arousal alone does not account for sexual offending. Deviant sexual arousal occurs also with non-sex offenders. The deviant sexual arousal must be accompanied by other cognitive and emotional factors to result in sexual aggression. Some of these factors include anger, low self-esteem, alcohol use, negative mood, the need for power and control, and deviant sexual preference. It is a constellation of factors which occur together with deviant sexual arousal that produces sexual offending (Blader and Marshall, 1989; Yates, 2003).

Schwartz (1997) published a summary of 21 theoretical approaches to sexual violence, from single-factor theories to integrated models like that of Marshall and Barbaree cited above. She also noted that even after 90 years of work on the topic, there still remains a hot debate on whether or not sexual offending is a form of mental illness or not.

Bartol concludes that, of the available theories, "none can account for the multiple causes and the full range of learning experiences, beliefs, motivations and attitudes of pedophiles" (1999, p. 307). Concerning rapists, Marshall notes that only a small percentage of rapists find their way to prison, yet virtually all of the research and theorizing is based on them. "The majority of the data available on rapists, then, represents a distorted picture but it is, unfortunately, the only picture we have" (Marshall, 2004, p. 149).

Assessment

Most experts in the field of sex offender research agree that assessment is the area in which we have made the most progress so far (Miner and Coleman, 2001). Actuarial risk assessment predicts the dangerousness and risk of reoffending of a sex offender. An additional or second type of assessment is to determine treatment needs and goals.

In risk assessment, the offender is usually assessed as low, moderate, or high risk for reoffending and knowing the circumstances under which an offender is most likely to reoffend is especially useful. Factors which are related to sexual reoffending, like risk factors for any criminal recidivism, are of two types: static and dynamic. Static risk factors are those which cannot be changed, such as past criminal history. Dynamic risk factors are those which can be changed, such as unemployment or substance abuse. Static factors which have been found to affect risk for sexual reoffending include victim gender and relationship to the offender, nonsexual criminal history, prior sexual offenses, age, anger problems, past failure to complete treatment, mental disorder, marital status, personality disorder, history of diverse sex crimes, bad childhood environment, and deviant sexual preference. Dynamic factors include unemployment, substance abuse, poor social adjustment, tolerant attitudes towards sex offenses, poor coping skills, low self-esteem, access to potential victims, negative attitudes toward treatment, uncooperativenss with supervision, and exacerbation of symptoms of a severe mental disorder (Hanson and Bussiere, 1998; Clipson, 2003).

The most often-used instruments for evaluating risk are the PCL-R, the STATIC-99, and the SORAG. The Psychopathy Checklist–Revised (PCL-R) is a 20-item list which was originally designed to measure the degree of psychopathy, or criminality, in an individual (Hare, 1993). Scores on this test are associated with criminal recidivism of all types, including sexual offender recidivism. The STATIC-99 is an easily scored 10-item scale developed by Hanson and Thornton (1999) and combines items from earlier attempts to predict recidivism. It provides levels of risk assessment and estimates of violent recidivism at 5-, 10-, and 15-year intervals. The Sex Offender Risk Appraisal Guide (SORAG) provides a score that can be placed in one of nine risk levels (Quinsey, Rice, Harris, and Cormier, 1998). The SORAG and the STATIC-99 predict sexual reoffending with at least modest accuracy (Barbaree, Seto, Langton, and Peacock, 2001; Hanson and Thornton, 2000).

If the purpose of the assessment is to evaluate treatment needs and set treatment goals, a more extensive assessment is necessary. This type of assessment should include: (1) an extensive clinical interview, which includes especially details of the offender's version of his sex offense and his empathy for the victim(s) as well as a complete medical, social, legal, sexual, and psychiatric history; (2) a review of all existing information, including especially official crime versions, victim statements, and criminal records, and previous treatment and evaluations, if conducted; (3) psychological testing, which may include a measure of intellectual functioning, a personality measure, and offense-specific measures, such as the Multiphasic Sex Inventory (Nichols and Molinder, 1984) or the Hanson Sexual Attitudes Questionnaire (Hanson et al., 1994); (4) interviews with significant others in the offender's life is also recommended (see Clipson, 2003, for an excellent discussion of assessment).

Sex-offender treatment programs often assess sexual attraction using penile plethysmography (PPG), also known as phallometry. The penile plethysmograph is a machine for measuring changes in the circumference of the penis. A stretchable band with mercury in it is fitted around the subject's penis. The band is connected to a machine with a video screen and data measures and records penile erection as various visual or auditory stimuli are presented. These stimuli may be slides or videos of naked children or adults, and auditory stimuli may be recorded descriptions of sexual acts (consenting or coerced) involving adults and/or children. Any changes in penis size, even those not felt by the subject, are recorded. Computer software is used to develop graphs showing the degree of arousal to each stimulus. The machine was first developed in Czechoslovakia by Dr. Kurt Freund to prevent draft dodgers from claiming they were gay just to avoid military duty (Carroll, 2004). The plethysmograph is used not only to identify those offenders who are sexually attracted to minors, but also to determine whether their attraction has been reduced or eliminated by treatment.

The appropriateness and efficacy of the PPG have been widely debated. Criticisms include that there is no evidence that strong arousal to pictures or sounds is reliably related to sexual offending, or that weak arousal is related to nonoffending, and that there are no standard stimulus materials for the PPG. There is also the ethical problem that visual and auditory depictions of nude women and children engaging in nonconsensual sex acts may seem to legitimize sexual deviance and further stimulate the sex offender. Research studies have shown that the PPG has reliably separated sex offenders from non–sex offenders, but there are also studies which fail to find this result (Barbaree, Baxter, and Marshall, 1989; Hudson and Ward, 1997; Ward, Hudson, and Keenan, 2004).

The reliability and validity of the PPG have not been well established and "clinical experience suggests that subjects can simulate response by manipulating mental images" (DSM-IV-TR, 2000). It is not hard to fake the PPG with conscious control of erections. "In essence, the early promise of phallometry to discriminate between offenders and nonoffenders has generally not been sustained," though some authors recommend phallometric testing anyway, at least for child molesters, as it is the best available technique for them at present (Ward, Hudson, and Keenan, 2004, p. 165). The debate continues.

One of the major problems in assessing sex offenders is that they are often very deceptive about their behavior. Dealing with deception and denial is one of the principal tasks of evaluators and therapists. Nichols and Molinder (1984) discussed three types of deception common with sex offenders. Dishonesty, outright lies and significant omissions, is the first. Distortion is the second, in which offenders justify and rationalize, often blaming others for their behavior. Denial is the third. In denial, the offender is deceiving both others and himself about the nature and extent of his sexual problems and trying to convince himself, as well as others, that it will never happen again and nothing needs to be done about it. Evaluators and therapists need to compare data from different sources, such as interview data, psychometric data, official records and third-party data as checks against the three forms of deception. It can be very difficult to obtain a clear and accurate picture of an individual's sexual offending. Polygraph testing is recommended by some workers in the field as a check against deliberate deception (Emerick and Dutton, 1993). In their study, Emerick and Dutton compared information obtained from official records, information obtained from interview data, and information obtained from polygraph testing. Polygraph testing changed the data on a number of important variables, increasing the number of assaults, degree of intrusion (oral-genital, vaginal, rectal), degree of force used, and mean number of victims under ten years old. Others, however, argue that polygraph data is unreliable and has unproven accuracy rates (see Kokish, 2003, for a good discussion). Clark Clipson writes that "a combination of the techniques of confrontation, clarification, and confirmation of self report data are the clinician's best aids in addressing this thorny problem" (Clipson, 2003, p. 148).

Methods of Treatment

After a review of treatment programs, Prentky, Knight, and Lee (1997) wrote that sex offender treatment can be divided into four general types:

(1) evocative therapy, which includes individual and group counseling to help the offender to understand the causes and motives of his behavior, and to teach empathy for the victims; (2) psychoeducational counseling, which uses a class or group setting and provides education about such topics as anger management, relapse prevention, human sexuality, and relationships; (3) drug treatment, which may be antiandrogens or antidepressant medication; (4) cognitive behavior therapy. Prentky and his colleagues conclude that cognitive behavioral approaches, sometimes accompanied by medication, are the most effective techniques for the cessation of deviant behavior in motivated individuals.

Lester and Hurst (2000) offer another way of understanding treatment approaches. They argue against a single structured program for all sex offenders: "Those working with sex offenders now realize that they are treating a heterogeneous population requiring a multidimensional approach and a wider range of treatment approaches" (2000, p. 255). They suggest that therapists should individualize treatment programs using a variety of treatment strategies (Maletzky, 1991; Schorsch et al., 1990; Lester and Hurst, 2000). Available approaches include organic strategies, behavioral strategies, cognitive strategies, and relapse prevention strategies. Organic approaches have in the past included surgical castration and stereotactic brain surgery, which disconnects the sex drives (Schorsch et al., 1990). Today organic approaches are mostly restricted to medications, particularly antiandrogens and antidepressants. Antiandrogens reduce testosterone, decrease erections and ejaculations, decrease sexual fantasies, and reduce sexual interest in general. The antidepressants, in this case, the SSRIs, have produced decreased paraphilic fantasies and urges. It is not known if this is because of their sexual side effects or because of increased control of anxiety, depression, and obsessionality (Miner and Coleman, 2001).

Behavioral approaches most often employed include (1) aversion therapy, in which offenders learn to associate unpleasant stimuli, such as electric shock, or drugs that induce vomiting, or unpleasant odors or tastes, with deviant sexual thoughts and behavior; (2) covert sensitization, in which offenders learn to associate deviant fantasies and behaviors with imagined negative consequences, such as being arrested; and (3) masturbatory conditioning in which deviant fantasies are replaced with nondeviant fantasies during masturbation. The use of aversion therapy raised the objection of unethical and inhumane treatment and, in addition, did not seem very effective (Epps, 1996). Consequently, covert sensitization is more often used in sex offender programs.

Cognitive approaches, which seek to identify and correct errors and distortions in an offender's thinking, include cognitive restructuring, empathy training, role playing, and social skills training. In cognitive therapy, attitudes, beliefs, and thoughts which support, rationalize, or justify sexual aggression are identified, confronted, and replaced with thoughts, beliefs, and attitudes which are supportive of nondeviant sexual behavior.

Relapse-prevention principles are taught to sex offenders. These principles help the offender to recognize high-risk situations (high risk for relapse into deviant sexual fantasies and behavior) and to identify and respond appropriately to early warning signals of relapse. Relapse for sex offenders seems to follow a sequence of events, which the offender can learn to recognize and correct, or avoid, early in the sequence. Pithers (1990) found that rapists are often angry and use alcohol or drugs prior to an act of sexual aggression. Pedophiles, on the other hand, usually experience anxiety and depression before seeking a child. Offenders can be taught to recognize the early warning signs and take corrective action before sexual offending occurs (George and Marlatt, 1989).

An example of a sex offenders treatment program is that presented by Ward, Hudson, and Keenan (2004), which was originally developed by Hudson et al. (1995). It is organized into seven modules, and incorporates and integrates the best techniques and strategies. The treatment is conducted over a 31-week period with a group of eight offender pedophiles and one therapist. The modules are as follows:

Module 1: Norm Building
Module 2: Understanding Offending (Cognitive Restructuring)
Module 3: Arousal Reconditioning
Module 4: Victim Impact and Empathy
Module 5: Mood Management
Module 6: Relationship Skills
Module 7: Relapse Prevention

Some additional treatment considerations are that group treatment is preferred over individual treatment because it is a more efficient use of available resources, but also because it has increased efficacy. Credible challenges and confrontation from other group members and vicarious learning can occur in the group setting but not in individual therapy (Ward, Hudson, and Keenan, 2004). Mathis and Collins (1970) found that open-ended groups in which offenders were at different stages of treatment were helpful and they also recommended the use of male and female co-therapists for the group treatment. Peer counselors are also frequently used in sex offender treatment.

Most sex offender treatment programs are for adult men with normal intelligence who agree to treatment and do not deny their offenses. There are four other special populations of sex offenders that have received far less attention, but who have definite treatment needs. These are juvenile sex offenders, developmentally disabled sex offenders, female sex offenders, and what Miner and Coleman call "sexually reactive youth," by which they mean prepubescent children who have sexually coerced other children (Miner and Coleman, 2001).

Research on Effectiveness

A warning shot was fired across the bow of sex offender treatment programs by Furby, Weinrott, and Blackshaw in 1989. After a thorough review of the research, they concluded that there was no scientific basis that sex offender treatment worked to reduce recidivism: "there is as yet no evidence that clinical treatment reduces rates of sex offending" (p. 27). Their study set off a debate about the effectiveness of sex offender treatment which continues today. Some researchers have pointed out results which are more optimistic than Furby, Weinrott, and Blackshaw's, particularly with certain treatment methods, while others agree with Furby et al. that the research has been inadequate and the case remains unproven. For example, Ward, Hudson, and Keenan argue that "there is evidence that comprehensive cognitive behavioral programmes, and those that combine antiandrogens with psychological treatment, are associated with ecologically significant reductions in recidivism for treated sex offenders" (2004, p. 164). Most researchers do agree that treatment is somewhat less effective with rapists than with pedophiles (Marshall and Pithers, 1994). One study found that 19 percent of sex offenders who completed treatment recidivated while 29 percent of offenders in comparison groups did (Hall, 1995). Hanson and his colleagues (2002) reported in a meta analysis of 43 recent studies that the sexual offense recidivism rate for treated sexual offenders was 9.9 percent as compared to 17.3 percent for untreated sexual offenders, and the general recidivism rate (all types of offences) was reduced from 51 percent to 32 percent with treatment (primarily cognitive behavioral treatment).

On the other hand, Quinsey and his colleagues concluded that the evidence for effective treatment is sparse and based on inadequately designed studies (Quinsey, Harris, Rice, and Lalumiere, 1993; Quinsey et al., 1998). Miner and Coleman report: "In all areas, the research has been lacking and inadequate" (Miner & Coleman, 2001, p. 11). Clipson (2003) argues that, despite a large body of research on sexual offense recidivism (Hanson and Bussiere, 1998), the conclusions of these efforts often appear conflicting. The problems are ones which plague most research on the effectiveness of interventions with criminal populations and are the results of the differences in individual studies which make them hard to compare. These differences include those in research designs, in the populations studied, in the definitions of recidivism, and in the length of the follow-up periods. Another problem is that the treatments which have been studied are often not well defined or described and are hard to compare to each other. In other words, some negative results may be obtained because the treatment was of poor quality, incompetently implemented, not appropriate for the population to which it was applied, or otherwise not in accordance with the principles of effective correctional intervention (Gendreau, 1996; Andrews and Bonta, 1998). Another problem is that random-assignment studies, which would be definitive, but are hardly ever conducted, may be unethical because they would require that high-risk sex offenders receive no treatment and then be released into the community (Marshall and Anderson, 1998).

Miner and Coleman (2001) suggest that the major challenge for sex offender treatment in the future is a stronger empirical base for treatment effectiveness. Meanwhile, Marshall (1992) has employed a cost-benefit analysis in which he demonstrated that eliminating the risk to reoffend in just one or two sexual offenders out of 100 treated is enough to cover the costs of treatment. And continuing to do treatment is the only way to develop more effective treatments (Marshall, 2004). Marshall was echoing Nicholas Groth, who wrote over 25 years ago:

That we do not have a cure does not mean, however, that we should abandon the idea of rehabilitating offenders. Some offenders are undoubtedly helped by such services. Even more important, such efforts offer the opportunity to increase our knowledge about the sexual offender and his offenses. This knowledge not only may be of benefit in helping victims but also may contribute to preventing the development of future offenders [Groth, 1979, p. 223].

This is a point of view as solid now as it was then. Undoubtedly, the debate will follow us into the next decade.

Female Offenders

In 2002, there were an estimated 2.2 million arrests of women in the United States, accounting for about 23 percent of all arrests that year. The proportion of inmates in that year who were women was 7 percent in Federal prisons, 6 percent in state prisons, and 12 percent in local jails. While female criminals are a small group compared to male criminals, the number of female defendants convicted of felonies in state courts has grown at more than two times the rate of increase in male defendants since 1990 (U.S. Department of Justice, 2002). Some researchers assert that a fundamental change has occurred in the nature and extent of female offending (Sommers and Baskin, 1992, 1993). Others have argued that the increase in offenses by women may be accounted for by increases in petty income-generating crimes and drug offenses, which are mainly a result of the crack epidemic (Coontz and Sevigny, 2003). Meda Chesney-Lind and Lisa Pasko (2004) have argued that there has been no fundamental change in female offending, but that women's imprisonment has greatly increased because of society's change in perspective on drug crimes, which has resulted in both more arrests and harsher punishment for female drug offenders than in the past. "[I]n essence, the war on drugs has become a largely unannounced war on women, particularly women of color" (Chesney-Lind, 1998, p. xiv).

The "typical" female offender in American prisons is aged 25–29, unmarried, with one to three children, is likely a victim of sexual abuse as a child, and is a victim of physical abuse, has current substance-abuse problems, was first arrested around age 15, is a high school dropout on welfare, has low skills, and has held mainly low-wage jobs (Brennan and Austin, 1997, p. 3). Bloom and Covington characterize females in the correctional system as "mostly young, poor, and undereducated women of color who have complex histories of trauma and substance abuse" (1998, p. 4).

Why do women commit crimes? Female criminality has been related, though not very convincingly, to abnormal chromosomal configurations, body fat, the castration complex, menstruation, and the onset of puberty. In *The Unadjusted Girl*, published in 1923, Thomas argued that female delinquency begins with the wish for new experience and excitement. Girls learn that they can have these by manipulating their "capital," that is their sexuality. According to this line of thought, it was primarily lower-class girls who were amoral and who learned to use their sexuality for personal excitement and perceived gain in status.

Current explanations for female criminality tend to emphasize social learning and gender roles over innate biological characteristics, though sometimes in unusual ways. For example, Pollak argued that the difference in male and female criminality is only an apparent difference because female criminality is hidden by gender roles (1950). Another line of argument begins with the shift in the 1970s towards increased participation in the labor force for women. This change resulted in greater opportunities for women to commit crimes and also greater exposure to the frustration and stress of the workplace. It also led, as the argument goes, to increased imitation of male behavior. The feminist view is that female delinquency is a defensive reaction to male efforts to control and dominate women's lives economically, emotionally, and/or physically.

Females are freer to engage in delinquency when the mother is working. Hagan and his colleagues studied patriarchal families, in which the father worked but the mother did not, egalitarian families, in which both parents worked, and mother-only, single-parent families. They omitted single-parent families where the father was the head of household because they could not find enough of these to study. Their research confirmed the prediction that female delinquency would be higher and more similar to male delinquency in the egalitarian and mother-only households than in the patriarchal families. In other words, in family structures in which the females had more opportunity to engage in delinquent behavior, more of them did so (Hagan, 1989).

Daly (1992) identified five pathways to female offending as a result of her analysis of federal court presentence investigation reports: (1) *the street woman*, who supports a drug habit with stealing, drug dealing, or prostitution; (2) *the harmed and harming woman*, who commits violent crimes, usually under the influence of drugs and/or alcohol and who usually has a history of being abused; (3) *the battered woman*, who has attacked or killed a violent man; (4) *the drug connected woman*, who uses or sells drugs as a result of her intimate relationships; (5) *other women*, who commit economically motivated crimes from greed or from poverty.

Moffitt, Caspi, Rutter, and Silva have published interesting research on gender differences in antisocial behavior from the Dunedin Multidisciplinary Health and Development Study. The Dunedin study is a 26-year-old longitudinal study of 1,000 male and female subjects born in Dunedin, New Zealand, in 1972–1973. The subjects were followed from age 3 to age 21 in their research, published in 2001, though the study is continuing. Moffitt and her colleagues argued that there are two distinct groups of delinquents, those whose antisocial behavior is limited to their adolescent years and those who persist in antisocial behavior throughout their life course. They found that these two distinct groups existed for girls as well as for boys. They also report that almost all females who engage in antisocial behavior fall into the adolescence limited group, with a sex ratio of 1.5 males to 1.0 females in that group. The life course persistent antisocial female is extremely rare, with only 1 in 100 females falling into this group. The sex ratio in this group is 10 males to 1 female. The males and females in the life course persistent group are very similar in terms of cognitive deficit, personality, and social environment. "Why do fewer females than males suffer the primary individual level risk factors for life course persistent antisocial behavior?" The researchers consider this to be "an unanswered question" (2001).

Two books published in 1975 addressed "the emancipation thesis," sometimes called "the opportunity thesis," the proposition that the women's liberation movement of the 1970s, while providing greater equality and freedom for women, would also increase the female crime rate. Freda Adler proposed in her book, *Sisters in Crime*, that as women began to move out of traditional homemaking roles and into the competitive marketplace, they would become more masculine in orientation and that they would acquire more masculine qualities, including, among other characteristics, criminality. Liberated women would become "as capable of violence and aggression as any man" (Adler, 1975). In *Women in Crime*, Rita Simon wrote that, as women moved into the marketplace and into positions of more power, they would have greater opportunities to commit economic and white-collar crimes and that this increase in opportunity would lead to a larger number of offenses committed by women (Simon, 1975). These two books stimulated much study and debate about women and crime. Since then, the data have indicated that Simon's theory had the greater validity, that is, there were larger increases in property offenses for women than there were increases in violent crimes committed by women, as Adler had suggested. But, overall, as Coontz and Sevigny report, the increase in female arrest rates in the last decade is more likely due to the war on drugs than to women's liberation. The increase in the female arrest rate is "largely confined to petty income generating offenses" committed by women who are multiple drug users in need of treatment. Coontz and Sevigny suggest that we need to address how gender affects both involvement in crime and involvement in drugs (Coontz and Sevigny, 2003).

It may be seen that many of these explanations really address the *increase* in female criminality in the last years of the 20th century but do not address the fundamental difference that has always existed between male and female criminality. In addition, some of these are really explanations for juvenile delinquency rather than explanations for adult criminality. These are not the same thing and the same explanations do not always apply. Even so, the above are a fair sample of explanations available for the gender difference in crime. They show collectively that we don't know very much about it.

Are the explanations for female criminality the same as explanations for male criminality, or do different explanations apply? This quandary is called the *generalizability problem* and it has important implications for treatment. If the explanations for male and female crime are essentially the same explanations, then treatment methods and programs may not need to consider gender. However, if the causes of crime are different for women than for men, gender-specific programs may be needed. Another consideration is the *responsivity principle*, proposed by the advocates of effective correctional programming (Andrews and Bonta, 1998; Gendreau, 1996)

149

which says that offenders respond best to programs tailored especially for their needs, a principle which could be applied in favor of gender-specific programs. Proponents of gender-specific programs argue that programs developed for males do not seem to work for females.

Steffensmeier and Allan (1998) argue that women's routes to crime differ from those of men. The ways in which these pathways are different include the victimization of women by male violence and the responses of women to being victimized, the demands of motherhood and child care, the exclusion of women from the most lucrative crime opportunities, and the ability of women to exploit sexual activity as an illegal moneymaking service. They also cite the "centrality of relational concerns among women," by which they mean the degree to which women are pulled into crime by the criminal activities of the men in their lives. The vast majority of female offenders are mothers and their relationship with their children is one of the major differences between them and male offenders who are often not involved to any great extent with their children (Zaplin and Dougherty, 1998). Bloom and Covington (1998) conclude that an effective program for female offenders should address addiction issues, women's development issues, and trauma recovery issues.

Gender-specific programming is more than just a program for females only. It must address issues unique to the female experience and perspective. The Juvenile Justice Evaluation Center of the Justice Research and Statistics Association (Office of Juvenile Justice and Delinquency Prevention, 2005) reports that the research literature suggests the following principles for gender-specific programming: tailoring programs to the unique needs of girls; involving girls in service decisions; using female staff; connecting girls with mentors; providing staff training on gender-specific programming; addressing the needs of pregnant or parenting girls; defining gender-specific programming; using local data to develop approaches; considering issues with rural jurisdictions.

Recommended treatment components that are consistent with the research so far include: concentration on relationship building, addressing mental health issues, focusing on maturation and development, treating sexual abuse, and addressing family issues.

One program considered a model for female offender programs is the STEP Program. STEP was begun in New York City, originally implemented for male offenders, but was adapted for African American female offenders. STEP is based on a three-step empowerment process that teaches participants to assume responsibility for their lives, to gain an understanding of "roadblocks" that hinder success, and to become active and supportive in the empowerment of others. The program has an institutional component and an aftercare component. The institutional component is a ten-week intensive learning program which includes academic education, vocational training, parenting, domestic violence issues, substance-abuse intervention (using counselors who are exaddicts and exoffenders), and group and individual counseling. The aftercare component provides voluntary group and individual counseling to graduates of the program who have been released from the Department of Correction using peer counselors as models (see Henriques and Jones-Brown, 1998).

The evaluation research on programs for female offenders is not conclusive. Though large numbers of process evaluations have been conducted and reviewed, outcome studies are relatively rare. For example, Koons, Burrow, Morash, and Bynum (1997) reviewed 67 programs but only six reported outcome measures. Austin, Bloom, and Donahue (1992) surveyed 100 operating programs but only four of them had been evaluated. The National Council on Crime and Delinquency conducted an outcome evaluation of the Reaffirming Young Sisters Excellence (RYSE) program. The researchers looked at 191 cases with an 18-month follow-up. They found no significant difference between the treatment group and a random control group on measures of completion of probation, time to completion of probation, time to completion of community service, and time to completion of restitution (National Council on Crime and Delinquency, 2001). Evaluations of programs for female offenders are still "relatively uncommon" (Office of Juvenile Justice and Delinquency Prevention, 2005). Zaplin concludes: "it is still not completely known what factors lead women and girls to criminal activity, and how interventions can be designed to mitigate these factors effectively" (Zaplin, 1998, p. 383). Gender-specific programming does appear to be increasing in the correctional system and perhaps we will have, in the near future, more conclusive evidence as to its effectiveness in reducing female offending.

Chapter Eight

Faith-Based Programs

I was in prison and ye came unto me.
— Matthew 25:26

Prison and prison imagery appear in the Bible often enough for us to suppose that imprisonment was a familiar and readily understood condition in ancient times. For example, in the book of Genesis, Joseph is cast into prison by Potiphar. In the Psalms, "The Lord sets the prisoners free." And, in the book of Isaiah, "He has sent me to bind up the broken hearted, to proclaim freedom for the captives, and release for the prisoners." In the New Testament, in Hebrews, Christian believers are enjoined to "Remember those in prison," and, in Matthew, Jesus says, "I was in prison and you came to visit me." This last has been the impetus for much visiting of prisoners by people of the Christian faith. St. Cyprian, bishop of Carthage in the third century, ordered the Christian clergy to visit prisoners in response to the Gospel of St. Matthew. In the fourth century, the Nicene Council initiated an organization of prison visitors (Eriksson, 1976).

However, it was not until the Enlightenment in the 18th century that the idea of imprisonment as a means of bringing about salvation was widely discussed. In 1776, Jonas Hanway published a book in England, *Solitude in Imprisonment*, in which he argued for the importance of reforming the prisoner and by "reforming," he meant religious conversion (McGowen, 1995). "The walls of his prison will preach peace to his soul and he will confess the goodness of his Maker, and the wisdom of the laws of his country" (quoted in McGowen, 1995, p. 78). Hanway was proposing the use of solitary confinement in prisons, but he was also expressing the idea that the reformation of the offender should be a principal goal of the imprisonment. He had precursors, of course, for example, the Benedictine monk Pater Jean Mabillon, who had written and published in 1724 a specific plan to apply the monastic life to criminal offenders. Mabillon proposed that the basic tenets of reforming the criminal offender were isolation, work, silence, and prayer (cited in Eriksson, 1976).

Religious programs are among the oldest and most commonly found prison programs. There is no doubt that religion is widely practiced in prison as nearly every prison has at least one chaplain and many have several. Religious services are one of the oldest and most common of prison programs. A 1991 survey found that 32 percent of prison inmates participated regularly in some form of religious programming (U.S. Department of Justice, 1993). Interest in faith-based programs for criminal offenders and the growth of faith-based prison units in some states has increased recently due to a renewed focus on restorative justice as opposed to retributive justice and to the activity and interest in faith community partnerships engendered by the administration of President Bush. Interest has also been stimulated by the fact that religious programming is dramatically less expensive than other types of offender treatment. One study estimated $150–$250 per inmate per year for religious programs versus $24,000 per inmate per year for other types of program (O'Connor and Pallone, 2002).

O'Connor has developed a model for effective religious programming for the Oregon Department of Correction which outlines five target areas:

(1) *pastoral administration*: working together with the institution and its program, keeping up good communication and research;

(2) *volunteerism:* coordinating the various volunteers, both individuals and groups, who want to help the inmates;

(3) *inmate spiritual needs*: conducting regular worship services, new inmate orientations, and spiritual "check ups" for inmates;

(4) *community*: developing a community of believers and partners who do something at least once a year to benefit and improve the community or improve interpersonal relations;

(5) *ethics:* conducting and enhancing the discussion and considera-

tion of ethics, justice, and a sense of right and wrong within the prison (O'Connor, 2005).

Example Programs

Modern faith-based programs include initiatives like RESTART, a comprehensive program operated by the Maryland Department of Correction, which offers secular drug treatment and counseling but also includes a volunteer-driven program based on the best-selling religious book, *The Purpose Driven Life*. RESTART also includes *Rights of Passage*, a Christian life skills program and two other religious programs which have been adapted for all faiths. Faith-based prison programs have been promoted in California, Florida, Iowa, Ohio, and South Carolina (Dishneau, 2005). Florida and Indiana operate residential prison religious programs where inmates live in segregated housing units, keep journals, attend small-group discussions, and attend regular worship services.

Twelve-step programs, such as Alcoholics Anonymous (AA), Narcotics Anonymous, and Gamblers Anonymous, which have been in prisons a long time, may be considered faith-based programs because they rely on a "higher power." These programs are nondenominational and nonsectarian. AA members say that AA is a spiritual program but not a religious one. By this declaration, they mean that twelve-step programs do appeal to a person's spirituality but do not promote any particular religious faith. They consider this distinction important to the broad appeal and success of these programs.

The Prison Fellowship is one of the largest and best known of the modern faith-based programs. It was founded in 1975 by Charles Colson. Colson spent seven months in federal prison on a one- to three-year sentence for obstruction of justice during the Watergate era of the Nixon administration. He was essentially a "dirty tricks" staffer who had gravitated "from surly frat boy to hard drinking marine to amoral political operative" (Cohen, 2005). "In the midst of his travails, Mr. Colson found religion," writes Cohen, and Colson then started an evangelical prison ministry. He also took on the role of prison reformer. The Prison Fellowship works with local churches to bring a Christian ministry to prisoners. Colson said "The biblical model says the way you deal with offenders is to redeem them" (quoted in Cohen, 2005, p. 2). He sees religious conversion as the key to restorative justice. He also founded the Justice Fellowship, which works to improve prison conditions, to help inmates with jobs and job training, and to assist newly released inmates. There is a recent biography by Jonathan Aitken, *Charles Colson: A Life Redeemed* (2005).

Circles of Support and Accountability were started by Harry Nigh, a Mennonite minister in 1994 (Morgan, 2005). Nigh had met a developmentally delayed pedophile who was released from prison and a Correctional Service Canada (CSC) psychologist had asked for Nigh's help with the case. So the first "circle" was Nigh, the released pedophile, and a small group of church volunteers. The circle assisted Taylor with every aspect of his life, including housing and health care. The circle volunteers were available to him by phone around the clock and they had a formal visit with him once a week to solve problems, celebrate small victories, and to hold him accountable for any risky actions or decisions, such as moving in with people who were a negative influence. They were also ready and willing to report him to the police if necessary. Today there are a hundred circles across Canada run by 20 organizations (Morgan, 2005). And the concept is being copied in other countries as well. A study by Wilson, a Canadian psychologist, showed that offenders receiving support from a circle were 70 percent less likely to reoffend than were other sex offenders (cited in Morgan, 2005).

There are certainly more possibilities than the traditional Christian services. Bo Lozoff started the Prison Ashram Project in 1973 and it can now be found in prisons across the nation and in other countries (Lozoff, 2006). Native American religions have appeared in prison settings, for example, the ancient faith of Hawaii. In a muddy prison yard near Watonga, Oklahoma,

> a group of men greeted the sun and prayed to Lono, the Hawaiian god of agriculture, fertility, and peace. About 100 prisoners were silent as a conch shell sounded. They followed a leader for chanting and prayers in the Hawaiian language, welcoming the day and pleading for wisdom and forgiveness [Downes, 2005, p. 1].

After a two-year legal battle, the Native Hawaiian Legal Corporation sued on behalf of 33 Hawaiian inmates who were confined at the Diamondback Correctional Facility in Oklahoma, accusing officials of denying their constitutional rights. A federal judge allowed the two rites celebrating Makahiki and a settlement was worked out by the two sides. The inmates had argued that the worship services helped them to restore a sense of *ho'o-ponopono*, or righteousness, in their lives. Their religious group enforced strict rules of attendance and respect, and a rejection of alcohol, drugs, gangs, and violence.

Probably one of the most widely known of all religious groups in prison are the Black Muslims, who have become a recognized and permanent part of American corrections, even though, in the beginning, they were considered a threat to the order and safety of the prison. That the black Muslims have survived so long as a viable and valuable prison religious group is due to the intersection of race, religion, and inmate culture, according to Felicia Dix-Richardson and Billy Close. Islam has prevailed in American prisons over the last six decades because it addresses the economic, social, and political inequalities experienced by African Americans (Dix-Richardson and Close, 2002). Religion has always been a significant part of African American culture and it compensates for the some of the deprivations of prison. "Islam has been able to capture the imagination of the African American male because it has the ability to draw upon this past and specifically address issues of immediate concern," such as oppression racism, spirituality, manhood and self empowerment (Dix-Richardson and Close, 2002, p. 101).

Since many African Americans brought Islam with them to the western hemisphere, it is likely that the Muslim religion has always been in American prisons to some degree. But Dix-Richardson and Close point to the 1940s and the emergence of Elijah Muhammad and the Nation of Islam as the essential starting point. In the beginning, the Nation of Islam was resisted and oppressed by prison administrators who feared it would disrupt the prison. In a landmark court decision, *Cooper v. Pate* (1967), the court held that the Nation of Islam was indeed a religion and must be recognized and treated as such. It also found that Muslims must be allowed to practice their religion in prison. Since then, and since the split within the Nation of Islam, Islamic diversity has increased among the African American prison population, but, as Dix-Richardson and Close point out, this probably means more Islamic converts and adherents in prisons, not less.

The importance of Islam to young black males has been recounted by many famous authors and public figures including James Baldwin, Malcolm X, Louis Farrakhan, C. Eric Lincoln, and Muhammad Ali. Since there are such large numbers of young black men in prison, it is not surprising that the Black Muslims have an important and permanent foothold there. Dix-Richardson and Close write: "Research regarding Islam within the prison system generally concluded that Islam promotes morality, conformity, self-esteem, responsibility, productivity, and a desire for spiritual and intellectual growth (2002, p. 103; see also Atkins and Glick, 1972; Sharif, 1981). The Black Muslims will most likely continue to grow and develop within prison walls across America.

Example Research

What is the relationship between religion and the rehabilitation of inmates, if there is one? (O'Connor and Perreyclear, 2002). It is hard to say what the rehabilitative effects of religious programming really are since there are few studies and those often have serious methodological flaws. These flaws include lack of random sampling, measurement error, and lack of a control group or appropriate comparison group. However, in all fairness, much of the correctional research has the same deficiencies. Johnson, Larson, and Pitts (1997) point out that there is so little research on religion and recidivism because religious staff are untrained in research or uninterested in research while social scientists have carried a broad bias against the relevance and importance of religious programming. This bias was introduced by Hirschi and Stark (1969) in a landmark study in which they questioned the efficacy of religion as a social control mechanism. They administered a self-report survey to 4,077 adolescents and found that there was no significant difference in reported deviant behavior between church attendees and nonattendees. Hirschi and Stark suggested that religion was not an inhibitor of deviance. This suggestion was generally accepted and led to a paucity of research about religion and rehabilitation of inmates. Benda and Toombs (2002) have argued that the importance of religiosity in criminology was an important and discussed topic until it was dismissed as a factor in the late 1960s and early 1970s by social scientists who accepted

Hirschi and Stark's conclusion. Now it seems to have revived as a factor worthy of scientific study. Since at least 1984, researchers have noted the neglect of religion as a variable in studies about prison adjustment and recidivism: "only a few studies have examined religious participation as an important indicator of either prison adjustment or post release adjustment" (Clear and Sumter, 2002, p. 131). Clear reports some indications of an inverse relationship between religion and deviance in two studies (Clear et al., 1992; Johnson et al., 1997). O'Connor (2002) reports that some strong correlations have been found between prison religiosity and prison behavior while some other studies have found a relationship between religiosity and recidivism but not with prison rule infractions. Following are some examples of the research so far on religious programming.

(1) Johnson, Larson, and Pitts (1997) studied religious programs, institutional adjustment, and recidivism. The religious program they examined was Charles Colson's Prison Fellowship (PF). They used two matched groups of inmates from four adult male prisons in New York. The subjects in one group (n = 201) had all participated in some Prison Fellowship programming (PF) and the members of the second, matched group (n = 201) had no involvement with Prison Fellowship (non–PF). The two groups were matched on the seven variables that were most likely to predict participation in PF: age, race, religious denomination, county of residence, military discharge, minimum sentence, and initial security classification. There were no significant differences between the two groups on measures of general and serious prison rule violations, and no significant difference on the measure of recidivism, which was arrest during a one-year follow-up period. When the PF group was divided into three levels of involvement in PF programs, (1) In Prison Seminars; (2) Life Plan Seminars; and (3) Bible studies, high participants in Bible studies (n = 22) were less likely to be arrested during the follow-up period than were the subjects of the other groups. The short follow-up period, the non random selection of PF participants, and overrepresented Hispanic inmates (who are as a group less likely to recidivate) were weaknesses in the study. Also there is some circularity in the findings here since the high-participant Bible studies group may have been people least likely to recidivate whether they participated in PF or not.

(2) O'Connor and Perreyclear (2002) studied a large medium/maxi-

mum security prison in South Carolina with 1,759 inmates. They found that 49 percent of the inmates attended at least one religious activity or program in a one-year period of time. Controlling for a number of demographic and criminal history risk factors, they found an inverse relationship between intensity of religious involvement (number of religious activities attended) and prison rule infractions. They also found that religious programming at the prison was extensive, varied, and inexpensive compared to other types of programming because so much of it was conducted by volunteers. Another interesting finding was that inmates in the religious group generally had a more serious criminal record than did inmates in the "nonreligious" group. They did not collect data on involvement in other programs which may have been an important factor in influencing prison rule violations. Prison rule violations is important but is not considered predictive of future criminal behavior after release from prison.

(3) Benda and Toombs (2002) studied 326 males aged 14 to 24 from 25 classes of boot camp in Arkansas. They studied a number of factors related to drug use among this population including attachment, beliefs, religiosity, physical abuse, peer association and use of excuses for illicit drug use. They found that religiosity is a major factor in explaining illicit drug use, though it is an indirect relationship, as religiosity influenced peer association which in turn influenced drug use very strongly. They conclude that "religiosity, beliefs, attachment to caregivers, and abuse are factors which help to explain why some youths differentially associate with peers who are involved in illicit acts" [Benda and Toombs, 2002, p. 176].

(4) Clear and Sumter (2002) administered a self-report questionnaire to 769 inmates in 20 prisons from 12 states. They used a recently developed scale of religiousness, originally developed by King and Hunt in 1975 (as described in Clear and Sumter, 2002). The scale measures overall religious beliefs and practices. The results indicated that there is a significant relationship between inmate adjustment to prison and measures of an inmate's religiousness. Interestingly, this relationship may exist in some institutions but not in others. The authors did not draw a random sample and were unable to determine the characteristics of the institutions where the hypothesized relationship existed and where it did not.

Conclusion

Grimesrud and Zehr (2002) argue for offender treatment programs based on a restorative model of justice rather than a retributive model. This approach is, in their view, a more biblical approach to both justice and treatment. Restorative justice focuses more on restoring the victim than on punishing the offender. They propose that restorative rehabilitation should be based on the following guidelines (2002, p. 282):

(1) it should be victim focused;

(2) treatment is not an entitlement but is a part of the accountability required of the offender;

(3) treatment focuses on integration into the community and strengthening social bonds rather than isolation from the community;

(4) interventions are individualized, matching risk and intensity of services;

(5) interventions are designed to address criminogenic needs and use cognitive behavioral methods. (These last two come from the "what works" literature, discussed at length in chapter five.)

They conclude that such a peacemaking approach to criminology is needed and is most consistent with the "deepest roots of Western theology, found in the Bible" [Grimesrud and Zehr, 2002, p. 283].

Grimesrud and Zehr also describe three forms of faith-based treatment based on the restorative justice model:

(1) *Victim Offenders Reconciliation Programs*: VORPs have been operated in North America and are usually implemented by a nonprofit organization in cooperation with the courts. Initially they were for property offenders and still are for the most part, though they have been used increasingly with more serious offenses. A volunteer mediator meets with the victim and the offender. The case is fully explored and feelings are expressed. They all must agree on a written restitution contract that becomes a condition of probation.

(2) *Family Group Conferences*: This approach originated in New Zealand in response to the Maori population. Youthful offenders (except

for a few, serious, violent offenders) are assigned a youth justice coordinator who facilitates a series of conferences with victims, their families, and offenders and their families. A youth advocate looks out for the rights and concerns of the offender. This group must come up with a complete solution to the case and must do so by consensus. And most of them do! (McElrea, 1994; Grimesrud and Zehr, 2002).

(3) *Sentencing Circles*: These "circles" were developed first among native American people in Canada but have been applied in other places (Ross, 1996; see also above discussion of circles for sex offenders). They take a variety of forms, but in general they develop sentencing plans in close coordination with the courts. They design plans which address community and victim concerns and problems. Emphasis is placed more on healing the victim more than on punishing the offender. This focus helps to heal individuals and communities, which ultimately prevents future crime.

Critics of faith-based programs, including civil libertarians and church-state separatists, argue that such programs give preferential treatment based on religion while subjecting other inmates to unwanted, government-supported religious messages. Some object to the government, federal or state, providing only faith-based programs to inmates (Johnson, 2006).

There is some evidence that religious programs make better-adjusted inmates with improved prison behavior, but they have no proven effect on recidivism so far. One problem to be addressed is that of defining religiosity operationally, that is, of defining it in a way that it can have some meaning and can be reliably measured. It is usually measured as number of religious services attended, but as some researchers have noted, this is quite a superficial way of conceptualizing it (see O'Connor and Pallone, 2002).

It has been shown that people attend church for many reasons such as familial pressure and fear of eternal damnation (see Benda & Toombs, 2002). Gorsuch (1988) has argued that the complexity of religiosity is not easily represented or accurately represented by single, simple measures like church attendance.

De Tocqueville and de Beaumont (1833), a keen observer, among other things, of American prisons, wrote that rehabilitation and reformation are two different things. Rehabilitation, whether the offender commits more crimes, can be measured, but reformation, whether the offender has truly changed, cannot. Faith-based programs are seeking the reformation of the offender, but his reformation is not a scientific question. Einstein was said to have remarked, "Not everything that counts can be counted." Many faith-based program advocates feel no need to justify their programs with scientific data, and, to be fair, many nonreligious programs for offenders have not been supported with data either. On the other hand, the rehabilitation of the offender through religious programs can be subjected to scientific scrutiny. Such efforts will likely enhance our knowledge of offender treatment and crime prevention, though we can, at the same time, acknowledge that not all of the important questions are scientific ones.

Chapter Nine

The Science of Sin: Correctional Treatment in the 21st Century

[T]he United States now has a punishment system that no one would knowingly have chosen.
— Michael Tonry, 2004.

Here in the final chapter, after having reviewed the history of the treatment of offenders, and after having seen illustrated in the history of prisons our deeply conflicted thinking about punishment and treatment, we will address two final questions: (1) Do correctional programs work? and (2) What should we try to do now?

Do Correctional Programs Work?

The current thinking on the efficacy of correctional treatment is sharply divided. An illustration of this debate can be seen in the work of Aos, Miller, and Drake and the work of David Farabee. Aos, Miller, and Drake (2006) asked the question, "Are there any adult corrections programs that work?" Or, stated in a more precise way, "What works, if anything, to lower the recidivism rates of adult offenders?" (p. 2) They surveyed all program evaluations conducted over the last 40 years in the United States and other

English-speaking countries. Their survey included many types of programs such as drug courts, boot camps, sex offender treatment programs, and work programs. They found 291 evaluations with sufficiently rigorous methodology to be included. The criterion for inclusion was the use of a well-matched non treatment comparison group. Meta analysis, as described by Lipsey and Wilson (2001), was used to analyze the data. The results are summarized in the table below.

Category or Type of Program	No. of Evaluations	Reduction in Recidivism
Programs for Drug-Involved Offenders	91	Yes (5–11%)
Programs for Offenders with Co-occurring Disorders	11	No
Programs for the General Offenders Population	25	Yes (8%)
Programs for Domestic Violence Offenders	9	No
Programs for Sex Offenders	16	Yes (0–31%)
Intermediate Sanctions	74	Yes (0–22%)
Work and Education Programs for the General Offender Population	30	Yes (5–13%)

Under Programs for Drug-Involved Offenders, the most effective were drug treatment in the community (12 percent) and drug courts (11 percent).

Under Intermediate Sanctions are included programs like electronic monitoring, boot camps, intensive supervision, both treatment and surveillance oriented, and restorative justice for low-risk offenders. In this category, only intensive supervision which was treatment oriented had an effect on recidivism (22 percent).

Under Programs for Sex Offenders, cognitive behavioral treatment in the community (31 percent) and cognitive behavioral treatment in prison (15 percent) had effects on recidivism. Psychotherapy programs and behavioral programs for sex offenders did not affect recidivism rates significantly.

Under Programs for the General Offenders Population, the authors reviewed 25 well-researched cognitive behavioral programs for general adult offenders. With an eight-year follow-up, there was a reduction in recidivism from 49 percent to 45 percent for the treatment group. Three of the better-known cognitive behavioral programs were Reasoning and Rehabilitation (R&R), Moral Reconation Therapy (MRT), and Thinking for a Change (T4C), all of which were discussed in chapter five.

Aos and his coworkers (2006) placed in a final, eighth category programs needing more research before any conclusions can be reached. Many areas need additional research, including therapeutic community programs for the mentally ill, domestic violence courts, work-release programs, intensive supervision of sex offenders in the community, Circles of Support and Accountability (COSA, faith-based supervision of sex offenders, which was discussed in chapters seven and eight), medical treatment for sex offenders, and case management in the community for drug offenders.

Aos, Miller, and Drake propose that future correctional policy should focus on proven evidence-based approaches. Even a small reduction in recidivism rates can be very cost-beneficial. For example, a 5 percent reduction in recidivism of high-risk offenders can produce significant savings for taxpayers and crime victims (Aos and his colleagues plan to publish a second part of their study which estimates cost-benefit ratios for the programs which were reviewed in the first part of the study). However, they did not address whether the inmate participants in the studies reviewed were high-risk offenders or not. An additional point is that if the cost of a particular program is less than the cost of the alternative, it is worthwhile to implement it even if the program has no effect on recidivism. For example, jail diversion programs which cost considerably less than long-term incarceration in the jail are worth implementing, even though they may have no measurable effects on the recidivism of the program participants.

Are there any adult correctional programs that work? Aos, Miller, and Drake conclude that some do and some don't; some treatment programs are effective in reducing recidivism for some offenders. Smith, Gendreau, and Goggin (in press) contend that a "huge" evaluation literature exists with at least three dozen quantitative reviews of this literature available and that these reviews include approximately 1,000 studies. It was this literature which produced the principles of effective intervention which were thoroughly discussed in chapter six. Summarizing across all evaluation studies, regardless of their nature, it has been reported that about 64 percent of the programs studied reduced recidivism, with average reduction being 10 percent. Programs with appropriate interventions produce 25–30 percent reductions (appropriate treatments are those outlined in detail in chapter six). Programs with optimal therapeutic integrity have shown reductions in recidivism in the range of 20–35 percent. Therapeutic integrity requires four features: (1) the program is designed and evaluated by individuals who are well qualified and versed in the behavioral literature; (2) the program is operated by staff who have at least a four-year degree in a helping profession; (3) the staff is specifically trained in the program design, underlying theory, and procedures, and keeps to them; (4) the program provides very intensive service.

But the reality of treatment in corrections is that high-quality programs with appropriate treatment procedures and therapeutic integrity are rarely found. The research of Paul Gendreau and his colleagues with the Correctional Program Assessment Inventory (also discussed in chapter six) shows that the most often encountered deficiencies are:

(1) poor implementation, with program staff not familiar with the literature in their field and without training and experience in successful programs;

(2) not using an actuarial system of assessment;

(3) dosage level is often insufficient, that is to say the treatment is not intensive or sufficiently long to have a therapeutic effect. which is not the same as saying it doesn't work;

(4) relapse prevention strategies underutilized;

(5) no treatment manual;

(6) no meaningful system of reinforcers;

(7) no evaluation practices;

(8) staff do not provide referral to appropriate and available follow-up services in the community;

(9) do not utilize therapeutic techniques that are known to be effective with offenders.

Thus, in answer to the question, "Do any adult correctional programs work?" Aos and his colleagues answer, "Some do and some don't." Gendreau and his colleagues add that the difference between those that do and those that don't is good program implementation, using the principles of effective intervention. Rhine, Mawhorr, and Parks (2006) write that the bane of effective correctional rehabilitation has been poor implementation and poor program integrity. They contend that the failure to implement correctly is largely due to organizational and fiscal constraints which compromise the principles of effective intervention. They argue that what we are seeing is the failure of poorly implemented programs and that these failures have considerably dampened enthusiasm for rehabilitation.

Douglas Marlowe, in his introduction to David Farabee's book, sees a quite different picture: "I wish it were otherwise, but scientific evidence is sorely lacking to support the effectiveness of rehabilitation programs for criminal offenders" (Farabee, 2005, p. ix). Farabee also quotes a study released by the National Research Council: "However, research conducted to date has not yet convincingly demonstrated the effectiveness of prison treatment programs" (Manski, Pepper, and Petrie, 2001, p. 260).

Farabee proposes that the reasons for this situation are (1) poor quality of research, (2) poor program implementation, and (3) false assumptions about correctional treatment. In his monograph, Farabee examines the common problems plaguing criminal justice research including, as we have seen in chapter one, lack of random assignment, incongruent follow-up periods, use of dropouts as comparison subjects, failure to use appropriate statistical controls, failure to account for aftercare, selection bias, and poor followup rates for interviews. Other sources of bias include funding related bias and publishing bias, by which he means the "publish or perish" dictum that haunts academia and greatly discourages publication of negative results. As Tetlock and Mitchell (1993) observed: "given the lack of standardized, widely accepted research methods and given the difficulty of replication in soft psychology, there are plenty of opportunities for unintentional biasing of results at the individual level of study" (p. 236).

"Another important reason for the lack of rigor in criminal justice treatment research relates to the relatively independent evolutions of criminal justice (the practice) and criminology (the science)" (Farabee, 2005, p. 23). Practitioners and researchers have historically not communicated with each other very much or very well, thus neither is informed by the other. And, finally, Farabee states: "What is even more disconcerting is that many of the experts charged with evaluating these programs are themselves emotionally and professionally tied to demonstrating their effectiveness" (p. 7).

Farabee reviewed the research in several categories, which included general reviews, prison visitation (such as "Scared Straight" programs), substance-abuse treatment, education, employment, life skills, cognitive behavioral programs, and faith-based programs. Most of the evaluations, he concluded, were not of sufficient quality to allow formal conclusions. "At best, their effects appear to be modest and short-lived. The many plausible reasons for these poor results can be reduced to two general categories: the quality of program implementation, and the assumptions upon which these programs are based" (p. 37). The misguided assumptions to which he refers include:

(1) the causes of crime can be traced to a single explanation;

(2) co-occurring behaviors must be causal, such as substance abuse but also other mental disorders;

(3) offenders have had blocked access to opportunities, so we should provide those opportunities in prison;

(4) a program can produce significant, long-term change in an offender's life. As Farabee states, "offenders will not change as a result of workbooks, videos, or talk therapy" [p. 55].

Crime is a choice and is not the result of a deficit in social services. The risk of getting caught is in fact very low. Farabee claims that we have emphasized severity rather than certainty and thereby rendered our sytem of punishment much less effective than it might be.

> [T]he vast majority of programs currently operating in our prison systems have never been subjected to rigorous evaluation. We have also seen that most programs that have been evaluated appear to have had little or no measurable effect, and, among those that did, the effects have tended to be modest and brief" [p. 48].

Yet he does not turn away entirely from rehabilitation; he thinks it can be achieved, but by system wide correctional practices, not by individual rehabilitation programs.

Lattimore (2006) believes that Farabee and Aos et al. could both be right. She and Ann Witte questioned the theoretical bases for correctional programs as far back as 1985, and argued for the "the fidelity of implementation." In an article they subtitled "We Don't Know Nothing Works" (Lattimore and Witte, 1985), they pointed out the poor quality of the evaluations that showed that "nothing works." Now Lattimore, along with Christy Visher, are co-principal investigators for the Multi-site Evaluation of the Serious and Violent Offender Reentry Initiative (SVORI). SVORI is a $150-million-dollar federal program with 89 sites across the United States (and the Virgin Islands). The 89 sites are operated by 69 grantee agencies who offer various combinations of prerelease and postrelease services for "serious and violent" offenders. The matching of needs and services is individualized. Lattimore and Visher will be conducting the impact evaluations in 14 states and are scheduled to complete follow-up interviewing in April, 2007. "The impact evaluation will focus on assessing the impact of SVORI on a number of intermediate outcomes — employment, family, and community involvement, housing, mental health, physical health, and substance abuse — that were specifically indicated by the federal sponsors of the SVORI initiative. In addition, we will examine a variety of recidivism indicators — self-report from interviews, probation/parole violation or revocation, arrest, and reincarceration" (Lattimore, 2006, p. 4). The results of these planned evaluations of SVORI may be very informative for the debate on correctional programs. "That both Aos and Farabee could be correct, which I believe, suggests how few breakthroughs have been made in identifying "what works" (2006, p. 4). Aos et al. could be right in identifying some programs that do work to reduce recidivism and Farabee could be right that we have had a lot of poorly implemented programs and poor quality evaluations which don't tell us very much and that we need systemic change. "One of the 'lessons learned' from our evaluation of control oriented and intermediate sanctions during the 1980s and 1990s was that both treatment and control (formal and informal) needed to be key program features if offender change was the outcome of interest.... Ultimately, our choice of crime control policies should reflect our recognition of the inexorable link between individual and community change" (Byrne and Taxman, 2005, p. 305). But, Lattimore continues, "I (and I expect others would agree) remain to be convinced that we have made sufficient, good faith effort over the last 25 years to forego rehabilitation as a goal" (Lattimore, 2006, p. 4).

There are clearly two points of view in this debate about the value of correctional programs, but there is also an important point of agreement and, perhaps, it is just here that we should be concentrating. There is strong general agreement that correctional program implementation is generally poor and that quality evaluations are not conducted often enough to reach any solid conclusions, even for programs with reasonably good implementation. Implementation is a continuing problem. Here is a recent example.

Wilson and Davis (2006) conducted an evaluation of Project Greenlight. Greenlight is an intensive short-term intervention for inmates during the transition period prior to release. It lasts for 8 weeks. The program is multimodal and utilizes the cognitive behavioral Reasoning and Rehabilitation Program (R & R), family counseling, behavioral techniques, and other community services. The evaluators found that program participants actually had higher recidivism than did controls. The study authors speculated that the reasons for this failure were a combination of implementation difficulties, program design, and a mismatch between the targeted offender population and the program. Visher (2006) says that the main lesson from the Greenlight evaluation is that, if an intervention is poorly conceived and/or poorly implemented, the program is likely to be unsuccessful. This is an old lesson.

Marlowe (2006) refers to programs like Greenlight as "kitchen sink" interventions. He complains also that critics of correctional programming are often dismissed as unnecessarily negative. He calls this being branded with a scarlet M (for Martinson)! Marlowe criticizes the evidence that the interventions used by Greenlight had empirical support in the first place, such as R & R. He writes that "the literature is so rife with 'noise' touting unproven interventions that practitioners and policy makers have difficulty separating the wheat from the chaff. It is difficult to discern which interventions are, in fact, evidence based and worthy of implementation, and which should be consigned to the scrap pile. As a result, the field does not learn from its mistakes and continuously reinvents unworthy paradigms" (2006, p. 339). He also points out that the program participants in Greenlight were generally noncompliant with treatment services. How could such an intervention reduce recidivism if the inmates do not participate?

Visher has said that "there is no consensus answer to the question 'Do prisoner reentry programs work?'" (2006, p. 299). Petersilia (2004) studied the literature exhaustively and noted the paucity of quality evaluations with which to reach any conclusions. If significant results are found the reduction in recidivism is small (Farrington and Welsh, 2005; Weisburd, Lum, and Petrosino, 2001; Farabee, 2005).

Perhaps the best summary is from Francis Cullen, who writes that the challenge for criminologists "will be to construct a knowledge base . . . which provides clearer guidance both on 'what works' and on strategies to implement such principles in the real world. The challenge for policy makers and practitioners will be to become more willing partners with criminologists in the development of effective programs, both receiving and helping to create new offender-treatment technology" (2002, p. 47).

What Should We Try to Do Now?

What we encounter again and again as we try to make criminology scientific are the ethical and practical problems that emerge when we try to employ true experimental designs that will provide definitive answers to scientific questions about crime and criminals. We attempt to cope with this problem by developing designs and methods which resolve some of the ethical concerns and practical problems, but the meaning of the results produced by these designs and methods are often debatable. With the data from such flawed studies, we descend into a tangled wilderness of technical and inconclusive debate about what the data "mean," providing ample opportunity for anyone to accumulate "scientific evidence" for just about anything. Foucault refers to this situation as "the chatter of criminology." Our best attempt so far to address this problem is the concept of convergent validity and the technique of meta analysis. Meta analysis, as we have seen in chapter one, is a method of summing the results of a large number of studies in order to express an overall result. Convergent validity is the concept that, if a number of studies, all of which are flawed, but not with same flaw, point to the same conclusion, then that conclusion is likely the right one.

Bushway and Weisburd (2006) suggest the direction to take for improving measurement in criminology. They point out that 80 percent of all articles in the journal *Criminology* rely on statistical models, indicating how much we rely on statistical techniques and their concomitant problems of selection bias. In addition, "problems develop when researchers apply the 'appropriate' technique in a mechanistic manner without truly understanding the underlying structure of the model or estimator in question" (2006, p. 3).

They propose that we focus on the three I's of quantitative criminology: (1) importation of techniques from other disciplines; (2) introspection in regard to the appropriate use of them in criminology; (3) innovation in the development of new techniques. "All social sciences face a consistent challenge to Import, Introspect, and Innovate in order to better answer the questions of interest to the field" (2006, p. 1).

In a technical sense, there are some areas of agreement about what should be done to improve correctional treatment: (1) good program implementation; (2) utilization of evidence-based techniques and methods; (3) good quality evaluations, and more of them; and (4) more collaboration between researchers, practitioners, and policymakers. But technical problems are not what is holding us back in the field of correctional treatment; it is not a lack of knowledge that is preventing our progress.

A central point of this book, and the reason that an historical perspective is important, is that we keep repeating ourselves, recycling old ideas as if they were brand new, and then discarding them before we have found out if they are effective or not. So we never really learn from them. We act like this because we are, as a culture, deeply conflicted about punishment and treatment.

Beyond the technical recommendations, there are plenty of suggestions about what is wrong and what to do about it. For example, Elliott Currie, in *Crime and Punishment*, writes: "a society that incarcerates such a vast and rapidly growing part of its population — but still suffers the worst violent crime in the industrial world — is a society in trouble, one that, in a profound sense, has lost its bearings (1998, p. 8). He also points out the growing reliance on prison and jails as a de facto mental health system. Currie is concerned to argue against conservative criminologists like James Q. Wilson and John Diuilio who have written about the success of prison and the inevitability of high crime rates in a free society. Currie discusses the "prison myths" which, he contends, have justified and perpetuated our enormous investment in imprisonment: (1) the myth of leniency, that the problem with our crime rate is that the punishments have been too lenient, when they are already the most severe in the Western world; (2) the myth of efficacy, that incarceration is working to reduce crime; (3) the myth that prison pays, that its savings in crime is worth its expense; and (4) the myth that there are no credible alternatives to what we are doing now. He asserts that the United States is "a country that, though generally quite wealthy, is also far more unequal and far less committed to including the vulnerable into a common level of social life than are other developed nations" (p. 120), and that "Countries where there is a wide gap between rich and poor routinely show higher levels of violent crime — which helps explain why the world's worst levels of violence have been found in places like Colombia, Venezuela, South Africa, and Mexico, where inequalities are even harsher and more consequential than in the United States" (p. 125).

In the 1960s, Currie argued, we were at a crossroads in our view of the criminal justice system in America. Prestigious and thoughtful groups like the Kerner Commission and the President's Crime Commission advocated one road to reduce recidivism: a balanced approach to crime, including better management of the criminal justice system and a commitment to reintegrating offenders into the community. But a second road, based on the assumptions that we had become insufficiently punitive, that most rehabilitative efforts were useless, and that the social conditions thought to be related to crime were not important, was to increase the use of incarceration. We chose the second one.

Once again Currie proposes, we are at a crossroads in our view of the criminal justice system. We can continue with more and more incarceration or we can "make the social investments that would lessen our need for a bloated correctional system" (p. 186). By this, he means child protection, job creation, family support, and community policing. "In a civilized society what matters is not just whether we reduce crime, but how" (p. 193).

David Farabee, in *Rethinking Rehabilitation* (2005), argues that what we need are correctional *practices*, not correctional *programs*. We need a paradigm shift, away from short-term, quick-fix programs based on single-item explanations of crime, towards long-term practices with consistent standards, while placing the responsibility for rehabilitation where it belongs — on the shoulders of the offenders themselves (2005, p. 49). He suggests that it is time to turn away from rehabilitation and concentrate on increasing the certainty of bad consequences for committing offenses.

The correctional practices that he recommends are:

(1) deemphasize prison as a sanction for nonviolent reoffenses and increase the use of intermediate sanctions;

(2) use prison programs to serve as institutional management tools, not as instruments for rehabilitation;

(3) mandate experimental designs for all program evaluations;

(4) establish evaluation contracts with independent agencies;

(5) increase the use of indeterminate community supervision, requiring three consecutive years without a new offense or violation;

(6) Reduce parole caseloads to fifteen to one, and increase the use of new tracking technologies.

Michael Tonry, in his *Thinking About Crime* (2004), proceeds from a stunning fact: "From capital punishment to three strikes and you're out to the highest imprisonment rates in the Western world *by a factor of five* [italics added], the United States stands alone in what it does to its citizens to prevent crimes and punish criminals" (p. vii). "Other countries experienced crime rises in the 1970s and 1980s, followed by declines in the 1990s, the same patterns the United States experienced, but did not adopt penal policies of unprecedented severity. Why did the United States?" (p. 98). The decline in the 1990s was not the result of more aggressive law enforcement and putting more people in prison because crime rates declined in every Western country. Cities and states in the United States that did not change their laws or policies also experienced a decline.

Why then were such harsh expressive policies adopted? "Because the groups most affected [by the punishment] lack political power and are widely regarded as dangerous and undeserving; because the groups least affected could be reassured that something is being done and lawlessness is not tolerated; and because few politicians are willing to oppose a policy when there is so little political advantage to be gained by doing so" (Garland, 2001, p. 132).

Tonry goes on to argue that

> complex, regularly recurring, but poorly understood interactions among crime trends, public attitudes, and policy making shape our sensibilities and through them our thought, policy debates, and policies. A succession of upsetting incidents has produced a series of moral panics that, among other things, has led to artificially heightened anxieties and fierce

overreactions. Current policies are an understandable but regrettable result" [p. 25].

Tonry believes that the public sensibilities entered a cycle of intolerance which coincided with a period of moral panics to produce an overreaction to the problem of crime, resulting in public support for severe punishment. By *sensibility*, he means "the ethos or zeitgeist of a moment that influences but does not determine what most people think and believe about a particular subject" (p. 70). He draws upon Stanley Cohen's theory of moral panic (1972). According to Cohen, a moral panic is "something negative, irrational, and regrettable; shocking or frightening incidents occurred, raw emotions took over, fears magnified, panic set in inhibitions weakened, and public officials overreacted" (cited in Tonry, 2004, p. 86). Examples of moral panics include the Salem witch trials, the Clacton riots which magnified the dangers of youth gangs in England, and recent child abuse and predator laws in the United States.

Tonry has his prescriptions, too: he listed nine altogether that consisted mainly of eliminating mandatory minimum sentences, mandating impact evaluations when new laws are proposed, adding sunset provisions to new sentencing laws, which will require their periodic review, and addressing racial disparities.

If we accept Tonry's argument about sensibilities, we should want to know how to affect public sensibilities. It seems that it would take more than a few sentencing policy changes to turn the situation around. Other than calling for less emotional reactions to crimes and criminals, Tonry offers us little else to help us affect public sensibilities about the problems of punishment and treatment, so this could be a fruitful area of work for criminologists. Public education about crime and criminals appears to be one of our weakest points.

If we are, as Currie has proposed, at a crossroads again, and perhaps on the verge of choosing more incarceration, it is worth remembering the work of our most incisive prison analysts. Michael Ignatieff, in *A Just Measure of Pain* (1978), emphasized the complex, and conflicted, motives of the religious and philosophical reformers who succeeded in replacing corporal punishment with imprisonment as the major punishment for crimes in the late 18th and 19th centuries. And there is David Rothman, who, in *The*

Discovery of the Asylum (1971), showed us how the 19th-century asylum brought together the concept of rehabilitation with the concept of incarceration, a link which we have been unable to break, even after many decades of failing to rehabilitate offenders.

Stanley Cohen, in *Visions of Social Control* (1985), wrote of the Great Incarcerations of the nineteenth century, "thieves into prisons, lunatics into asylums, conscripts into barracks, workers into factories, children into schools" (p. 25). Cohen cogently summed up our situation in the latter part of the 20th century:

> Take for example, the specific issue of programmes aimed at treating and rehabilitating offenders in the wake of the "nothing works" critique. For law and order conservatives the message was "we told you so" — criminals cannot be changed, we must protect the public through hard punishment, deterrence, incapacitation. For tender hearted liberals and technocratic criminologists: rehabilitation hasn't really been tried properly, if our present techniques don't work we should try to devise others. For tough minded liberals: this shows that you must distrust benevolence, let us abandon rehabilitation and substitute less ambitious goals. For civil libertarians and the justice lobby: treatment is an attack on civil rights and an extension of the therapeutic state and a violation of the norms of justice and proportionality. For Marxists: treatment obviously won't work because it is just an ideological tool to focus on the individual thus mystifying the real causal connection with the larger social and economic structure. For Foucault (and similar theorists), the whole idea of treatment working is absurd — it is simply another twist in the self contained spiral of power, classification, and knowledge [1985, pp. 35–36].

And then there is Michel Foucault who, in *Discipline and Punish* (1975), wrote of the "carceral system" and the social power that it exercised in the service of the emergent capitalist class. Before dismissing him too quickly as a class-struggle theorist, consider some of his incisive comments. Foucault points out that

> for the past 150 years the proclamation of the failure of the prison has always been accompanied by its maintenance. The only alternative actually envisaged was deportation, which England abandoned at the beginning of the nineteenth century and which France took up under the

Second Empire, but rather as a rigorous and distant form of imprisonment" [p. 272].

"Prisons do not diminish the crime rate: they can be extended, multiplied or transformed, the quantity of crime and criminals remains stable or, worse, increases" (p. 265). Foucault argues that this has always been the case with imprisonment and quotes a French newspaper from February, 1842:

> In France, one calculates at about 108,000 the number of individuals who are in a state of flagrant hostility to society. The means of repression at one's disposal are: the scaffold, the iron collar, three convict ships, 19 maisons centrales, 86 maisons de justice, 362 maisons d'arrêt, 2,800 cantonal prisons, 2,238 cells in police stations. Despite all these, vice goes unchecked. The number of crimes is not diminishing . . . the number of recidivists is increasing, rather than declining [cited in Foucault, 1975, p. 265].

The prison, instead of reducing crime, maintains delinquency, encourages recidivism, transforms the occasional offender into an habitual offender delinquent, and promotes a delinquent prison subculture. Foucault maintains that "in the multiple mechanisms of incarceration, ... we must hear the distant roar of battle" (p. 308). Here he means class warfare and before we turn too quickly aside from this type of analysis, we should remember that the distant roar of battle may be heard in our present language about crime. We commonly use the metaphor of war: the war against crack, the war against crime, the war on drugs, etc. It seems that the main casualties of the war on crack have been women of color, who are filling our prisons at an unprecedented rate (Coontz and Sevigny, 2003).

None of these analysts of "the great incarceration" has the solution to our present dilemma, but they offer perspectives important to consider. Keeping their perspectives in the background of our picture of punishment and treatment, we may be able to avoid focusing too exclusively on the search for what Lattimore has called "the aluminum bullet" of correctional treatment. She suggests that we are diligently seeking the programmatic equivalent of an aluminum bullet, one which works for everyone, is cheaper than silver, and is recyclable, because we don't want to spend for high-quality programs which have a chance at rehabilitation, but which can be expensive (Lattimore, 2006, p. 4).

It will take more than data collection and journal articles to rehabilitate offenders because it is not just a lack of knowledge that is hampering us. We are locked into a regularly revolving cycle because of our deeply conflicted views as a people about punishment and treatment. Should we make offenders suffer or should we help them? Which is the most effective for ensuring our safety? Which is more just? Which is more humane? Can we do both at once, as some have claimed?

David Farrington, one of our best criminologists, writes recently:

"The good news is that many programs are effective in preventing future offending. My conclusion is that early interventions, which target children under age 12, are particularly needed. It is surely better to intervene early in criminal careers rather than to wait until many people have been victimized. Hence, early identification and preventive intervention seems likely to be an effective strategy to prevent crime. As with public health, prevention is better than cure" [2005, p. 244].

This recommendation needs no further proof to support it and we have known it at least since 1764, when Cesare Bonesana, the Marchese di Beccaria, and the father of criminology, wrote: "It is better to prevent crimes than to punish them." A full forty years ago Karl Menninger wrote:

These and a great many other questions remain to be solved by the patient methods of scientific investigation. But, in the meantime, we need not wait for results of the new research findings. For we have at hand great quantities of research findings which clearly indicate what we should be doing. Much indeed we don't now, but we are not doing one tenth of what we should about what we already know" [Menninger, 1966, p. 277].

We often complain that it is lack of knowledge which prevents our progress in reducing crime and recidivism, but it is, instead, our deeply conflicted feelings about punishment and treatment which impede us. We must move this great debate beyond the primitive urge for revenge and place it above the poisoned dialogue of partisan politics. We have had, from the beginning, more light than we have used and perhaps we will not be gaining any new insights until we have learned to use what we already know.

References

Abel, G.G., Becker, J.V., Cunningham-Rathner, J., Mittleman, M.S., Murphy, M.S., and Rouleou, J.L. (1987). Self reported crimes of nonincarcerated paraphiliacs. *Journal of Interpersonal Violence, 2*, 3–25.

Abel, G.G., Mittleman, M.S., and Becker, J.V. (1985). Sexual offenders: Results of assessment and recommendations for treatment. In H.H. Ben-Aron, S.I. Hucker, and C.D. Webster (Eds.), *Clinical Criminology.* Toronto: MM Graphics.

Abel, G.G., Rouleau, J.L., and Cunningham-Rathner, J. (1986). Sexually aggressive behavior. In W. Curran, A.L. McGarry, and S.A. Shah (Eds.) *Forensic psychiatry and psychology: Perspectives and standards for interdisciplinary practice* (pp. 289–313). Philadelphia: Davis.

Adams, R., and Vetter, H.J. (1981). Social structure and psychodrama outcome: a ten year follow up. *Journal of Offender Counseling Services and Rehabilitation, 6*, 111–119.

Adler, F. (1975). *Sisters in crime.* New York: McGraw Hill.

Aitken, J. (2005). *Charles Colson: A life redeemed.* New York: Doubleday.

Alexander, F., and Healy, W. (1935). *The roots of crime.* New York.

Alexander, F., and Parsons, B.V. (1982). *Functional family therapy.* Monterey, CA: Brooks/Cole.

Alexander, F., and Staub, H. (1931). *The criminal, the judge, and the public.* New York: Macmillan.

Amen, D. (1999). *Firestorms in the brain.* Newport Beach, CA: Mindworks Press.com.

American Psychiatric Association (2000). *Diagnostic and statistical manual of mental disorders, text revision* (4th Ed.). Washington, DC: American Psychiatric Association.

Andrews, D., Zinger, I., Hoge, R., Bonta, J., Gendreau, P., and Cullen, F. (1990). Does correctional treatment work? A clinically relevant and psychologically informed meta-analysis. *Criminology, 28*, 369–404.

Andrews, D., and Bonta, J. (1994, 1998). *The psychology of criminal conduct* (1st and 2nd eds.). Cincinnati, OH: Anderson Publishing Company.

Aos, S., Miller, M., and Drake, E. (2006). *Evidence based adult corrections programs: What works and what does not.* Olympia, WA: Washington State Institute for Public Policy.

References

Armstrong, T.A. (2003). The effect of Moral Reconation Therapy on the recidivism of youthful offenders. *Criminal Justice & Behavior, 30* (6), 668–687.

Associated Press (2005). Nation's inmate population increased 2.3 percent last year. *The New York Times,* April 25, 2005.

Atkins, B.M., and Glick, H.R. (1972). *Prison, protest, and politics.* Englewood Cliffs, NJ: Prentice Hall.

Aurelius, M. (2003). *Meditations.* Translated by Gregory Hays. Modern Library: New York, NY.

Austin, J., Bloom, B., and Donahue, T. (1992). *Female offenders in the community: Analysis of innovative strategies and programs.* Washington, DC: National Institute of Corrections, National Council on Crime and Delinquency.

Ayllon, T., and Azrin, N.H. (1968). *The token economy.* New York: Appleton Century.

Bacchus, L., Strang, J., and Watson, P. (2000). Pathways to abstinence: Two year follow up data on 60 abstinent former opiate addicts. *European Addiction Research, 6,* 141–7.

Bandura, A. (1977). Self efficacy: Toward a unifying theory of behavioral change. *Psychological Review, 94,* 191–215.

Bank, L., Marlowe, J., Reid, J., Patterson, G., and Weinrott, M. (1991). A comparative evaluation of parent training interventions for families of chronic delinquents. *Journal of Abnormal Child Psychology, 19,* 15–33.

Barbaree, H., Baxter, D.J., and Marshall, W.L. (1989). The reliability of the rape index in a sample of rapists and nonrapists. *Violence and Victims, 4,* 299–306.

Barbaree, H., Seto, M., Langton, P., and Peacock, R. (2001). Evaluating the predictive accuracy of six risk assessment instruments for adult sex offenders. *Criminal Justice & Behavior, 28,* 490–521.

Barovick, H. (1999). Bad to the bone. *Time Magazine,* December 27, 1999.

Barry, J.G. (1958). *Captain Maconochie of Norfolk Island.* Oxford: Oxford University Press.

Bartol, C.R. (1999). *Criminal behavior.* Upper Saddle River, NJ: Prentice-Hall.

Bazelon, D. (1977). Street crime and correctional potholes. *Federal Probation, 42,* 3.

Beaumont, J.G. (1983). *Introduction to neuropsychology.* Oxford: Blackwell.

Beccaria, Cesare. (1996). *Of crimes and punishments.* Marsilio Publishers: New York.

Beck, A.T. (1970). Cognitive therapy: Nature and relation to behavior therapy. *Behavior Therapy, 1,* 184–200.

Beck, A.T. (1976). *Cognitive therapy and the emotional disorders.* New York: International Universities Press.

Beier, E.G. (1952). Client centered therapy and the involuntary client. *Journal of Consulting Psychology, XIV,* 332–337.

Benda, B., and Toombs, N. (2002). Religiosity and drug use among inmates in boot camp: Testing a theoretical model with reciprocal relationships. In T.P. O'Connor and N.J. Pallone (Eds.). *Religion, the community, and the rehabilitation of criminal offenders* (pp. 161–184). New York: The Haworth Press.

Berne, E. (1961). *Transactional analysis in psychotherapy.* New York: Grove Press.

Berne, E. (1964). *Games people play.* New York: Grove Press.

Bierne, Piers. (1993). *Inventing criminology.* Albany: State University of New York Press.

Birk, L. (1973). *Biofeedback: Behavioral medicine.* New York: Grune and Stratton.

Bixby, F.L. (1951). Short term treatment of youthful offenders. *Focus, 30,* 33–36.

References

Blader, J.C., and Marshall, W.L. (1989). Is assessment of sexual arousal in rapists worthwhile? A critique of current methods and the development of a response compatibility approach. *Clinical Psychology Review, 9,* 569–587.

Bloom, B., and Covington, S. (1998). *Gender specific programming for female offenders: What is it and why is it important?* Paper presented at the 50th Annual Meetings of the American Society of Criminology, November 11–14 1998, Washington DC.

Bourduin, C.M., Mann, B.J., Cone, L.T., Henggeler, S.W., Fucci, B.R., Blaske, D.M., and Williams, R.A. (1995). Multisystemic treatment of serious juvenile offenders. *International Journal of Offender Therapy and Comparative Criminology, 34,* 105–113.

Bowen, M. (1978). *Family therapy in clinical practice.* New York: Aronson.

Bradford, J.McD.W., and Pawlek, A. (1993). Double blind placebo crossover study of cyproterone acetate: a single case study. *Canadian Journal of Psychiatry, 32,* 22–30.

Bratter, T. (1974). Helping those who do not want to help themselves. *Corrective and Social Psychiatry, 20,* 23–30.

Brennan, T., and Austin, J. (1997). *Women in jail: Classification issues.* Washington DC: US Department of Justice, National Institute of Corrections.

Bromberg, W. (1975). *From Shaman to psychotherapist.* Chicago: Henry Regnery Company.

Bromberg, W., and Franklin, G. (1952). The treatment of sexual deviates with group psychodrama. *Group Psychotherapy, 4,* 274–292.

Bronfenbrenner, U. (1979). *The ecology of human development: Experiment by nature and design.* Cambridge, MA: Harvard University Press.

Bruton, J. (2004). *The big house.* Stillwater, MN: Voyageur Press.

Burke, H., and Hart, S.D. (2000). Personality disordered offenders: conceptualization, assessment, and diagnosis of personality disorder. In S. Hodgins and R. Muller-Isberner (Eds.), *Violence, crime, and mentally disordered offenders.* New York: John Wiley & Sons, Ltd.

Burkhead, M.D. (2006). *The search for the causes of crime.* Jefferson, North Carolina and London: McFarland.

Bush, J., and Bilodeau, B. (1993). *OPTIONS: a cognitive change program.* Washington, DC: National Institute of Corrections.

Bushway, S., and Weisburd, D. (2006). Acknowledging the centrality of quantitative criminology in criminology and criminal justice. *The Criminologist, 31* (4) 1–5.

Butler, B., Long, A., and Rowsell, P. (1977). *Evaluative study of the social therapy unit Oak Ridge Division. Report to the Ombudsman of Ontario.* Unpublished Report. Cited in Quinsey, V.L., Harris, G.T., Rice, M.E., and Cormier, C.A. (2003). *Violent Offenders.* Washington, DC : American Psychological Association.

Byrne, J., and Taxman, F. (2005). Crime (control) is a choice: Divergent perspectives on the role of treatment in the adult corrections system. *Criminology and Public Policy,* 4 (2), 291–310.

Carey, B. (2005). Can brain scans see depression? *The New York Times,* October 18, 2005.

Carroll, R. (2004). The plethysmograph. In R. Carroll (Ed.), *The Skeptics Dictionary.* Hoboken, NJ: John Wiley and Sons.

Cautela, J. (1967). Covert sensitization. *Psychological Record, 20,* 459–468.

Chaiken, J.M., and Chaiken, M.R.(1983). Crime Rates and the Active Criminal in J.Q. Wilson (Ed.), *Crime and Public Policy.* San Francisco: Institute for Contemporary Studies.

References

Chesney-Lind, M. (1998). Foreword. In R.T. Zaplin (Ed.), *Female offenders: Critical perspectives and effective interventions* (pp. xiii–xv). Gaithersburg, MD: Aspen Publishers.

Chesney-Lind, M., and Pasko, L. (2004). *The female offender* (2nd Ed.). Thousand Oaks: Sage Publications.

Citrome, L., and Volavka, J. (2000). Pharmacological treatments for psychotic offenders. In S. Hodgins and R. Muller-Isberner (Eds.). *Violence, crime, and mentally disordered offenders* (pp. 153–176). New York: John Wiley and Sons.

Clark, D.H. (1965). The therapeutic community: Concept, practice, and future. *British Journal of Psychiatry, 11,* 947–954.

Clear, T., Stout, B., Dammer, H., Kelly, L., Hardyman, P., and Shapiro, C. (1992). Prisons, prisoners, and religion: Final report. Newark, NJ: School of Criminal Justice, Rutgers University.

Clear, T., and Sumter, M. (2002). Prisoners, prison, and religion: Religion and adjustment to prison. In T.P. O'Connor and N.J. Pallone (Eds.). *Religion, the community, and the rehabilitation of criminal offenders* (pp. 127–160). New York: The Haworth Press.

Cleckley, H. (1988). *The Mask of Sanity* . Augusta, Georgia: Emily S. Cleckley, Publishers. Originally published in 1941 by C.V. Mosby Company.

Clemmer, D. (1958). *The prison community.* New York: Holt, Rinehart, & Winston.

Clipson, C.R. (2003). Practical considerations in the interview and evaluation of sexual offenders. In R. Geffner, K.C. Franey, T.G. Arnold, and R. Falconer (Eds.), *Identifying and treating sex offenders* (pp. 127–174), New York: Haworth Press.

Cohen, A. (2005). *Charles Colson and the mission that began Watergate.* The New York Times, July 25, 2005.

Cohen, L.E., and Felson, M. (1979). Social change and crime rate trends: A routine activity approach, *American Sociological Review,* 44:588–608.

Cohen, S. (1972). *Folk devils and moral panics.* New York: St. Martin's Press.

Cohen, S. (1985). *Visions of social control.* New York: Basil Blackwell.

Connor, D.F., and Steingard, R.J. (1996). A clinical approach to pharmacotherapy of aggression in children and adults. In C.F. Ferris, T. Grisso, et al. (Eds.), Understanding aggressive behavior in children. *Annals of the New York Academy of Sciences.* New York: New York Academy of Sciences.

Cooke, D.J. (1989). Containing violent prisoners: An analysis of Barlinnie Special Unit. *British Journal of Criminology, 129,* 129–143.

Coontz, P., and Sevigny, E. (2003). Revisiting the rise of the violent female offender: Drugs and violent crime. University of Pittsburg, Graduate School of Public and International Affairs, February, 2003.

Cooper, A.J. (1981). A placebo controlled trial of the androgen cyproterone acetate in deviant hypersexuality. *Comprehensive Psychiatry, 22* (5), 458–465.

Cooper, A.J., and Cernovsky, Z. (1992). The effects of cyproterone acetate on sleeping and waking penile erections in pedophiles: possible implications for treatment. *Canadian Journal of Psychiatry, 32* (8), 738–740.

Corsini, R. (1947). Nondirective vocational counseling of prison inmates. *Journal of Clinical Psychology, 3,* 96–100.

Corsini, R. (1951). The method of psychodrama in a prison. *Group Psychotherapy, 3,* 321–326.

Craft, M., Stephenson, G., and Granger, C. (1964). A controlled trial of authoritarian and self governing regimes with adolescent psychopaths. *American Journal of Orthopsychiatry, 34,* 543–554.

Cullen, F. (1993). The Grendon reconviction study, Part 1. *Prison Service Journal, 90,* 35–37.

Cullen, F. (1994). Grendon: the therapeutic prison that works. *Therapeutic Communities, 15* (4), 301–311.

Cullen, F. (2002). Rehabilitation and treatment programs. In J.Q. Wilson and J. Petersilia (Eds.), *Crime: Public policies for crime control.* Oakland, CA: ICS Press.

Cullen, F., and Gendreau, P. (1989). The effectiveness of correctional rehabilitation: Reconsidering the "nothing works" debate. In L. Goodstein and D. MacKenzie (Eds.), *American prisons: Issues in research and policy* (pp. 23–44). New York: Plenum.

Currie, E. (1998). *Crime and punishment in America.* New York: Henry Holt.

Daly, K. (1992). Women's Pathways to Felony Court: Feminist Theories of Law Breaking and Problems of Representation. *Review of Law and Women's Studies 2,* 11–52.

Davis, G.E., and Leitenburg, H. (1987). Adolescent sex offenders. *Psychological Bulletin, 101,* 417–427.

De Leon, G. (1983). The next therapeutic community: Autocracy and other notes toward integrating old and new therapeutic communities. *Therapeutic Communities, 4* (4), 249–261.

Denno, D.W., and McClelland, R.C. (1986). Longitudinal evaluation of a delinquency prevention program by self report. *Journal of Offender Counseling, Services, and Rehabilitation, 10,* 59–82.

Dishion, T., and Andrews, D. (1995). Preventing escalation in problem behavior with high risk young adolescents: intermediate and one year outcomes. *Journal of Consulting and Clinical Psychology, 63,* 538–548.

Dishneau, D. (2005). Prisoners' rights of passage. Center on Juvenile and Criminal Justice. Associated press. Retrieved from http://www.cjcj.org/press/prisoners_rights.html. 6/14/2006.

Dix-Richardson, F., and Close, B. (2002). Intersections of race, religion, and inmate culture: the historical development of Islam in American corrections. In T.P. O'Connor and N.J. Pallone (Eds.). *Religion, the community, and the rehabilitation of criminal offenders* (pp. 87–108). New York: The Haworth Press.

Dolan, B. (1998). Therapeutic community treatment for severe personality disorders. In T. Millon, E. Simonsen, M. Birket-Smith, and R.D. Davis (Eds.), *Psychopathy: Antisocial, criminal, and violent behavior* (pp. 407–430). New York: The Guilford Press.

Doren, D.M. (2002). *Evaluating sex offenders: A manual for civil commitment and beyond.* Thousand Oaks: Sage Publications.

Dostoevsky, F. (1986). *The house of the dead.* Penguin Books: London, England.

Downes, L. (2005). *The blessings of Lono: A vision of paradise in Oklahoma.* The New York Times, 2/15/2005.

Drapkin, I. (1989). *Crime and punishment in the ancient world.* Lexington, MA: Lexington Books.

Driver, E.D. (1973). Charles Buckman Goring. In H. Mannheim (Ed.), *Pioneers in criminology.* Montclair, New Jersey: Patterson Smith.

Eaves, D., Tien, G., and Wilson, D. (2000). Offenders with major affective disorders. In S. Hodgins and R. Muller-Isberner (Eds.). *Violence, crime, and mentally disordered offenders* (pp. 131–152). New York: John Wiley & Sons.

References

El-Hai, J. (2004). *The lobotomist.* Hoboken, NJ: John Wiley & Sons, Inc.

Eliasoph, E. (1955). Concepts and techniques of role playing and role training utilizing psychodramatic methods in group therapy with adolescent drug addicts. *Group Psychotherapy, 8,* 308–315.

Ellis, A. (1962). *Reason and emotion in psychotherapy.* Secaucus, NJ: Lyle Stuart.

Ellis, A. (1973). *Humanistic psychotherapy.* New York: Julian.

Emerick, R., and Dutton, W. (1993). The effect of polygraphy on the self report of adolescent sex offenders. *Annals of Sex Research, 6,* 83–103.

Epps, K. (1996). Sex offenders. In C. Hollin (Ed.) *Working with offenders.* New York: John Wiley & Sons.

Eriksson, T. (1976). *The reformers.* New York: Elsevier Scientific Publishing Company, Inc.

Eysenck, H.J. (1977). *Crime and personality* (2nd Ed.). London: Routledge and Kegan Paul.

Farabee, D. (2005). *Rethinking rehabilitation.* Washington, DC: The AEI Press.

Farrington, D. (1989). Early Predictors of Adolescent Aggression and Adult Violence. *Violence and Victims, 4,* 79–100.

Farrington, D. (2005). Early identification and preventive intervention: How effective is this strategy? *Criminology and Public Policy, 4* (2), 237–248.

Farrington, D, and Welsh, B.C. (2005). Randomized experiments in criminology: What have we learned ion the last two decades? *Journal of Experimental Criminology, 1,* 19–38.

Federal Bureau of Prisons (2006). Retrieved from http//www.bop.gov. July 31, 2006.

Federoff, J.P. (1993). Serotonic drug treatment of deviant sexual interests. *Annals of Sex Research, 6,* 105–121.

Feldman, L.H. (1991). Evaluating the impact of intensive family preservation services in New Jersey. In K. Wells and D.E. Beigel (Eds.), *Family preservation services: research and evaluation* (pp. 33–47). Newbury Park, CA: Sage.

Feldman, M.P. (1977). *Criminal behavior: A psychological analysis.* London: Wiley.

Feldman, P. (1993). *The psychology of crime.* Cambridge: Cambridge University Press.

Feldman, R.P., and Goodrich, J.T. (2001). Psychosurgery: a historical overview. *Neurosurgery, 48* (3), 647–659.

Fink, L., Derby, W.N., and Martin, J.P. (1969). Psychiatry's new role on corrections. *American Journal of Psychiatry, 126,* 124–128.

Finkelhor, D., and Araji, S. (1986). Explanations of pedophilia: a four factor model. *The Journal of Sex Research, 22,* 145–161.

Finkelhor, D., Hotaling, G., Lewis, I.A., and Smith, C. (1990). Sexual abuse in a national survey of adult men and women: Prevalence, characteristics, and risk factors. *Child Abuse and Neglect, 14,* 19–28.

Finkenaur, J.O. (1982). *Scared Straight! and the panacea phenomenon.* Englewood Cliffs, NJ: Prentice-Hall.

Fixsen, D.L., Phillips, E., Harper, D.S., Mesigh, J., Timbers, G.D., and Wolf, M.M. (1972). *The teaching family model of group home treatment.* Paper read at the American Psychological Association Annual Convention. Cited in Feldman, P. (1993). *The psychology of crime.* Cambridge: Cambridge University Press.

Fletcher, B., and Chandler, R. (2006). *Principles of drug abuse treatment for criminal justice populations.* Washington, DC: National Institute of Drug Abuse, NIH Publication No. 06-5316.

References

Foucault, M. (1975). *Discipline and punish*. London: Penguin Books, Ltd.

Freud, S. (1961). The ego and the id. In *The complete psychological works of Sigmund Freud, 19*, London: Hogarth.

Freud, S. (1948). Psycho-analysis and the ascertaining of truth in courts of law. *Collected Papers, 2*, London: Hogarth.

Furby, L., Weinrott, M., and Blackshaw, L. (1989). Sex offender recidivism: a review. *Psychological Bulletin, 105*, 3–30.

Garland, D. (2001). *The culture of control: Crime and social order in contemporary society*. Chicago, IL: University of Chicago Press.

Garrett, C. (1985). Effects of residential treatment on adjudicated delinquents: a meta-analysis. *Journal of Research in Crime and Delinquency, 22*, 287–308.

Geffner, R., Franey, K.C., and Falconer, R. (2003). Adult sexual offenders: current issues and future directions. In Geffner, R., Franey, K.C., Arnold, T.G., and Falconer, R. (Eds.) *Identifying and treating sex offenders* (pp. 1–16). New York: the Haworth Maltreatment and Trauma Press.

Gendreau, P. (1996). The principles of effective intervention with offenders. In A. Harland (Ed.). *Choosing correctional options that work* (pp. 117–130). Thousand Oaks, CA: Sage.

Gendreau, P., and Andrews, D. (1994). *The correctional program assessment inventory* (5th Ed.). Saint John: University of New Brunswick.

Gendreau, P., and Goggin, C. (2000). Correctional treatment: Accomplishments and realities. In P. Van Voorhis, M. Braswell, and D. Lester (Eds.). *Correctional counseling & rehabilitation* (pp. 289–297). Cincinnati, OH: Anderson Publishing Company.

Gendreau, P., and Ross, R. (1979). Effective correctional treatment: Bibliotherapy for cynics. *Journal of Research in Crime & Delinquency, 25*, 463–489.

Gendreau, P., and Ross, R. (1987). Revivification of rehabilitation: evidence from the 1980's. *Justice Quarterly, 4*, 349–407.

George, W.H., and Marlatt, G.A. (1989). Introduction. In D.R. Laws (Ed.), *Relapse prevention with sex offenders*. New York: Guilford Press.

Gibbs, J., and Goldstein, A. (1995). *The EQUIP program: teaching youth to think and act responsibly through a peer helping approach*. Champaign, IL: Research Press.

Glasser, W. (1965). *Reality therapy*. New York: Harper and Row.

Glick, B., Bush, J., and Taymans, J. (2001). *Thinking for a change*. Washington, DC: National Institute of Corrections.

Glover, E. (1960). *The roots of crime*. New York: International Universities Press.

Goddard, H.H. (1920). *Human efficiency and levels of intelligence*. Princeton: Princeton University Press.

Goldstein, A. (1988). *Prepare curriculum*. Champaign, IL: Research Press.

Goldstein, A., and Glick, B. (1987). *Aggression replacement training*. Champaign, IL: Research Press.

Goldstein, A., Glick, B., and Gibbs, J. (1998). *Aggression replacement training: A comprehensive intervention for aggressive youth* (Rev. ed.). Champaign, IL: Research Press.

Gordon, D.A., Andrews, D.A., Hill, J., and Kurkowsky, P. (1992). *Therapeutic integrity and the effectiveness of family therapy: a meta-analysis*. Unpublished manuscript, available from D.A. Andrews, Carleton University.

Gorsuch, R.L. (1988). Psychology of Religion. *Annual Review of Psychology, 39*, 201–221.

187

References

Gottfredson, M., and Hirschi, T. (1990). *A General Theory of Crime*. Stanford, CA: Stanford University Press.

Green, R. (2002). Is pedophilia a mental disorder? *Archives of Sexual Behavior, 31* (6), 467–471.

Greenfeld, L. (1997). *Sex offenses and offenders*. Washington, DC: Bureau of Justice Statistics.

Greenwald, H. (1973). Direct decision therapy. San Diego, CA: Edits.

Grimesrud, T., and Zehr, H. (2002). Rethinking God, justice, and treatment of offenders. In T.P. O'Connor and N.J. Pallone (Eds.). *Religion, the community, and the rehabilitation of criminal offenders* (pp. 259–286). New York: The Haworth Press.

Groth, A.N. (1979). *Men who rape*. New York: Plenum Press.

Groth, A.N. (1978). Patterns of sexual assault against children and adolescents. In A. Burgess, A.N. Groth, L. Holstrom, and S.M. Sgroi (Eds.) (pp. 3–24). *Sexual assault of children and adolescents*. Lexington, MA: Lexington Books.

Groth, A.N., Burgess, A., and Holmstrom, L. (1977). Rape, power, anger, and sexuality. *American Journal of Psychiatry, 134* (11), 1239.

Hagan, J. (1989). *Structural criminology*. New Brunswick, NJ: Rutgers University Press.

Haley, J. (1976). *Problem solving therapy*. San Francisco: Jossey-Bass.

Hall, G. (1995). Sexual offender recidivism revisited: A meta analysis of recent treatment studies. *Journal of Consulting and Clinical Psychology, 63*, 802–809.

Halleck, S. (1988). *The mentally disordered offender*. Washington, DC: American Psychiatric Publishing.

Halleck, S., and Witte, A. (1977). Is rehabilitation dead? *Crime & Delinquency, 23*, 372–382.

Hanson, R.K., and Bussiere, M.T. (1998). Predicting relapse: A meta analysis of sexual offender recidivism studies. *Journal of Consulting and Clinical Psychology, 66*, 348–362.

Hanson, R.K., Gizzarelli, R., and Scott, H. (1994). The attitudes of incest offenders: Sexual entitlement and acceptance of sex with children. *Criminal Justice and Behavior, 21*, 187–202.

Hanson, R.K., Gordon, A., Harris, A.J., Marquis, J., Murphy, W., Quinsey, V.L., and Seto, M.C. (2002). First report of the collaborative data outcome project on the effectiveness of psychological treatment for sex offenders. *Sexual Abuse: A Journal of Research and Treatment, 14* (12), 169–194.

Hanson, R.K., and Thornton, D. (1999). *Static-99: Improving actuarial risk assessments for sex offenders*. User Report 99–02. Ottawa, Ontario: Department of the Solicitor General of Canada.

Hanson, R.K., and Thornton, D. (2000). Improving risk assessment for sex offenders: a comparison of three actuarial scales. *Law and Human Behavior, 24*, 119–136.

Hare, R.D. (1993). *Without conscience*. New York: The Guilford Press.

Haskell, M. (1959). Role training and job placement of adolescent delinquents. *Group Psychotherapy, 12*, 250–257.

Haskell, M., and Weeks, H. (1960). Role training as preparation for release from a correctional institution. *Journal of Criminal law, Criminology, and Police Science, 50*, 441–447.

Hawking, S. (1998). *A brief history of time*. New York: Bantam Books.

Hendren, R.L. (1999). *Disruptive behavior disorders in children and adolescents*. Washington, DC: American Psychiatric Press.

References

Henggeler, S.W., and Bourdin, C.M. (1990). Family *therapy and beyond: a multisystemic approach in treating the behavior problems of children and adolescents.* Pacific Grove, CA: Brooks/Cole.

Henggeler, S.W., Melton, G.B., and Smith, L.A. (1992). Family preservation using multisystemic therapy: An effective alternative to incarcerating serious juvenile offenders. *Journal of Consulting and Clinical Psychology, 60,* 953–961.

Henriques, Z.W., and Jones-Brown, D. (1998). Self taught empowerment and pride: A multimodal/dual empowerment approach to confronting the problem of African American female offenders. In R.T. Zaplin (Ed.), *Female offenders* (pp. 307–330). Gaithersburg. MD: Aspen Publisher, Inc.

Hirschi, T. (1969). *Causes of delinquency.* Berkeley, CA: University of California Press.

Hirschi, T., and Hindelang, M. (1977). Intelligence and delinquency: A revisionist view. *American Sociological Review, 42,* 571–587.

Hirschi, T., and Stark, R. (1969). Hellfire and delinquency. *Social Problems, 17,* 202–213.

Hodges, A. (2000). *Alan Turing: The enigma.* New York: Walker & Company.

Hodgins, S. (2004). Offenders with major mental disorders. In C. Hollin (Ed.), *Offender assessment and treatment,* West Sussex: John Wiley & Sons, Inc.

Hodgins, S., and Cote, G. (1990). The prevalence of mental disorders among penitentiary inmates. *Canada's Mental Health, 38,* 1–5.

Hodgins, S., and Muller-Isberner, R. (Eds.). (2000). *Violence, crime, and mentally disordered offenders.* New York: John Wiley & Sons.

Holland, A. (2004). Criminal behavior and developmental disability: an epidemiological perspective. In W.R. Lindsay, J.L. Taylor, and P. Sturmey (Eds.).(2004). *Offenders with developmental disabilities* (pp. 23–34). West Sussex: John Wiley & Sons.

Hollin, C. (Ed.). (2004). *Offender assessment and treatment.* West Sussex: John Wiley & Sons, Inc.

Homant, R.J., and Osowski, G. (1982). The politics of juvenile awareness programs: a case study of Jolt. *Criminal Justice and Behavior, 9,* 55–68.

Hough, M. (1996). *Drugs misuse and the criminal justice system: A review of the literature.* London: Home Office, Drugs Prevention Initiative.

Howells, K., and Hollin, C. (1989). An introduction to concepts, models, and techniques. In K. Howells and C. Hollin (Eds.) *Clinical approaches to violence* (pp. 3–22). Chichester: Wiley.

Hudson, B. (2002). Punishment and Control. In M. Maguire, R. Morgan, and R. Reiner (Eds.), *The Oxford Handbook of Criminology* (3rd Ed.), Oxford: Oxford University Press.

Hudson, S.M., Marshall, W.L., Ward, T., Johnston, P.W., and Jones, R.L. (1995). Kia Marama: A cognitive-behavioral programme for incarcerated child molesters. *Behavior Change, 12,* 69–80.

Hudson, S.M., and Ward, T. (1997). Rape: Psychopathology and theory. In D.R. Laws and W. O'Donohue (Eds.) *Sexual deviance: Theory, assessment, and treatment* (pp. 332–355). New York: Guilford.

Ignatieff, M. (1978). *A just measure of pain: The penitentiary in the industrial revolution.* New York: Pantheon.

Irwin, J., and Cressey, D. (1962). Thieves, convicts and the inmate culture. *Social Problems, 19,* 142–155.

Jacoby, J. (Ed.). (1994). *Classics in Criminology.* Prospect Heights, IL: Waveland Press.

References

Jeffrey, C.R. (1973). The Historical Development of Criminology. In Hermann Mannheim (Ed.), *Pioneers in Criminology*. Montclair, NJ: Patterson Smith.

Johnson, B.R., Larson, D.B., and Pitts, T.C. (1997). Religious programs, institutional adjustment, and recidivism among former inmates in prison fellowship programs. *Justice Quarterly*, 14 (1), 1–21.

Johnson, H.A., and Wolfe, N.T. (2003). *History of criminal justice*. Cincinnati: Anderson Publishing Company.

Johnson, L. (2006). *Religion today*. The San Francisco Chronicle, October 6, 2005. Retrieved from http://www.sfgate.com/cgi-bin/article.cgi?file 6/14/2006.

Justice Policy Institute (2005). Quoted in the Associated Press. Nation's Inmate Population Increased 2.3 Percent Last Year. New York: *The New York Times*, April 25, 2005.

Kernberg, O.F. (1998). The psychotherapeutic management of psychopathic, narcissistic, and paranoid transferences. In T. Millon, E. Simonsen, M. Birket-Smith, and R.D. Davis (Eds.), *Psychopathy: antisocial, criminal, and violent behavior*. New York: The Guilford Press.

Kilpatrick, D.G., Best, C.L., Saunders, B.E., and Veronen, L.J. (1988). Rape in marriage and in dating relationships: How bad is it for mental health? In R.A. Prentky and V.L. Quinsey (Eds.) *Human sexual aggression: Current perspectives*. New York: New York Academy Sciences.

Kirigin, K.A., Braukman, C.J., Attwater, J.D., and Wolf, M.M. (1982). An evaluation of the teaching family (Achievement Place) group homes for juvenile offenders. *Journal of Applied Behavior Analysis*, 15, 1–16.

Knight, R.A., Warren, J.I., Reboussin, R., and Soley, B.J.(1998). Predicting rapist type from crime scene variable. *Criminal Justice & Behavior*, 25 (1), 46–80.

Knorring, L., and Ekselius, L. (1998). Psychopharmacological treatment and impulsivity. In T. Millon, E. Simonsen, M. Birket-Smith, and R.D. Davis (Eds.), *Psychopathy: Antisocial, criminal, and violent behavior*. New York: The Guilford Press.

Kohlberg, L. (1976). Moral stages and moralization. In T. Lickona (Ed.), *Moral development & behavior*. New York: Holt, Rhinehart, & Winston.

Kokish, R. (2003). The current role of post conviction sex offender polygraph testing in sex offenders treatment. In R. Geffner, K.C. Franey, T.G. Arnold, and R. Falconer (Eds.), *Identifying and treating sex offenders* (pp. 175–194). New York: Haworth Press.

Koons, B., Burrow, J., Morash, M., and Bynum, T. (1997). Expert and Offender Perceptions of Program Elements Linked to Successful Outcomes for Incarcerated Women. *Crime and Delinquency*, 43, 512.

Korn, R., and McCorkle, L. (1959). *Criminology and penology*. New York: Henry Holt.

Koss, M.P., Gidyez, C.A., and Wisniewski, N. (1987). The scope of rape: incidence and prevalence of sexual aggression and victimization in a national sample of higher education students. *Journal of Consulting and Clinical Psychology*, 55, 162–170.

Kurtines, W.M., and Szapocznik, J. (1996). Family interaction patterns: structural family therapy within contexts of cultural diversity. In E.D. Hibbs and P.S. Jensen (Eds.), *Psychosocial treatments for child and adolescent disorders*, pp. 671–697. Washington, DC: American Psychological Association.

Lang, P.J. (1970). Stimulus control, response control, and the desensitization of fear. In D.J. Levis (Ed.). *Learning approaches to therapeutic behavior*, pp. 148–173. Chicago IL: Aldine Press.

References

Langan, P.A., and Levin, D.J. (2002). *Recidivism of Prisoners Released in 1994*. Bureau of Justice Statistics Special Report. Washington: U.S. Department of Justice.

Lattimore, P.K. (2006). Reentry, reintegration, rehabilitation, recidivism, and redemption. *The Criminologist, 31* (3), 1-6.

Lattimore, P.K., and Witte, A. (1985). Programs to aid ex-offenders: We don't know nothing works. *Monthly Labor Review*, April, 1985, 46-48.

Lazarus, A. (1971). *Behavior therapy and beyond*. New York: McGraw Hill.

Lester, D. (2000). Group and milieu therapy. In P. Van Voorhis, M. Braswell, and D. Lester (Eds.) (pp. 193-224). *Correctional counseling & rehabilitation* (4th Ed.). Cincinnati, OH: Anderson Publishing Company.

Lester, D., and Hurst, G. (2000). Treating sex offenders. In P. Van Voorhis, M. Braswell, and D. Lester (Eds.) (pp. 251-264). *Correctional counseling & rehabilitation* (4th Ed.) Cincinnati, OH: Anderson Publishing Company.

Lester, D., and Van Voorhis, P. (2000). Psychoanalytic therapy. In P. Van Voorhis, M. Braswell and D. Lester (Eds.) (pp. 111-128). *Correctional counseling & rehabilitation* (4th Ed.). Cincinnati, OH: Anderson Publishing Company.

Liddle, H.A. (1995). Conceptual and clinical dimensions of a multidimensional, multisystemic engagement strategy in family based adolescent treatment. *Psychotherapy, 32*, 39-58.

Liddle, H.A., and Dakof, G.A. (1995). Efficacy of family therapy for drug abuse: Promising but not definitive. *Journal of Marital and Family Therapy, 21*, 511-543.

Liddle, H.A., Dakof, G.A., and Diamond, G. (1991). Adolescent substance abuse: Multi dimensional family therapy in action. In E. Kaufman and P. Kaufman (Eds.), *Family therapy with drug and alcohol abuse* (pp. 120-171). Boston, MA: Allyn & Bacon.

Lindsay, W.R., Taylor, J.L., and Sturmey, P. (Eds.) (2004). *Offenders with developmental disabilities*. West Sussex: John Wiley & Sons.

Lipsey, M. (1992). Juvenile delinquency treatment: a meta-analytic inquiry into the variability of effects. In T. Cook, D. Cordray, H. Hartmann, L. Hedges, R. Light, T. Louis, and F. Mosteller (Eds.), *Meta-analysis for explanation* (pp. 83-127). New York: Russell Sage.

Lipsey, M., and Wilson, D.B. (2001) *Practical meta-analysis*. Thousand Oaks: Sage.

Little, G.L. (2000). Cognitive-behavioral treatment of offenders. *Addictive Behaviors Treatment Review, 2* (1) 12-21.

Little, G.L. (2001). Meta-analysis of MRT recidivism research on post-incarceration adult felony offenders. *Cognitive-Behavioral Treatment Review, 10*, 4-6.

Little, G.L., Robinson, K.D., and Burnette, K.D. (1993). Cognitive-behavioral treatment of felony drug offenders: A five year recidivism report. *Psychological Reports, 73*, 1089-1090.

Losel, F. (1995). Increasing consensus in the evaluation of offender rehabilitation? Lessons from recent research synthesis. *Psychology, Crime, & Law, 2*, 19-39.

Lowenkamp, C.D. (2004). *A program level analysis of the relationship between correctional program integrity and treatment effectiveness*. Unpublished doctoral dissertation, University of Cincinnati, Ohio.

Lozoff, B. (2006). The prison ashram project. Retrieved from http://humankindness.org, 7/31/2006.

Lykken, D. (1995). *The Antisocial Personalities*. Hillsdale, New Jersey: Lawrence Erlbaum Associates.

References

MacKenzie, D., Brame, R., McDowall, D., and Souryal, C. (1995). Boot Camp Prisons and Recidivism in Eight States. *Criminology*, 33:327–358.

Main, T. (1946). The hospital as a therapeutic institution. *Bulletin of the Menninger Clinic, 10*, 66–68.

Maletsky, B.M. (1991). *Treating the sexual offender.* London: Sage.

Manski, C., Pepper, S., and Petrie, C.V. (Eds.) (2001). *Informing America's policy on illegal drugs: What we don't know keeps hurting us.* Washington, DC: National Academy Press.

Markovitz, P.J. (1995). Pharmacotherapy of impulsivity, aggression, and related disorders. In E. Hollander and D. Stein (Eds.), *Impulsivity and aggression.* New York, Wiley.

Marshall, W.L. (1988). The use of sexually explicit stimuli by rapists, child molesters, and nonoffenders. *The Journal of Sex Research, 25,* 267–288.

Marshall, W.L. (1992). The social value of treatment for sexual offenders. *Canadian Journal of Human Sexuality, 1,* 109–114.

Marshall, W.L. (2004). Adult sexual offenders against women. In C. Hollin (Ed.), *Offender assessment and treatment* (pp. 147–162). West Sussex: John Wiley & Sons, Inc.

Marshall, W.L., and Anderson, D. (2000). Do relapse prevention components enhance treatment effectiveness? In D.R. Laws, S.M. Hudson, and T. Ward (Eds.), *Remaking relapse prevention with sex offenders* (pp. 39–55). Thousand Oaks, CA: Sage.

Marshall, W.L., and Barbaree, H.E. (1990). An integrated theory of the etiology of sexual offending. In W.L. Marshall, D.R. Laws, and H.E. Barbaree (Eds.), *Handbook of sexual assault: Issues, theories, and the treatment of the offender* (pp. 257–275). New York: Julian Press.

Marshall, W.L., and Barrett, S. (1990). *Criminal neglect: Why sex offenders go free.* Toronto: Doubleday.

Marshall, W.L., and Pithers, W.D. (1994). A reconsideration of treatment outcome with sex offenders. *Criminal Justice and Behavior, 21,* 10–27.

Martinson, R. (1974). What works? Questions and answers about prison reform. *Public Interest, 35,* 22–54.

Martinson, R. (1976). California research at the crossroads. *Crime & Delinquency, 22,* 178–191.

Martinson, R. (1979). New findings, new views: A note of caution regarding sentencing reform. *Hofstra Law Review, 7,* 243–258.

Mathis, J., and Collins, M. (1970). Progressive phases in the group therapy of exhibitionists. *International Journal of Group Psychotherapy, 20,* 163–169.

Maultsby, M. (1975). Rational behavior therapy for acting out adolescents. *Social Casework, 56,* 35–43.

McConville, S. (1995). The Victorian prison: England, 1865–1965. In N. Morris and D.J. Rothman (Eds.), *The Oxford history of the prison.* New York: Oxford University Press.

McCord, J. (1978). A thirty year follow up of treatment effects. *American Psychologist, 33,* 284–289.

McCorkle, L., Elias, A., and Bixby, F. (1958). *The Highfield story.* New York: Holt.

McElrea, F.W.M. (1994). Restorative justice in practice. In J. Barnside and N. Baker (Eds.) *Relational justice: Repairing the breach.* Winchester, UK: Waterside Press.

McGowen, R. (1995). The well ordered prison: England, 1780–1865. In N. Morris and

References

D.J. Rothman (Eds.), *The Oxford history of the prison*. New York: Oxford University Press.

McMurran, M. (2004). Offenders with personality disorders. In C. Hollin (Ed.), *Offender assessment and treatment*, West Sussex: John Wiley & Sons, Inc.

McMurran, M., Egan, V., and Ahmadi, S. (1998). A retrospective evaluation of a therapeutic community for mentally disordered offenders. *Journal of Forensic Psychiatry, 9*, 103–113.

Mears, D.P. (2006). Evaluating the effectiveness of supermax prisons. National Institute of Justice, Rockville, MD: US Department of Justice. NCJ 211971.

Meichenbaum, D.H. (1975). Self-instructional methods. In F.H. Kanfer and A.P. Goldstein (Eds.), *Helping people change: A textbook of methods* (pp. 357–391). New York: Pergamon.

Meloy, J.R. (1988). *The psychopathic mind: Origins, dynamics, and treatment*. North Vale, NJ: Jason Aronson.

Menninger, K. (1968). *The crime of punishment*. New York: the Viking Press, Inc.

Miller, W., Brown, J., Simpson, T., Handmaker, N., Bien, T., Luckie, L., Montgomery, H., Hester, R., and Tonigan, J. (1995). What works? A methodological analysis of the alcohol treatment outcome literature. In R. Hester and W. Miller (Eds.) *Handbook of alcoholism treatment approaches*, Boston, MA: Allyn & Bacon.

Millon, T. (2004). *Masters of the mind*. Hoboken, NJ: John Wiley & Sons, Inc.

Millon, T., Simonsen, E., Birket-Smith, M., and Davis, R.D. (1998). *Psychopathy: Antisocial, criminal, and violent behavior*. New York: The Guilford Press.

Miner, M.H. (1997). How can we conduct treatment outcome research? *Sexual Abuse: A Journal of Research and Treatment, 9*, 95–110.

Miner, M.H., and Coleman, E. (2001). *Sex offender treatment*. New York: Haworth Press.

Minuchin, S. (1974). *Families and family therapy*. Cambridge, MA: Harvard University Press.

Minuchin, S., and Fishmann, H.C. (1981). *Family therapy techniques*. Cambridge, MA: Harvard University Press.

Mitchell, J., and Palmer, E.J. (2005). Evaluating the Reasoning and Rehabilitation Program for young offenders. *Journal of Offender Rehabilitation, 39*, 31–45.

Moffitt, T., Caspi, A., Rutter, M., and Silva, P.A. (2001). *Sex differences in antisocial behavior*. Cambridge: Cambridge University Press.

Monahan, J., and Steadman, H.J. (1983). Crime and mental disorder: an epidemiological approach. In M. Tonry and N. Morris (Eds.), *Crime and justice: An annual review of research* (pp. 145–189). Chicago: University of Chicago Press.

Money, J. (1986). *Lovemaps: Clinical concepts of sexual/erotic health & pathology, paraphilia, and gender transposition in childhood, adolescence & maturity*. Buffalo: Prometheus.

Moreno, J. (1934). *Who shall survive?* Washington, DC: Nervous and Mental Disease Publishing Co.

Moreno, J. (1946) *Psychodrama*. New York: Beacon House.

Morgan, J. (2005). *A circle of tough love*. Utne, July-August, 2005, 17–18.

Morris, N. The contemporary prison: 1965 to present. In N. Morris and D.J. Rothman (Eds.), *The Oxford History of the Prison*. New York: Oxford University Press.

Morris, N. (2002) *Maconochie's gentlemen*. Oxford: Oxford University Press.

Muller-Isberner, R., and Hodgins, S. (2000). Evidence based treatment for mentally

References

disordered offenders. In S. Hodgins and R. Muller-Isberner (Eds.). *Violence, crime, and mentally disordered offenders* (pp. 1–38). New York: John Wiley & Sons.

Murchison, C. (1926). *Criminal intelligence.* Worcester.

National Council on Crime and Delinquency (2001). *Evaluation of the RYSE: A report prepared for the Alameda County Probation Department.* Oakland, CA: National Council on Crime and Delinquency.

Nelson, K.E. (1990). Family based services for juvenile offenders. *Children and Youth services Review, XII*, 193–212.

Nesovic, A. (2003). Psychometric evaluation of the correctional program assessment inventory. *Dissertation Abstracts International*, 64(09),4674B. (UMI No. AATNQ 83525).

Nichols, H.R., and Molinder, I. (1984). *Multiphasic sex inventory manual.* Tacoma, WA: Nichols and Molinder.

Noble, J.H., and Conley, R.W. (1992). Toward an epidemiology of relevant attributes. In R.W. Conley, R. Luckasson and G. Bouthilet (Eds.) *The criminal justice system and mental retardation.* Baltimore, MD: Paul Brookes.

Novaco, R. (1979). The cognitive regulation of anger and stress. In P. Kendall and S. Hilton (Eds.). *Cognitive-behavioral interventions: Theory, research, and procedures.* New York: Academic Press.

Nurco, D., Ball, J., Shaffer, J., and Hanlon, T. (1985). The criminality of narcotic addicts. *The Journal of Nervous and Mental Disease, 173*, 94–102.

O'Connor, T.R. (2005). Religion as a factor in rehabilitation. Retrieved from http://faculty.ncwc.edu/toconnor/294/294lect08.htm. 8/27/2005.

O'Connor, T.R., and Pallone, N.J. (Eds.). (2002). *Religion, the community, and the rehabilitation of criminal offenders.* New York: The Haworth Press.

O'Connor, T.R., and Perreyclear, M. (2002). Prison religion in action and its influence on offender rehabilitation. In T.P. O'Connor and N.J. Pallone (Eds.). *Religion, the community, and the rehabilitation of criminal offenders* (pp. 11–34). New York: The Haworth Press.

Office of Juvenile Justice and Delinquency Prevention (2005). Gender specific programming. Retrieved from http://www.jrsa.org/jjec/programs/gender/state of evalaution.html, 6/4/2005.

Palmer, T. (1975). Martinson revisited. *Journal of Research in Crime and Delinquency, 12*, 133–152.

Palmer, T. (1992). *The re-emergence of correctional intervention.* Lexington, MA: D.C. Heath.

Palmer, T. (1996). Programmatic and non-programmatic aspects of successful intervention. In A. Harland (Ed.). *Choosing correctional options that work* (pp. 131–182.). Thousand Oaks, CA: Sage.

Parker, S. (1995). *Collins eyewitness science: Medicine.* Sydney: HarperCollins Publishers.

Partridge, G.E. (1930). Current conceptions of psychopathic personality." *American Journal of Psychiatry, 10*: 53–99.

Patterson, G. (1982). *A social learning approach: Coercive family process.* Eugene, OR: Castalia.

Patterson, G. (1986). Performance models for antisocial boys. *American Psychologist, 42*, 432–44.

Penrose, L. (1939). Mental disease and crime: Outline of a comparative study of European statistics. *British Journal of Medical Psychology, 18*, 1–15.

References

Peters, E.M. (1998). Prison before the prison. In N. Morris and D.J. Rothman (Eds.), *The Oxford History of the Prison*. New York: Oxford University Press.

Petersilia, J. (1996). Improving corrections policy: The importance of researchers and practitioners working together. In A. Harland (Ed.). *Choosing correctional options that work* (pp. 223–231). Thousand Oaks, CA: Sage.

Petersilia, J. (2004). What works in prisoner reentry? Reviewing and questioning the evidence. *Federal Probation, 68*, 4–8.

Phillips, E.L. (1968). Achievement Place: Token reinforcement procedures in a home style rehabilitation setting for "pre-delinquent" boys. *Journal of Applied Behavior Analysis, 1*, 213–23.

Pithers, W.D. (1990). Relapse prevention with sexual aggressors: A method for maintaining therapeutic gain and enhancing external supervision. In W.L. Marshall, D.R. Laws, and H.E. Barbaree (Eds.), *Handbook of sexual assault: Issues, theories, and treatment of the offender.* (pp. 343–361). New York: Plenum.

Pithers, W.D. (1997). Maintaining treatment integrity with sexual abusers. *Criminal Justice and Behavior, 24*, 34–51.

Pollak, O. (1950). *The criminality of women*. Philadelphia: University of Pennsylvania Press.

Preble, E., and Casey, J. (1969). Taking care of business: The heroin user's life on the street. *International Journal of the Addictions, 4* (1), 1–24.

Prendergast, M., Anglin, D., and Wellisch, J. (1995). Treatment of drug abusing offenders under community supervision. *Federal Probation, 59*, 66–75.

Prentky, R.A., Knight, R., and Lee, A. (1997). Risk factors associated with recidivism among extra familial child molesters. *Journal of Consulting and Clinical Psychology, 65*, 141–149.

Pressman, J. (2002). *Last resort: Psychosurgery and the limits of medicine*. Cambridge: Cambridge University Press.

Project MATCH Research Group (1997). Matching alcoholism treatment to client heterogeneity: Project MATCH post treatment drinking outcomes. *Journal of Studies on Alcohol, 58*, 7–29.

Quackenbush, R.A. (2003). The role of theory in the assessment of sex offenders. In Geffner, R., Franey, K.C., Arnold, T.G., and Falconer, R (Eds.) *Identifying and treating sex offenders* (pp. 77–102). New York: the Haworth Maltreatment and Trauma Press.

Quay, H.C. (1987). Institutional treatment. In H.C. Quay (Ed.), *Handbook of juvenile delinquency* (pp. 244–265). New York: Wiley.

Quinsey, V.L. (1998). Comment on Marshall's "monster, victim, everyman." *Sexual Abuse: A Journal of Research and Treatment, 10*, 65–69.

Quinsey, V.L., Harris, G.T., Rice, M.E., and Cormier, C.A. (1998). *Violent Offenders*. Washington, DC : American Psychological Association.

Quinsey, V.L., Harris, G.T., Rice, M.E., and Lalumiere, M.L. (1993). Assessing treatment efficacy on outcome studies of sex offenders. *Journal of Interpersonal Violence, 10*, 85–105.

Raine, A. (1993). *The Psychopathology of Crime*. San Diego: Academic Press.

Raymond, N., Robinson, B., Kraft, C., Rittberg, B., and Coleman, E. (2001). Treatment of pedophilia with leuprolide acetate: A case study. In Miner, M.H., and Coleman, E. (2001). *Sex Offender Treatment*. New York: Haworth Press.

Rector, M. (1967). *President's commission on law enforcement and administration of*

References

justice, task force report on corrections. Washington, DC: Government Printing Office.

Reid, A., Lindsay, W.R., Law, J., and Sturmey, P. (2004). The relationship of offending behavior and personality disorder in people with developmental disabilities. In W.R. Lindsay, J.L. Taylor, and P. Sturmey (Eds.) (pp. 289–304). *Offenders with developmental disabilities* (pp. 23–34). West Sussex: John Wiley & Sons.

Reid, S. (1994). *Crime and criminology* (7th Ed.). Chicago: Brown and Benchmark.

Rhine, E., Mawhorr, T., and Parks, E. (2006). Implementation: The bane of effective correctional programs. *Criminology and Public Policy, 5* (2), 347–358.

Rice, M.E., Harris, G.T., and Cormier, C. (1992). Evaluation of a maximum security therapeutic community for psychopaths and other mentally disordered offenders. *Law and Human Behavior, 16,* 399–412.

Riggs, P.D. (1998). Clinical approach to the treatment of ADHD in adolescents with substance use disorders and conduct disorder. *Journal of the American Academy of Child and Adolescent Psychiatry, 37* (3): 331–332.

Riggs, P.D., Leon, S.L., Mikulich, S.K., and Pottle, L.C. (1998). An open trial of bupropion for ADHD in adolescents with substance abuse disorders and conduct disorder. *Journal of the American Academy of Child and Adolescent Psychiatry, 37* (12): 1271–1278.

Robertson, G., and Gunn, J. (1987). A ten year follow up of men discharged from Grendon Prison. *British Journal of Psychiatry, 151,* 674–678.

Robinson, D., and Porporino, F. (2004). Programming in cognitive skills: The reasoning and rehabilitation programme. In C. Hollin (Ed.), *Offender assessment and treatment* (pp. 63–78). West Sussex: John Wiley & Sons, Inc.

Robinson, W., and Rezendes, M. (2003). Abuse scandal far deeper than disclosed, report says: Victims of clergy may exceed 1,000, Reilly estimates. *The Boston Globe,* July 24, 2003, A1.

Rogers, C. (1951). *Client centered therapy.* Boston, MA: Houghton-Mifflin.

Rogers, C. (1986). Reflection of feelings. *Person Centered Review, 1,* 125–140.

Romig, D.A. (1978). *Justice for our children.* Lexington, MA: Lexington Books.

Ross, R. (1996). *Returning to the teachings: Exploring aboriginal justice.* Toronto: Penguin.

Ross, R., and Ewles, C. (1988). Reasoning and rehabilitation. *International Journal of Offender Therapy and Comparative Criminology, 32,* 29–35.

Ross, R., and Fabiano, E. (1985). *Time to think: A cognitive model of delinquency prevention and offender rehabilitation.* Johnson City, TN: Institute of Social Science and Arts.

Rothman, D. (1971). *The discovery of the asylum: Social order in the new republic.* Boston, MA: Little, Brown.

Rothman, D. (1995). Perfecting the prison: United States, 1789–1865. In N. Morris and D.J. Rothman (Eds.), *The Oxford history of the prison.* New York: Oxford University Press.

Rotman, E. (1995). The failure of reform: United States, 1865–1965. In N. Morris and D.J. Rothman (Eds.), *The Oxford history of the prison.* New York: Oxford University Press.

Russell, D.E.H. (1984). *Sexual exploitation: Rape, child sexual abuse, and workplace harassment.* Newbury Park, CA: Sage.

Saleh, F.M., and Berlin, F.S. (2003). Sexual deviancy: diagnostic and neurobiological

References

considerations. In R. Geffner, K.C. Franey, T.G. Arnold, and R. Falconer (Eds.), *Identifying and treating sex offenders*, New York: Haworth Press.

Samenow, S. (1984, 2004). *Inside the Criminal Mind*. New York: Times Books.

Sandhu, H.S. (1970). Therapy with violent psychopaths in an Indian prison community. *International Journal of Offender Therapies, 14*, 138–144.

Satir, V. (1967). *Conjoint family therapy*. Palo Alto, CA: Science and Behavior Books.

Schmidt, P., and Witte, A. (1989). Predicting Criminal Recidivism Using "Split Population" Survival Time Models. *Journal of Econometrics, 40*, 141–59.

Schoenfeld, C. (1971). A psychoanalytic theory of juvenile delinquency. *Crime and Delinquency, 17*, 469–480.

Schorsch, E., Galedary, G., Haag, A., Hauch, M., and Lohse, H.(1990). *Sex offenders: Dynamics and psychotherapeutic strategies*. New York: Springer-Verlag.

Schrumski, T., Feldman, C., Harvey, D., and Holiman, M. (1984). A comparative evaluation of group treatments in an adult correctional facility. *Journal of Group Psychotherapy, Psychodrama, and Sociometry, 36*, 133–147.

Schwartz, B.K. (1997). Theories of sex offenders. In B.K. Schwartz and H. Cellini (Eds.), *The sex offender: New insights, treatment innovations, and legal developments* (pp. 2–32). Kingston, NJ: Civic Research Institute.

Seghorn, T.K., Prentky, R.A., and Boucher, R.J. (1987). Childhood sexual abuse in the lives of sexually aggressive offenders. *Journal of the American Academy of child and Adolescent Psychiatry, 26*, 262–267.

Sellin, T. (1944). *Pioneering in penology, the Amsterdam house of correction in the sixteenth and seventeenth centuries*. Philadelphia: University of Pennsylvania Press.

Sellin, T. (1953). Philadelphia prisons of the eighteenth century. *Transactions of the American Philosophical Society, 43* (1), 326–330.

Sewell, R., and Clark, C. (1982). An evaluation study of "The Annexe," a therapeutic community in Wormwood Scrubs prison. Unpublished report from the Home Office Prison Department.

Sharif, S.R. (1981). *Crime and corrections: An Al-Islamic perspective*. Chicago: Kazi Publications.

Simon, R. (1975). *Women in Crime*. Lexington, MA: Lexington Books.

Smith, A., Berlin, L., and Bassin, A. (1960). Group therapy with adult probationers. *Federal Probation, 24*, 15–21.

Smith, A., Berlin, L., and Bassin, A. (1965). Hostility and silence in client centered group therapy with adult offenders. *Group Psychotherapy, 18*, 191–198.

Smith, C., Algozzine, B., Schmid, R., and Hennly, T. (1990). Prison adjustment of youthful inmates with mental retardation. *Mental Retardation, 28*, 177–181.

Smith, P., Gendreau, P., and Goggin, C. (in press). Correctional Treatment: Accomplishments and realities. In P. Van Voorhis, M. Braswell, and D. Lester (Eds.) *Correctional counseling & rehabilitation* (5th Ed.). Cincinnati, OH: Anderson Publishing Company.

Snyder, J., and Patterson, G. (1987). Family interaction and delinquent behavior. In H.C. Quay (Ed.), *Handbook of Juvenile Delinquency* (pp. 216–243). New York: Wiley.

Soloff, P.H. (1998). Symptom oriented psychopharmacology for personality disorders. *Journal of Practical Psychiatry and Behavioral Health, 4*, 3–11.

Sommers, I., and Baskin, D. (1992). Sex, race, age, and violent offending. *Violence and Its Victims, 7* (3), 191–201.

References

Sommers, I., and Baskin, D. (1993). The situational context of violent female offending. *Crime and Delinquency, 30,* 136–162.

South, N. (2000). Drugs, alcohol, and crime. In M. Maguire, R. Morgan, and R. Reiner (Eds.). *The Oxford handbook of criminology* (3rd Ed.) (pp. 914–946). Oxford: Oxford University Press.

Spencer, H. (1862). *First principles.* London: William and Norgate.

Steffensmeier, D., and Allan, E. (1998). The nature of female offending: Patterns and explanation. In R.T. Zaplin (Ed.), *Female offenders* (pp. 5–30). Gaithersburg. MD: Aspen Publisher, Inc.

Stermac, L.E., and Quinsey, V.L. (1985). Social competence among rapists. *Behavioral Assessment, 8,* 171–15.

Stimson, G. (1998). Harm reduction inaction: Putting theory into practice. *International Journal of Drug Policy, 9* (6), 401–409.

Sutherland, E.H. (1931). Mental deficiency and crime. In K. Young (Ed.), *Social Attitudes.* New York: Henry Holt.

Sutherland, E.H., and Cressey, D. (1966). *The Principles of Criminology* (7th Ed.). Philadelphia: J.B. Lippincott and Company.

Swenson, C.C., Henggeler, S.W., and Schoenwald, S.K. (2004). Family based treatments. In C. Hollin (Ed.). *Offender assessment and treatment.* West Sussex: John Wiley & Sons, Inc.

Sykes, G. (1958). *The society of captives.* Princeton: Princeton University.

Taylor, J.L., Novaco, R.W., Gillmer, B., and Robertson, A. (2004). Treatment of anger and depression. In W.R. Lindsay, J.L. Taylor, and P. Sturmey (Eds.) (2004). *Offenders with developmental disabilities* (pp. 201–220). West Sussex: John Wiley & Sons.

Tetlock, P.E., and Mitchell, G. (1993). Liberal and conservative approaches to justice: conflicting psychological portraits. In B.A. Mellers and J. Baron (Eds.). *Psychological perspectives on justice* (pp. 234–55). New York: Cambridge University Press.

Teuber, N., and Powers, E. (1953). Evaluating therapy in a delinquency prevention program. *Proceedings of the Association for Research in Nervous and Mental Diseases, 3,* 138–147.

Thomas, W.I. (1923). *The unadjusted girl.* New York: Harper and Row.

Thorne, F.C. (1955). Directive and personality eclectic counseling. In J.L. McCray and D.E. Sheer (Eds.). *Six approaches to psychotherapy.* New York: The Dryden Press.

Thornhill, R., and Thornhill, N.M. (1987). Human rape: The strengths of the evolutionary perspective. In C. Crawford, M. Smith, and D. Krebs (Eds.). *Sociobiology and Psychology.* Hillsdale, NJ: Erlbaum.

Tiihonen, J. (2000). Pharmacological treatments for personality disordered offenders. In S. Hodgins and R. Muller-Isberner (Eds.). *Violence, crime, and mentally disordered offenders.* New York: John Wiley & Sons, Ltd.

Tjaden, P., and Thoennes, N. (2000). Prevalence and consequences of male to female and female to male intimate partner violence as measured by the National Violence Against Women Survey, *Violence Against Women,* 6 (2), 142–161.

Toch, H. (1982). The disturbed disruptive inmate: Where does the bus stop? *Journal of Psychiatry and Law, 10,* 327–349.

Tocqueville, A. de, and Beaumont, G. de (1833). *On the penitentiary system in the United States and France.* Translated by Francis Lieber. Philadelphia: Casey, Lea, and Blanchard.

References

Tonry, M. (2004). *Thinking about crime: Sense and sensibility in American penal culture.* New York: Oxford University Press.

Truax, C., Wargo, D., and Silber, L. (1966). Effects of group psychotherapy with high accurate empathy and nonpossessive warmth upon female institutionalized delinquents. *Journal of Abnormal Psychology, 71,* 267–274.

U.S. Department of Justice, Bureau of Justice Statistics (2006). Criminal offenders statistics. Retrieved from http://www.ojp.usdoj.gov/bjs/crimoff.htm

U.S. Department of Justice, Bureau of Justice Statistics (2005). *Prison and jail inmates at midyear 2004.* Washington: U.S. Government Printing Office 4/05, NCJ 208801.

U.S. Department of Justice, Bureau of Justice Statistics (1993). *Survey of state prisoners, 1991.* Washington, DC: U.S. Government Printing Office.

U.S. Department of Justice, Bureau of Justice Statistics (2004). *Sourcebook of criminal justice statistics, 2003.* Washington, DC: U.S. Government Printing Office.

U.S. Department of Justice, Bureau of Justice Statistics (2005). *Sourcebook of criminal justice statistics, 2004.* Washington, DC: U.S. Government Printing Office.

U.S. Department of Justice, Bureau of Justice Statistics (2006). www.ojp.usdoj.gov/bjs/dcf/duc.htm Retrieved 7/30/2006.

Valentine, E. (1986). *Great and desperate cures: The rise and decline of psychosurgery and other radical treatments for mental illness.* New York: Basic Books.

Van Dijk, J.J.M., and Mayhew, P. (1992). *Criminal victimization in the industrial world.* The Hague, Netherlands: Directorate for Crime Prevention.

Van Voorhis, P., and Hurst, G. (2000). Treating substance abuse in offender populations. In P. Van Voorhis, M. Braswell, and D. Lester (Eds.) (pp. 265–288). *Correctional counseling & rehabilitation* (4th Ed.). Cincinnati, OH: Anderson Publishing Company.

Van Voorhis, P., Braswell, M., and Lester, D. (2000). *Correctional counseling & rehabilitation* (4th Ed.). Cincinnati, OH: Anderson Publishing Company.

Van Voorhis, P., Braswell, M., and Morrow, B. (2000). Family therapy. In P. Van Voorhis, M. Braswell, and D. Lester (Eds.) (pp. 225–248). *Correctional counseling & rehabilitation* (4th Ed.). Cincinnati, OH: Anderson Publishing Company.

Visher, C. (2006). Prisoner reentry: Editorial introduction. *Criminology and Public Policy, 5* (2), 299–302.

Vorrath, H., and Brentro, L. (1985). Positive peer culture (2nd Ed.). Chicago, IL: Aldine.

Walker, N., and McCabe, S. (1973). *Crime and insanity in England,* I and II. Edinburgh: Edinburgh University Press.

Wanberg, K., and Milkman, H. (1998). *Criminal conduct and substance abuse treatment: Strategies for self improvement and change.* Thousand Oaks, CA: Sage.

Ward, T., Hudson, S.M., and Keenan, T.R. (2004). The assessment and treatment of sexual offenders against children. In C. Hollin (Ed.). *Offender assessment and treatment,* West Sussex: John Wiley & Sons, Inc.

Watson, J.B., and Raynor, R. (1920). Conditioned emotional reactions. *Journal of Experimental Psychology, 3,* 1–14.

Weinrott, M.R., Jones, R.R., and Howard, J.R. (1982). Cost effectiveness of teaching family programs for delinquents: Results of a national evaluation. *Evaluation Review, 6,* 173–201.

Weisburd, D., Lum, C., and Petrosino, A. (2001). Does research design affect study outcomes in criminal justice? *Annals of the American Association of Political and Social Science, 578,* 50–70.

References

Wexler, H.K. (1995). The success of therapeutic communities for substance abusers in American prisons (review). *Journal of Psychoactive Drugs, 27* (1), 57–66.

Wexler, H.K., and Lipton, D. (1993). From reform to recovery: Advances in prison drug treatment. In J. Inciardi (Ed.). *Drug treatment and criminal justice.* Newbury Park, CA: Sage Publications.

Wexler, S.K., Deleon, G., Thomas, G., Kressel, D., and Peters, J. (1999). The Amity Prison TC evaluation: Reincarceration outcomes. *Criminal Justice & Behavior, 26* (2), 147–167.

White, E. (2006). Country's prisons bursting at seams. Asheville, NC: *Asheville Citizen Times*, May 22, 2006.

White, R. (1956). *The abnormal personality* (2nd Ed). New York: The Ronald Press Company.

Wilkinson, J. (2005). Evaluating evidence for the effectiveness of the Reasoning and Rehabilitation Programme. *The Howard Journal of Criminal Justice, 44* (1), 70–85.

Wilson, J.A., and Davis, R.C. (2006). Good intentions meet hard realities: An evaluation of the Project Greenlight Reentry Program. *Criminology and Public Policy, 5* (2), 303–338.

Wilson, J.Q., and Herrnstein, R.J. (1985). *Crime and human nature.* New York: Simon and Schuster.

Winter, N., Holland, A.J., and Collins, S. (1997). Factors predisposing to suspected offending by adults with self reported learning disabilities. *Psychological Medicine, 27*, 595–607.

Wolfgang, M., Figlio, R.F., and Sellin, T. (1972). *Delinquency in a birth cohort.* Chicago, IL: University of Chicago Press.

Wolpe, J. (1958). *Psychotherapy by reciprocal inhibition.* Palo Alto, CA: Stanford University Press.

Yaralian, P.S., and Raine, A. (2001). The positive school of criminology: Biological theories of crime. In R. Paternoster and R. Bachman (Eds.). *Explaining criminals and crime.* Los Angeles: Roxbury Publishing Company.

Yates, P.M. (2003). Treatment of adult sexual offenders: A therapeutic cognitive-behavioral model of intervention. In R. Geffner, K.C. Franey, T.G. Arnold, and R. Falconer (Eds.), *Identifying and treating sex offenders* (pp. 195–232). New York: Haworth Press.

Yochelson, S., and Samenow, S. (1976). *The criminal personality, I.* New York: Jason Aronson.

Yochelson, S., and Samenow, S. (1977). *The criminal personality, II.* New York: Jason Aronson.

Yochelson, S., and Samenow, S. (1986). *The criminal personality, III.* New York: Jason Aronson.

Zaplin, R.T., and Dougherty, J. (1998). Programs that work: Mothers. In R.T. Zaplin (Ed.). *Female Offenders* (pp. 331–348). Gaithersburg. MD: Aspen Publisher, Inc.

Zeleney, L.D. (1933). Feeblemindedness and criminal conduct. *American Journal of Sociology, 38*, 564–578.

Index

Index

Index

Index